THE GREAT CENTURIES OF PAINTING

COLLECTION PLANNED AND DIRECTED BY

ALBERT SKIRA

*Translated by Stuart Gilbert*

Library of Congress Catalog Card Number: 56-9860

Printed in Switzerland

Distributed in the United States by
THE WORLD PUBLISHING COMPANY
2231 West 110th Street - Cleveland 2, Ohio

THE GREAT CENTURIES OF PAINTING

THE SIXTEENTH CENTURY

# FROM LEONARDO TO EL GRECO

TEXT BY LIONELLO VENTURI

SKIRA

*The colorplate on the title-page:*

Leonardo da Vinci (1452-1519). The Adoration of the Magi (detail), before 1482.
Uffizi, Florence.

Our purpose in this volume is to describe the various schools of European painting that flourished in the 16th century, to throw light on the underlying unity of those schools, and to show how that unity was realized in spite of the dramatic conflict between the Reformation and Roman Catholicism which divided Christendom against itself throughout the century and intensified the contrasts between the art traditions of the North and South of Europe.

The "twilight of the Middle Ages" lingered on in the Netherlands and the great Flemish tradition of painting that had held its ground so staunchly from Van Eyck to Gerard David did not surrender without a struggle to the new ideas filtering in from Italy; it was largely this sense of conflict that supplied the driving force of Brueghel's genius. In Germany, under the moral stimulus of the Reformation, artists were fired with a new enthusiasm and German painting rose to heights it had never yet attained; Grünewald's art, produced in a state of high emotional pressure, has the intensity of a mystic's vision, while that of Dürer is a conscious and successful effort to reconcile the religious ideals of Protestantism with the spirit of the Italian Renaissance, which Holbein, master of the objective portrait, effortlessly assimilated.

Italy followed in the path of Leonardo da Vinci, who combined a grace and beauty all his own with monumental form and movement. Raphael explored a realm of undreamt-of loveliness, and Michelangelo one of unprecedented grandeur and expressive power, while Correggio created an art of sensuous delight. Meanwhile in Venice Giorgione saw the world in terms of a poet's dream and Titian achieved that new synthetic vision of reality which led up to Tintoretto and Veronese. In that synthesis man was no longer an isolated unit but a participant in nature; this conception, transcending the Renaissance, opened the way to modern times and modern art.

Another art style known as Mannerism arose and spread over Europe. For these painters art was not the imitation of nature but a product of the thinking mind and a creation of the "inner eye." Mannerism led in two directions: towards the School of Fontainebleau with its ideal of courtly elegance and refinement, and towards that cult of form for its own sake sponsored by the Church Militant of the Counter-Reformation.

But both the pictorial and the spiritual aspirations of the 16th century found their supreme expression in Spain in the art of El Greco, whose masterpieces are a superb fusion of Byzantine abstractionism, the poetic realism of the Venetians, Roman mannerism and Spanish mysticism. And the union of these diverse elements cleared the stage for the art of the next century and the triumph of Baroque.

★

We take pleasure in tendering our most sincere and grateful thanks to all those who, with unfailing kindness, have contributed to the making of this book, in particular, the curators and directors of museums, the civil and religious authorities, and private collectors both in Europe and America.

THE SIXTEENTH CENTURY

# FROM LEONARDO TO EL GRECO

I

## THE RENAISSANCE IN ITALY
## FROM LEONARDO TO CORREGGIO

LEONARDO DA VINCI - BOLTRAFFIO - SOLARIO - PIERO DI COSIMO - FRA BARTOLOMEO
RAPHAEL - MICHELANGELO - CORREGGIO

2

## THE RENAISSANCE IN GERMANY
## FROM DÜRER TO HOLBEIN

GRÜNEWALD - DÜRER - HOLBEIN - CRANACH - BALDUNG GRIEN
MANUEL DEUTSCH - HANS LEU - ALTDORFER

3

## PAINTING IN THE NETHERLANDS
## FROM BOSCH TO BRUEGHEL

HIERONYMUS BOSCH - MASSYS - PATINIR - LUCAS VAN LEYDEN - SCOREL - BRUEGHEL

4

## PAINTING IN VENICE
## FROM GIORGIONE TO VERONESE

GIORGIONE - TITIAN - SEBASTIANO DEL PIOMBO - LOTTO
TINTORETTO - JACOPO BASSANO - VERONESE

5

## MANNERISM
## FROM PONTORMO TO EL GRECO

PONTORMO - ROSSO FIORENTINO - BRONZINO - BECCAFUMI - PARMIGIANINO - PRIMATICCIO
NICCOLÒ DELL'ABBATE - JEAN CLOUET - FRANÇOIS CLOUET - MASTER OF FLORA - CARON
SPRANGER - ANTONIO MORO - AERTSEN - CAMBIASO - EL GRECO

# THE RENAISSANCE IN ITALY

LEONARDO DA VINCI (1452-1519). PORTRAIT OF A LADY, CA. 1474. (16 ½ × 14 ½″)
COLLECTION OF THE PRINCE OF LIECHTENSTEIN, VADUZ.

# I

## FROM LEONARDO TO CORREGGIO

When a visitor to the Uffizi sees for the first time Leonardo's *Adoration of the Magi*, he is apt to be surprised by the dark, almost monochrome effect of the painting, in which rare glints of light strike through the shadows, no less than by the surging movement of the figures and the sense of mystery conveyed by purely plastic means. Alongside it the other contemporary Florentine paintings impress us with their bright precision and juvenile enthusiasm; whereas Leonardo seems strangely ageless, disillusioned, of no time and all time.

So dimly lighted are the Virgin and the Kings of the East that they look like phantoms. Around them all is plunged in shadows, a haunted dusk teeming with figures; some trying to break through the all-enveloping gloom; others responding to the divine summons. Among them we see an old man on the brink of death, his face twisted with emotion, a young man lost in meditation, St Joseph going about his humble tasks. A horse's head, much elongated, with quivering nostrils, is seen amid the crowd—a touch of fantasy to which the artist's creative imagination has somehow lent a curious plausibility. Behind these figures is a ruined palace with people on horseback and on foot moving to and fro, and beyond it a stretch of rocky country where mounted men are fighting a wild beast. A distant prospect summarily indicated in pale colors acts as a sort of backdrop to the action. The kings and their followers are crowding round the Madonna and Child. So much for the ostensible theme; the true significance of the picture lies elsewhere. What emerges from the shadows is an image of the tragic pathos of the human condition. Light, shade and movement conjure up forms hitherto unknown to art; line is implied rather than explicit, modeling is swept away on a tide of emotion, and space transformed into a fantastic vision in which all figurative elements are subordinated to psychological expression.

The *Adoration of the Magi* is unfinished. After making many studies of the lay-out and details in 1481, Leonardo ceased working on it when in the following year he was invited to Milan by the Duke Lodovico Sforza (il Moro). We may well believe that Leonardo was glad to leave this picture as it was; he had expressed, for himself and for posterity, all that he had to say and by the same token created a new style destined to shape all modern art. And to "complete" the picture at the bidding of others—in this case the monks of San Donato at Scopeto who had commissioned it—would have meant playing false to the creative urge behind it.

The *St Jerome* in the Vatican, another unfinished work, has all the remarkable qualities of the *Adoration of the Magi* and of certain drawings which reveal Leonardo's art at its best, since in them he could give free play to his imagination, untroubled by the exigencies of his public or his patrons.

He was twenty-nine when he painted the *Adoration of the Magi,* after working for several years in Andrea del Verrocchio's *bottega,* and though still a student had already gone far towards working out his personal style. To the *Baptism of Christ* (Uffizi), a work by his master, Leonardo contributed an angel very different from Verrocchio's angel in the same picture. The latter, shown full face, with the plastic values clearly rendered, is a young, healthy, rather material being with a childishly ingenuous gaze. Leonardo's angel is shown almost in back view, with the face turned in profile; in an attitude unknown to tradition and heightening the figure's expressive power. The cheek is slightly shadowed so as to round off the angles and add delicacy to the features, while soft lights play on the hair and some parts of the garment. This angel, too, is looking up, but there is nothing childish in his gaze, and the figure has a wistful charm, an almost feminine abandon. The freedom of the drawing and presentation and the spirituality of the face speak not only for Leonardo's rare creative genius but for a new moral outlook. Here beauty is replaced by grace.

The attribution of the *Portrait of a Lady* in the Liechtenstein Collection was long a moot point but today it is generally agreed that Leonardo was its maker, and this consensus of opinion testifies to the keener perception of the *quality* of a work of art that has, happily, developed among connoisseurs. For no man save Leonardo, in the decade from 1470 to 1480, was capable of creating a masterpiece of this order. The appeal of this portrait owes much to the cool, detached, disillusioned manner in which the young woman seems to be looking forth at the world; the face is noble, but without a trace of arrogance, the features are etherialized. One might almost see in this an *in memoriam* picture, the vision of a lovely lady in the land of Shades. Though her face is in some ways a reflection of the painter's mind, there is an antinomy between its physical features, whose sculpturesque volumes recall Verrocchio, and that very special attitude to life which was Leonardo's. Sometimes his creative vision outstripped the powers of his hand, great though these were. In any case the shadow on the cheeks attenuating their plastic structure, certain lights glancing across the woman's hair, the shape of the neck and the reddish-brown garments foreshadow unmistakably the style of his maturity. And it is fascinating thus to find the genius of Leonardo manifesting itself tentatively in a form he had not yet fully mastered.

Of this new form, which was to emerge in the *Adoration of the Magi,* there are early indications in several drawings, such as the pen-and-ink study of a *Madonna and Child* in the Louvre. The outlines of the bodies were treated sketch-wise and the numerous pentimenti, though they may look like "fumbling," were essential. The forms are not locked up within themselves but continuous, suggesting movement; they tighten or expand, merging into the shadows at the center, out of which the Child rises up, turning towards his Mother whose body, bent towards Him, is not delineated. Yet we

LEONARDO DA VINCI (1452-1519). STUDY FOR THE ANGEL IN THE "VIRGIN OF THE ROCKS." (7¼×6¼")
SILVER-POINT DRAWING ON YELLOW PAPER. BIBLIOTECA REALE, TURIN. (ENLARGED IN REPRODUCTION)

LEONARDO DA VINCI (1452-1519). THE ADORATION OF THE MAGI, BEFORE 1482.
(95 ½ × 96 ½″) UFFIZI, FLORENCE.

palpably sense its presence, intimated by the face and hands—a body of exquisite delicacy, aerial lightness. The line defining the Child's limbs melts away into a sudden, unexpected patch of black; indeed the whole design is a skein of brilliant improvisations, a complex of infinitely varied accents. Nothing definite is seen, only ever-changing movement, flecks of light and shade dappling a uniform greyish-brown ground —the void. Before and after Leonardo, whenever Florentine artists aimed at suggesting color or producing an effect of strangeness, they clearly demarcated certain elements, leaving others in suspense. But Leonardo ruled out all well-defined forms without exception; what he sought for was a vision self-sufficient, purged of all that was unessential, an art in which suggestion took the place of statement and material elements were submerged by light and movement. But besides its fine serenity and smoothly flowing movement, there is another quality distinctive of Leonardo's art: its grandeur, the effect of monumentality achieved by the suppression of extraneous details, avoidance of all over-emphasis and a telling synthesis of the lines of force.

The *Virgin of the Rocks* (Louvre) and the *Last Supper* (Santa Maria delle Grazie, Milan) are the only extant pictures made by Leonardo when he was attached to the court of Lodovico il Moro between 1482 and 1500. The composition of the former is governed by a single unifying principle, all the personages being interlinked by significant attitudes and gestures. The Virgin is gently urging the child St John towards the Christchild who is blessing him and behind whom the angel is pointing to St John. The lay-out is simple, forthright, well-nigh prosaic. Nevertheless the artist's handling of the scene is admirably free. Although the figures conform to a well-marked pyramidal schema, the dark central mass enables them to be spaced out. In short the picture reconciles two conflicting exigencies: the integration of the figures into an organic unity and their participation in the world of nature. As in the *Adoration of the Magi* the Virgin has the central place but instead of playing the leading part, she seems curiously aloof, absorbed in her musings, while the hands and faces of the others supply the "action." And the immateriality of her figure, lost in shadows, brings out the spiritual significance

LEONARDO DA VINCI (1452-1519).
THE VIRGIN OF THE ROCKS, 1483-1499.
(78 × 48″) LOUVRE, PARIS.

*Photographed after partial removal of the varnish.*

of the scene; after our eyes have vainly sought a resting-place on either side, they are drawn back irresistibly to the central figure, with its intimations of a mystery, its serene beauty and remoteness.

So as to fill the picture space in depth, the group is presented obliquely, but the linear pattern is also fully realized on the surface. The grotto acts as a background and the gentle light playing on the bodies ricochets on to the distant rocks. But everywhere shadow predominates, bathing the images in an atmosphere both meaningful and evocative. Discarding outright contrasts of light and shade, Leonardo has modulated the light throughout a long recession towards the shadows, in which all is modeled in a soft penumbra. The problem he set himself in this picture was one of reconciling contraries; of realizing a composition at once unified and dispersed, delineated on the surface yet suggesting depth; and of handling forms in such a way that, while having relief, they were absorbed into the atmosphere—a composition in which each detail was clearly stated yet subordinated to the general effect. A solution was provided by his famous *sfumato*, rippling like a fluid over surfaces and molding forms. And besides being a stylistic expedient, *sfumato* also served to realize the poetic ideal voiced by Leonardo in some well-known passages of his Treatise on Painting.

"Observe how in the evening, when the weather is rainy, the faces of the men and women you meet on the roads acquire a singular grace and gentleness..."

"A wonderfully soft play of light and shade can be seen on the faces of people sitting on the doorsteps of houses in the shade. Looking at them, you find that the shadowed portions of these faces are blurred by the shadows of the houses... and much beauty can be brought to features by a skillful heightening of this play of light and shade."

If for the doorsteps of houses at nightfall we substitute the mysterious grotto, we can see that Leonardo achieved his dream of beauty in the *Virgin of the Rocks*. His predilection for the soft, diffused light of the hour when the day is dying and night has not yet come prevented him from troubling overmuch about color. While in *sfumato* —the blending and softening of light tones into dark—form acquires a wonderful delicacy, colors tend to be submerged and here they are no more than tints having no local values and melting into the dusk of nightfall. Leonardo's light is functional to form, but not to color. When he applied himself to perfecting a picture such as this, the vision that held his gaze was one of perfect grace; what he aimed at was to conjure up out of an all-enveloping *sfumato* unforgettable faces, like those of the Virgin, St John and the angel. Buoyant forms, uninfluenced by the pull of gravity and so exquisitely fragile that they seem less like real beings than like the figures of a dream, they do not belong to Raphael's world of beauty, but to a world of heavenly grace.

In 1504 the Duchess Isabella d'Este Gonzaga wrote to Leonardo asking him to paint a picture of the Child Jesus endowed with "that suavity and sweetness in the expression which you alone can compass." This shows that it was to his "suavity and sweetness" that Leonardo owed his success in court circles, a success we can readily understand in the light of the *Virgin of the Rocks*. But eulogies of this kind must have struck the creator of the *Adoration of the Magi* and the *St Jerome* as involuntarily ironical.

True, with the *Virgin of the Rocks* he had proved to himself that, given time and with infinite pains, he could really "finish" an oil painting. But on this matter of "finish" he was always in two minds. He completed a picture in order to "triumph," as he put it; on the other hand, so far as his personal satisfaction was concerned, the sketch sufficed, since in a drawing he could express himself with perfect freedom. One reason for this attitude he shared with the greatest painters of the day; neither Michelangelo nor Giorgione greatly cared to "finish" their works. For this was a time when the distinction between the artist and the artisan was coming to the fore and the artist was impatient with what he looked on as manual labor, the craftsman's proper function. Moreover, Leonardo saw himself, and rightly so, as a pioneer in many fields; his was indeed a universal genius. This was recognized by his contemporaries who ascribed magical properties to his "inventions," but, aside from his discoveries in anatomy, hydraulics and many other branches of science, what grip the modern imagination are his anticipations of the future, his plans for submarines and airships. It has been said, correctly, that if these plans were never carried out, the fault lay entirely with the age he lived in. Actually, however, to Leonardo's thinking, the theoretical value of an invention lost nothing by remaining dormant in his notebooks; and he took much the same view as regards his activities in the field of art.

A long-standing practice of the art historian is that of attaching particular importance to works on which an artist has expended much time, which he has painstakingly brought to what is called perfection. Raphael is an obvious case in point; as between his small picture of *St George* and his big fresco, the *School of Athens,* the latter has always attracted more attention. But a discussion of the reasons behind this preference would take us too far afield. We will merely suggest that there are no substantial grounds for deploring the fact that, owing either to his temperament or to the circumstances of the age, Leonardo finished so few works. Indeed his failure to complete the *Adoration of the Magi* may well have been a blessing in disguise. Though the angel in the *Virgin of the Rocks* has more graciousness, more sweetness, as compared with the preliminary sketch (Turin), we find in the latter a more intense and mysterious vitality, superior creative power.

But have we here the true Leonardo, the man of heaven-scaling ambition, first great painter of light and a pathfinder of modern science both theoretical and applied? Put this way, our question suggests that ravishing as is the beauty of his angels, this represents but one facet of Leonardo's many-sided personality. His culture and, more particularly, the neo-Platonist influences then predominant in Florence led him to follow up this path, his immediate aim being to "triumph" (as he styled it) and to gratify Isabella d'Este or the King of France. Obviously this new grace was a notable discovery; which is why it had so many imitators. But Leonardo's ultimate goal lay elsewhere; he was in quest of something more deeply rooted in life, something exclusively his own —something which was never to be imitated.

Writing from Florence in 1501, Pietro da Novellara informed Isabella d'Este that Leonardo was working on his *St Anne,* and added: "He has done nothing else, except

LEONARDO DA VINCI (1452-1519). THE ADORATION OF THE MAGI (DETAIL), BEFORE 1482.
UFFIZI, FLORENCE.

sometimes touching up the portraits that two of his assistants are engaged on." Thus it is impossible to say if the many portraits that at one time or other have been ascribed to him are really by his hand—with the exception of the *Monna Lisa.* Moreover, the uniqueness of this picture, into which Leonardo poured his whole soul, makes it difficult for us to see him in other portraits. In any case his imagination was obviously too personal, too autonomous, for portrait-painting—as indeed is evidenced by the *Monna Lisa.* The intellectualism, the visionary remoteness we see in La Gioconda's gaze was Leonardo's, not his model's. His, too, that intimation of a mystery, an immemorial wisdom that "all the thoughts and experience of the world had etched and molded" in her face, hinted at not only by the enigmatic smile but also in the dim, fantastic

LEONARDO DA VINCI (1452-1519). THE ADORATION OF THE MAGI (DETAIL), BEFORE 1482.
UFFIZI, FLORENCE.

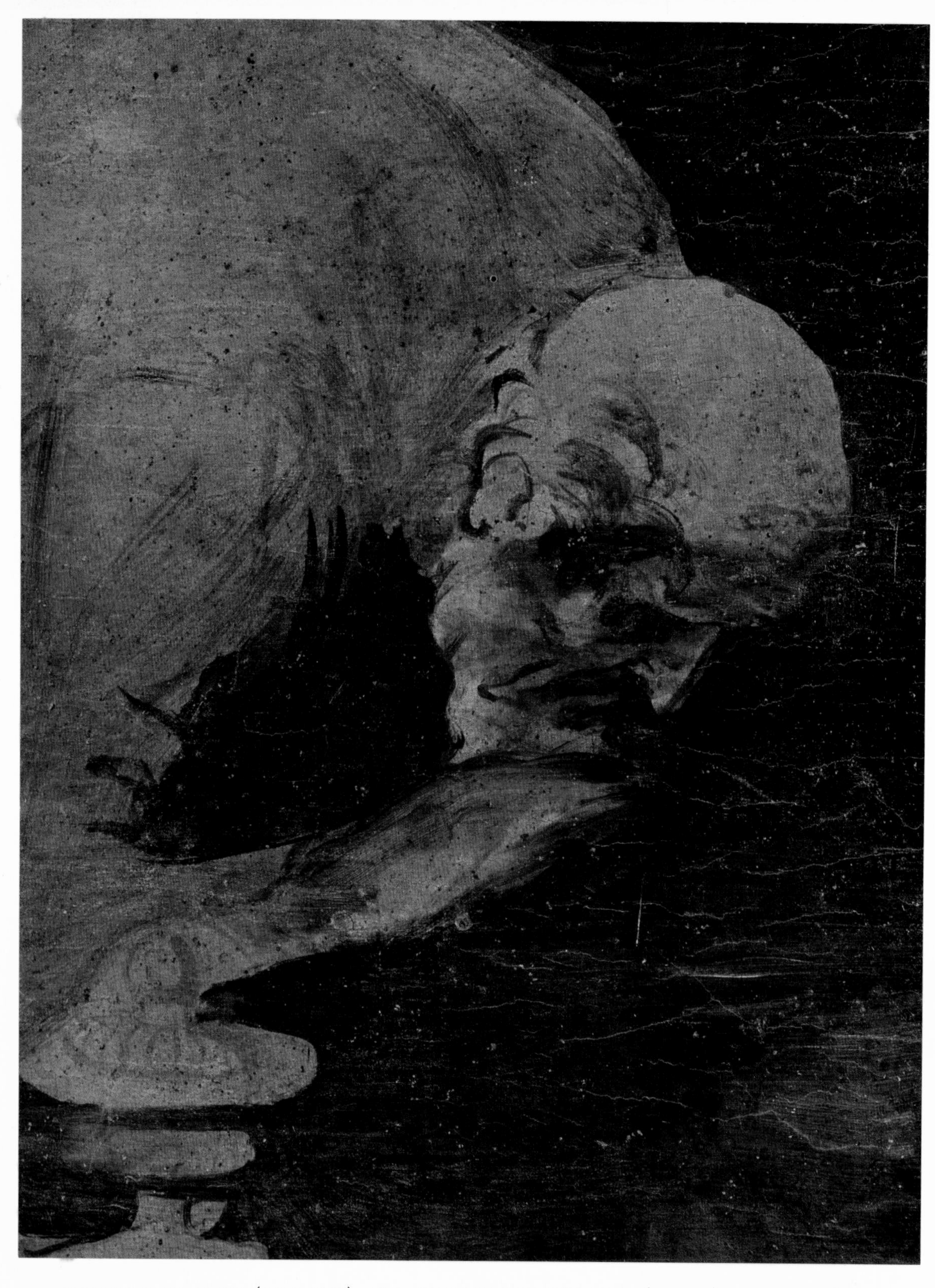

LEONARDO DA VINCI (1452-1519). THE ADORATION OF THE MAGI (DETAIL), BEFORE 1482.
UFFIZI, FLORENCE.

landscape; this is a Faustian face rather than a woman's. So multifarious are the allusions, so diverse the meanings behind meanings, that sometimes the beholder has almost an impression of a plethora of subtleties. Nevertheless despite its structural complexity, the artist has imparted to the picture itself a wonderful simplicity; here he brought off another "victory," but this seeming ease cost him infinite labor—extending, Vasari tells us, over many years.

The fact that we can trace the successive stages in the making of the *St Anne* enables us to follow the evolution of Leonardo's style during the last years of the century and up to 1506 or thereabouts. The earliest sketches show that he originally intended to depict the Holy Family in a very human, intimate way; but subsequently decided for a more monumental, fully plastic treatment. The final outcome was the picture in the Louvre, in which the movements and gestures of the figures are determined by the exigencies of a monumental lay-out. The composition is based on that dialectic relationship of masses known as *contrapposto,* being so disposed that a gesture on the right is promptly balanced by another on the left, the result being a dynamic symmetry wherein intellectual values are transmuted into art. Thus at the turn of the century Leonardo realized that monumentalism was to be the keynote of Cinquecento art and showed artists how it could be attained.

But beauty even when interpreted on monumental lines was for Leonardo only a milestone on the path he had mapped out for himself; he aspired to nothing short of imparting a new, revolutionary significance to the human situation, and the dramatic played a necessary part in it. While there had already been hints of this in the *Adoration of the Magi,* it comes out unmistakably in the *Last Supper* painted for Santa Maria delle Grazie in Milan and completed or almost completed in 1497. This picture is in a sadly damaged state and we have to refer to the drawing to get an idea of the expressions on the faces. Nevertheless the monumental grandeur of the ensemble can still be seen in the fresco. This effect is due both to the architectural framework rigidly enclosing gestures and to the rhythmical balancing of the groups of disciples on either side of Christ. Christ has just told them "One of you shall betray Me" and the disciples react to the tragic tidings each in his own manner and at successive intervals of time. Among those nearest Christ, John and Philip are overwhelmed by their emotion. Peter in a gust of apprehension thrusts Judas aside, Thomas and James the Greater make no secret of their horrified surprise and indignation, while on the two groups furthest from the Savior the effect of the announcement is less pronounced—as though attenuated or retarded by their distance from the central figure. Thus the expressive variety of gestures creates at once a sense of the lapse of time and a complex symmetry, adding spiritual overtones to the rendering of the scene.

Intended to decorate (in competition with Michelangelo) one of the walls of the Council Hall in the Palazzo Pubblico, Florence, the *Battle of Anghiari* would have displayed Leonardo's feeling for the dramatic at its apogee. But the mural was never completed, and all we have to go on are some sketches and a written description. Judging by the accounts of those who saw the cartoon, the central scene was a seething mêlée of men and horses whose frenzy seemed to electrify the surrounding atmosphere, laced with smoke and flames. In the sketches, the scope of the action is limited by considerations of a formal order. Yet no one before or after him has rendered the immediacy, speed and drive of headlong movement with such compelling power as in these drawings. In the picture he achieved not only perfect form but a remarkable compositional equilibrium. The battle is depicted in three episodes, as in a triptych. It begins with a combat between two men on horseback; in the central scene we see the terrific struggle for the colors which gave this work its alternative title the "Battle of the Standard"; and finally the cavalry held in reserve. Thus the composition included a sequence of events in time and space—though the latter was perforce constricted.

Basic to Leonardo's style was his *sfumato*, that fusion between form and color-light which made it possible to bathe the image in a "vapory" atmosphere and to body forth the conception of a world in which man was not, as in the 15th century, a protagonist, but an element of the universe on a par with earth and sky. Hence the importance Leonardo assigned to landscape, which, however fantastic or remote, sets what might be called the picture's moral tone. Far from wishing to limit painting to the portrayal of man and his activities, he sought to include all nature in his art—rain, sky and stars. For Leonardo perspective was no longer merely geometric, it could also be chromatic and convey the density of the atmosphere intervening between the beholder and the distant image, thus causing nature to play a part in the human situation.

Leonardo's conception of painting linked up with his scientific theories. It is hardly necessary to point out that he tackled many of the problems dealt with by modern science, and that he actually made blueprints of several inventions that have materialized in our time. In Florence throughout the 15th century science and religion had marched side by side and gradually the function of directing operations of the mind had been withdrawn from the latter and assigned to science. Leonardo, however, broke with the neo-Platonic tradition of the Quattrocento and, embracing Aristotelian realism, studied the world of nature without any idealistic bias. He believed like Aristotle that nature was guided by an inner Reason of her own that manifested itself in her operations and that what the scientific researcher had to do was, starting from the data of experience, to work back to the rational principles—of a mathematical order—that govern the phenomenal world. Pencil in hand, Leonardo embarked on this adventurous quest. The first truth he encountered on his path was that of beauty, the living poetry of graceful forms. Next he discovered the unity between force and movement and in this he saw a key to the tragic predicament, religious and political, of his time. Beyond these came pure science, and since this lay wholly outside the scope of the culture of his day, Leonardo transposed his ideas into the future, when thanks to science man would master his environment, just as Machiavelli projected into the future the political system he had set his heart on but could not get adopted. And both men sensed the poetry of the unfinished.

His contemporaries were alive to the grandeur of Leonardo's art and freely drew inspiration from his *sfumato*, his monumental vision and his feeling for movement.

LEONARDO DA VINCI (1452-1519). THE ADORATION OF THE MAGI (DETAIL), BEFORE 1482.
UFFIZI, FLORENCE.

LEONARDO DA VINCI (1452-1519). ST ANNE (DETAIL), 1501-1506.
LOUVRE, PARIS.

LEONARDO DA VINCI (1452-1519). ST ANNE (DETAIL), 1501-1506.
LOUVRE, PARIS.

They also exploited his knowledge of hydraulics and military engineering. But they felt that there was something faintly sinister about this man who so resolutely went his own way, whose knowledge was encyclopedic and whose capacity for invention seemed superhuman. The milieu he frequented was highly lettered, but Leonardo boasted of being "an unlettered man," and of preferring to be a painter, philosopher and scientist. After winning Isabella d'Este's enthusiastic patronage by the charm of his painting, instead of humoring his patroness, he promptly diverted his energies to inventing a new machine. In Rome Pope Leo X did not know what to do with him and finally Leonardo migrated to the court of Francis I in France, where he died in 1519. Perhaps the most striking thing about this man of many-sided genius was his amazing faculty of living in the future more than in the present.

**THE CRISIS OF THE RENAISSANCE**

It is common knowledge that the last decade of the 15th and the first three of the 16th century witnessed a wonderful flowering of painting and sculpture in Italy, an art whose classical perfection is comparable with that of the Golden Age of Greece. To this period belong the masterpieces of Leonardo, Raphael, Giorgione and Correggio; most of Michelangelo's and Titian's; and a host of epoch-making works. In other fields, Ariosto's *Orlando Furioso*, the political and historical speculations of Machiavelli and Francesco Guicciardini, and the discoveries of the great sea-captains contributed to the prodigious intellectual ferment prevailing in Italy during those crowded, colorful years. There was thus a striking contrast between the political, religious and economic calamities of the peninsula and its signal triumphs in the domains of art and the intellect.

The period between the French invasion under King Charles VIII in 1494 and the year 1530 which witnessed the downfall of the last Florentine republic was politically disastrous for Italy. Not only did the country come under foreign domination, destined to last three centuries, but it was ruined economically as well, and the triumphal progress of the Renaissance was brought virtually to a standstill. Nor did the Catholic Church of Rome fare much better; its authority was seriously undermined by the Reformation; in fact it seemed as if Savonarola's maledictions were being fulfilled and the Church being castigated for her all too obvious delinquencies.

To account for the anomaly between artistic achievement and political collapse we must bear in mind the relations then obtaining between the Church and the community, and the change of outlook that had taken place. In the Middle Ages the artist created for the glory of God; a cathedral or a fresco might be a work of art but its point of departure was an ideal concept stemming from a loftier source. It was only during the Renaissance that the work of art came to be viewed from the aesthetic angle, as something existing in its own right. There was no longer any question of transcendence; the artist could be a-moral without being immoral, and Machiavelli's ideal ruler was confessedly unscrupulous.

The myth of a "renewal" bulked large in the *Weltanschauung* of the Renaissance, and it was this yearning for a revival of the perfection they read into the arts of antiquity that led the 14th- and 15th-century Italians to hark back to the culture, prized so highly, of the Greeks and Romans, without however relinquishing their own Christian ideal. But the impulse to renewal was already flagging when the 16th century began; it might indeed be said that the Renaissance unwittingly transmitted this "revivalist" trend of thought to its arch enemy, the Reformation. Acting as its spokesman, Savonarola had launched a program of reform in Italy and though he failed, his ideal and his aspirations had survived his death (1498). During the 1529-1530 siege the heroic resistance of the Florentines was sustained by the proclamation of "Christ, King of Florence," in memory of Savonarola. But Malatesta Baglioni, after reviewing the military situation, was convinced that, notwithstanding the Florentines' faith in Christ the King, defeat was inevitable and, judging it expedient to surrender, secretly negotiated a treacherous agreement with the besiegers. Thus in this city which for over a century had led the way in European culture, their mystical faith enabled its inhabitants to perform feats of legendary valor; whereas rationalist logic, in the absence of a secular morality, led to an act of abject treachery. It was not until the Age of Enlightenment that a moral code based on purely secular principles came into being.

It is interesting to observe how the great Italian painters reacted to the political and social conditions of their day. Leonardo perfectly understood the nature of the change that was taking place. He was the first artist to humanize a scene like that in the *Adoration of the Magi*, and to dramatize the *Last Supper* to an extent unparalleled in any work of the previous century. Nevertheless Leonardo viewed the contemporary predicament with detachment; one has a feeling that his moral sense was not strong enough to prompt him to commit himself. It was, above all, scientific research that fired his enthusiasm; and by engrossing himself in that, he lived more in the future than in the present. Therein lay both his strength and his limitations. He built up an art of pure intelligence with scant regard to the material means employed—one of the results being that many of his paintings rapidly deteriorated. Art was for him the supreme truth, but he ranged beyond art, exploring many branches of science. Unfortunately the technical equipment he needed was lacking in his time.

In the early 16th century Florence still held the lead in the intellectual life of Italy, though now and again some of her greatest citizens were driven into exile. In 1505 the city called on Leonardo and Michelangelo to decorate the Hall of the Great Council in the Palazzo Pubblico, thereby demonstrating that Florence still could achieve what lay beyond the power of other cities. But neither artist did more than draw up some preliminary plans. The great days, in fact, were over and Rome now stepped into the place of Florence. In 1505 Pope Julius II summoned Michelangelo to Rome, and Raphael followed him three years later. They were employed on painting the Sistine ceiling and the Stanze of the Vatican, respectively. From 1508 to 1520 most of the art of Italy (with the exception of Venice) was produced at Rome under the auspices of Julius II and Leo X.

Raphael is one of the most popular artists of all ages and not without good reason. Still we cannot forget that he worked in something of a hot-house atmosphere and solely for an art-loving élite.

Julius II liked to do things in a big way, and, wishing to build for himself a colossal tomb, he called in Michelangelo who was no less enamored than he, perhaps even more enamored, of the impossible. When the project for the tomb fell through, the Pope commissioned Michelangelo to decorate the ceiling of the Sistine Chapel. For building the new St Peter's, the largest church in Christendom, he called in that architect of genius Bramante, who, an old legend has it, had announced the singular intention of making the road to Paradise passable for vehicles, once he was on the Other Side! The commission for the Stanze went to Raphael whose gift of imparting grace and charm even to the most grandiose conceptions commended him to Julius II. This great pope's predilection for huge monumental works of art was certainly motivated by the religious and political conditions of the age. Since there could now be no question of regaining the Franciscan virtues of humility, chastity and charity, the only alternative was to bolster up the prestige of the Church by a display of strength, beauty and grandeur. In short, the ideal of Julius II and his associates was to steal their thunder from the ancient Romans, and compete with them on their own ground.

Son of Lorenzo the Magnificent, Leo X was educated by Politian and liked to boast that he was "born in a library." He devoted even more time than Julius had to literature and art, his interest in culture and intellectual pursuits even leading him to neglect affairs of State. At his court the obsession with antiquity reached a point where Christ was assimilated to Apollo and the Virgin to Diana. Erasmus was scandalized by a Good Friday sermon preached by Cardinal Inghirami, who in the presence of the Pope discoursed eloquently on pagan subjects and completely forgot to make any reference to Christ's Passion.

Living in a constant round of festivals and banquets, Leo X failed to recognize the seriousness of Luther's revolt and its menace for the Holy See. On the other hand, he seems to have realized that Raphael's untimely death in 1520 spelt the end of his dream of a new golden age of art, and when the Romans one and all went into mourning he, like them, obscurely felt that the loss of their "divine painter" was a portent of decline. Leo X died next year and was succeeded by a Dutch pope who cared nothing for art. And only a few years later, in 1527, came the sack of Rome, prelude to the end of the Renaissance. Yet when we remember what was then happening throughout Europe and the calamities still to come, we can see that Rome was for some while yet a favored oasis, a refuge from the storm—and still capable of producing masterpieces.

### THE SCHOOL OF LEONARDO IN LOMBARDY AND TUSCANY

All Italian painting was influenced by the new ways of seeing and the aesthetic Leonardo had brought into the world. Generally speaking, the painters who worked in his immediate orbit are not greatly appreciated today (the same fate has befallen Raphael's, Michelangelo's and Correggio's satellites). It has been said that the Lombards oriented Leonardo's innovations towards a sentimental art, and the Florentines towards an academic classicism. There is some truth in this, yet it is only fair to recognize that a number of works exist which, if not wholly by the Master's hand (though he may well have had a share in them), rank among the finest creations of the Italian Renaissance.

For example we find Novellara writing in 1501 to Isabella d'Este about the two pupils who were making portraits in which the Master "sometimes helped them." True, as a result of modern research many works traditionally ascribed to Leonardo are now excluded from the canon ; but this does not detract in any way from their charm. Noteworthy examples are the *Portrait of a Musician* and *Woman in Profile* (Ambrosiana, Milan) and the *Portrait of a Nobleman with Long Hair* (Brera, Milan). The version of the *Virgin of the Rocks* in the National Gallery, London, was a joint work of Leonardo and De Predis. Here the monumental quality is more pronounced than in the Louvre version, but the latter has a more intense vitality. By and large it may be said that the Lombard painters successfully mastered the use of Leonardo's *sfumato*—they had already been initiated into it, to some extent, by Flemish painting—while keeping to the Quattrocento tradition of humanistic realism imbued with charm. What they failed to understand in Leonardo was the intellectual side of his art ; that he saw in art a means to the enlargement of knowledge.

Ambrogio De Predis was Leonardo's chief collaborator at Milan. De Predis was a miniaturist who in 1502—twenty years, that is, after Leonardo's coming to Milan—made his *Portrait of the Emperor Maximilian I* (Vienna) ; but in this picture, excellent in its way, the precise rendering of details is a far cry from Leonardo's art.

A painter of very different caliber was Antonio Boltraffio (1466/67-1516). His only master was Leonardo in whose studio he worked and whose technique he skillfully assimilated, but without effacing his own personality. The composition of his *Virgin and Child* (Poldi-Pezzoli Museum, Milan) is based on an harmonious relationship of contrasted masses, and the obscurity of the *sfumato* is happily allied with rich, resonant colors ; but most striking is the grace, at once discreet and noble, that sets this picture in a class apart. This delicate expressiveness, tinged with idealism, is also found in the *Portrait of a Man* (possibly Girolamo Casio of Bologna) in the National Gallery, London, while in the *Madonna of the Casio Family* (Louvre) the artist displays a keen feeling for architecturally ordered composition that, while deriving from the Quattrocento, has the new freedom of movement characteristic of the 16th century.

Bramante's pupil Bartolomeo Suardi, known as Bramantino (ca. 1480-ca. 1536), shows an admirable feeling for tectonic structure not only in his composition but also in his figures—an effect which is, however, weakened when he takes to displaying his mastery of *sfumato*. Of much interest, too, are the painters who, thanks to their familiarity with Venetian painting, breathed new life into traditional 15th-century Lombard art ; such men as Andrea Solario, Bartolomeo Veneto and Bernardino Luini.

Andrea Solario (op. 1493-1524) imparted to his Madonnas a look of motherly love that is infinitely touching. His famous *Vierge au coussin vert* (Louvre) has a charm all its own, spontaneous and sincere, if perhaps a little "bourgeois" in conception. He also painted some justly famous portraits, such as the *Chancellor Morone* (Duke Gallarati-Scotti Collection, Milan), remarkable both for the vigor of the treatment and its masterly design. In fact he had not only a personality differentiating him from his Leonardesque Milanese contemporaries, but also a turn of mind resembling Holbein's.

GIOVANNI ANTONIO BOLTRAFFIO (1466/67-1516). VIRGIN AND CHILD, 1490-1500.
(18 × 14 ¼″) MUSEO POLDI-PEZZOLI, MILAN.

ANDREA SOLARIO (OP. 1493-1524). PORTRAIT OF CHANCELLOR MORONE, CA. 1522.
(32¼ × 24¾″) COLLECTION OF DUKE GALLARATI-SCOTTI, MILAN.

Bartolomeo Veneto (op. 1502-1530) liked to describe himself as stemming from both Venice and Cremona in equal proportions. After painting in the manner of Giovanni Bellini he moved on to a Lombard style in which, besides Leonardo's influence, we seem to detect that of Raphael and Dürer. His most successful works were portraits, which while somewhat resembling Solario's have greater elegance and a more aristocratic grace.

Like Veneto, Bernardino Luini (op. 1507-1532) combined Foppa's tradition with the Venetian procedures of Cima da Conegliano and Alvise Vivarini. It is their slightly outmoded sweetness, delicate and unassuming, and an almost childish grace, that make his best works such as the La Pelucca frescos (now in the Brera, Milan) so attractive. Here it is evident that Luini was his simple self, uninfluenced by Leonardo. Yet even his much praised "grace," long regarded as the fine flower of the Lombard soul, tends to sickly-sweetness whenever Leonardesque sophistication enters into it.

Giovanni Antonio Bazzi, better known as Sodoma (1477-1549), studied from 1490 to 1497 in Spanzotti's *bottega* at Vercelli. However, his earliest dated works—produced at Siena soon after 1500—show the Leonardesque tendencies then prevailing at Milan ; hence the general belief that Sodoma spent the last three years of the century in that city. All that is best in this artist derives from Leonardo, as can be seen in his *Christ at the Column* (Pinacoteca, Siena) and *St Sebastian* (Uffizi). On the other hand, when he attempted to imitate Raphael, as in the Farnesina frescos (Rome), he never got beyond a superficial mannerism. For he lacked the insight needed to perceive the true secrets of Raphael's art, its harmony and ordered beauty.

Less refined and more spontaneous was Gaudenzio Ferrari (ca. 1471-1546), whose masterwork is the fresco sequence in the church at Varallo, near Novara. Trained at Milan, he familiarized himself with the methods of Bramantino and Leonardo, but his natural bent was towards a more popular type of art, realistic, verging on the Baroque. Nevertheless the immediacy of his responses, his practice of interpreting biblical incidents in terms of contemporary life (the Vercelli *St Christopher* is a case in point), his ingenious fusion of painting and sculpture (as in the Sacro Monte Chapel at Varallo) and, lastly, the liveliness of his color unclouded by *sfumato*—all these highly personal traits entitle him to a place apart in the annals of 16th-century Lombard painting. Indeed, given his temperament and his anticipations of Baroque, he might almost be styled a Rubens in advance of his time.

When reference is made to the "School of Leonardo," we think primarily of Lombard painters, but the Florentines, too, were much influenced by Leonardo—it might even be said that the true purport of his art was better understood in Florence. None the less there is no denying that "Leonardism" lasted longer in Lombardy than in Florence, where very soon it paled before the rising star of Michelangelo.

Florentine painting of the Quattrocento owes its greatness to a uniquely successful combination of tireless brainwork with strongly felt emotion. But after the deaths of Lorenzo the Magnificent and Savonarola its emotive drive tended to peter out, whereas the intellectual factor more than held its own—with the result that there was a gradual decline of the moral purpose in Florentine art.

PIERO DI COSIMO (1462-1521). VULCAN AND AEOLUS. (61 3/8 × 65″) NATIONAL GALLERY OF CANADA, OTTAWA.

Piero di Cosimo (1462-1521) stood outside the main current of Florentine painting in the 16th century, since in the great majority of his works the guiding spirit is obviously that of Quattrocento art. Though his debt to Leonardo is unmistakable, he cannot

PIERO DI COSIMO (1462-1521). A FOREST FIRE (LEFT SIDE), 1490-1500.
(OVER-ALL DIMENSIONS: 28 × 80″) ASHMOLEAN MUSEUM, OXFORD.

be regarded as a disciple or a mere epigone of the master; rather, he is a painter who, defying classification, opened vistas on the future. For he displays incomparable maestria in reconciling the facts of visual experience with the fantastic inventions of his prolific imagination and in co-ordinating the technique of Leonardo with his own creative impulse, based on an exceptional feeling for, and understanding of, the archetypal myths of remote antiquity.

His originality lay in his interpretation of these themes; nothing quite like this had been done before. Breaking up outlines, he achieved effects of light and shade rarely if ever found in the work of his Florentine contemporaries. His was a strikingly unorthodox approach; hence Vasari's allusion to his "bizarre type of mind." If his last works be excepted, we might say he demonstrated in his art an alternative to mannerism. For instead of starting out from a pre-selected group of forms, he had

PIERO DI COSIMO (1462-1521). A FOREST FIRE (RIGHT SIDE), 1490-1500.
ASHMOLEAN MUSEUM, OXFORD.

recourse to a world of fantastic imagery imbued with the sensuality which is one of his distinctive traits. And we can easily understand why our present-day surrealists voice an unqualified admiration of Piero di Cosimo.

A born colorist, a subtle and ingenious craftsman, with a gift for rendering poetic images with meticulous precision, he created imaginary landscapes in a singularly delicate technique. Examples are *A Forest Fire* (Ashmolean, Oxford), the *Death of Procris* (National Gallery, London) and the *Venus and Mars* (Berlin). That he was also a fine portraitist is proved by the two Amsterdam portraits. While following in the footsteps of the greatest Quattrocento painters, he also mastered the use of Leonardo's *sfumato,* adapting it both to the rendering of form and to elegant, discreetly subdued expression, as in his *Magdalen* in Rome. Yet one almost feels that this artist came too late; that his age lacked the spiritual maturity needed to sustain such splendid gifts.

PIERO DI COSIMO (1462-1521). PORTRAIT OF A FLORENTINE LADY AS ST MARY MAGDALEN, CA. 1505.
(28 ½ × 21″) GALLERIA NAZIONALE, ROME.

This may be why after taking refuge in a world of fantastic imagery of the kind we should nowadays describe as "surrealistic," he relapsed into a humdrum art and confined himself to unoriginal, pseudo-monumental forms.

Two Florentine painters, Fra Bartolomeo and Andrea del Sarto, may be described as victims of Leonardo's art; both were highly gifted men and both for one reason or another failed to "make the grade" one would have expected of them.

Soon after the tragic end of Savonarola (1498), to whom he had been greatly attached, Fra Bartolomeo (1475 ?-1517), a man of a naturally pious disposition, took monastic vows. Conceived on a small scale and sensitively rendered, his early works fell in line with the Quattrocento tradition, while their forms and colors were perfectly in keeping with the religious zeal inspiring them. Unfortunately, however, the times were not propitious for the expression of a belief so zealous and sincere as that of Fra Bartolomeo; it might almost be said that the devoutness behind these early works

FRA BARTOLOMEO (1475?-1517). PIETÀ, 1516. (62 × 78 ¼") PALAZZO PITTI, FLORENCE.

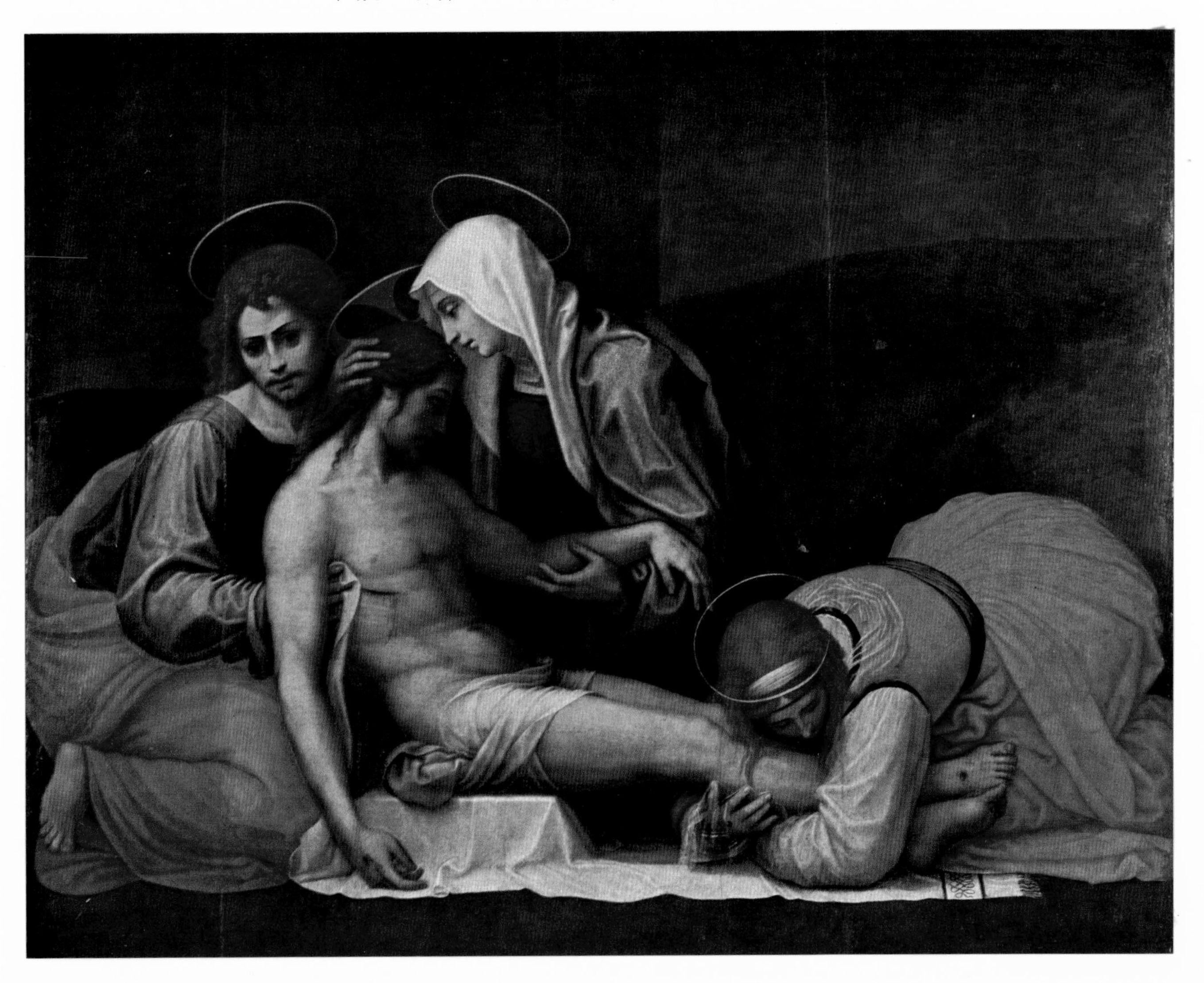

handicapped the artist. Like Savonarola, Fra Bartolomeo could be described as a victim of his age even though, instead of being burnt at the stake, he was loaded with honors. Being a painter born as well as a devout Christian, he could not fail to utilize Leonardo's great discovery. But *sfumato* was not intended for the expression of religious emotion, and, moreover, it led inevitably to what was known as *sprezzatura*, to architectonic composition and monumental effects more appropriate to secular than to Christian imagery. Hence the ambivalence we feel in Fra Bartolomeo's later work. The bright colors of his youth were overcast by chiaroscuro, while in many cases the free expression of his faith was sacrificed to studied monumentalism. Still there are some exceptions. The *Pietà* in the Pitti Palace, Florence, is a complete success, monumental without being rhetorical; its form is flawless, its emotion sincerely felt, nor does the *sfumato* devitalize its color. Only one objection might be made to this otherwise perfect work: the sepulchral coldness pervading the composition and making it look like an array of statues in tinted marble. Fra Bartolomeo's tragedy was that of a man who was not strong-minded enough to react against the culture of his age, and at the same time too scrupulous to compromise with it.

The problem of Andrea del Sarto (1486-1531), on the other hand, was not one of choosing between religious faith and the spirit of the Renaissance. He was a natural colorist, much more so than Fra Bartolomeo; yet he, too, thinned his color by an admixture of *sfumato*. It might be argued that, as a by-product of light and shade, *sfumato* can but intensify color. But the fact remains that Leonardo employed it as a means of rendering form and chiaroscuro, and it could never be transformed into those effects of light and shade produced by color *per se*, as found for instance in Venetian painting. Monumental and dynamic, Andrea del Sarto's form implements a composition that holds well together plastically and has great expressive power. For three centuries he ranked as one of the greatest Italian artists; today he has but few admirers. Vasari, perhaps, put his finger on the explanation when he said his art was "flawless." So long as writers on art set an overriding value on craftsmanship, Andrea was praised to the skies; but when stress came to be laid on the artist's "message," our flawless painter was dismissed as tedious. His method of handling color can be seen to advantage in the *Assumption* in the Pitti Palace. A patch of *sfumato* in the center at once gives a sense of depth and acts as a foil to certain colors—red, yellow, olive-green—which float on the surface without being eaten up by the chiaroscuro. Whereas in his famous *St John* (also in the Pitti) the beauty of the colors is marred by an over-emphasis on sculpturesque values, giving a curious lividity to the ensemble. In *Charity* (Louvre) the pyramidal structure is highly effective, vibrant like a tongue of fire, and one gets the feeling of an ingenious contrapposto between the figures which seem to be sinking down and the ascending drive of the plastic lines of force. Better perhaps than any of his coevals, Andrea del Sarto understood the nature and potentialities of Leonardo's *sfumato* and grasped the many opportunities it provided for experiments in style. But, little daring, he aspired to nothing higher than mere formal perfection. Thus he was the type figure of the virtuoso *à outrance*—a perfectionist too perfect to be "alive."

Though not born in Florence, Raphael and Michelangelo were trained there and so belonged to that Florentine school which held the lead in Italy for two centuries thanks to its boldness, intellectual range and active interest in all the art problems of the age.

Urbino, Raphael's birthplace, would have been little more than a drab provincial town remote from the art currents of the day had not Duke Federigo da Montefeltro converted it into a flourishing cultural center. The Ducal Palace, designed by Luciano Laurana, was originally decorated by Piero della Francesca, Uccello and Joos van Ghent ; later, by Melozzo da Forlì, Luca Signorelli and other celebrated artists. No less famous than its art treasures was the splendid library, one of the largest in Europe. Renowned for its elegance and erudition, Federigo's court provided a model for one of the most famous books of the Renaissance, Baldassare Castiglione's *Il Cortegiano* ("The Perfect Courtier"), published a generation later. That under the enlightened sway of a man like Duke Federigo this relatively obscure Italian town should have blossomed out into a center of art and learning need not, given the conditions of the age, greatly surprise us. The remarkable thing is that Urbino should have promptly given the world two artists of the very highest rank : Bramante and Raphael.

Raphael's father was a painter and a poet of no particular merit, but it is to his credit that he sensed the greatness of Leonardo and Perugino from the start. Raphael, who was only eleven when his father died in 1494, was sent to study under Perugino in the last years of the century, and took a hand in the decorations of the Scala del Cambio at Perugia, which were completed in 1500. Like Leonardo, Perugino had studied under Andrea del Verrocchio but, unlike him, had failed to realize the importance henceforth to be attached to movement, plastic vigor and monumental composition. On the contrary, he practised an art imbued with religious emotion in which woman's beauty and the glamour of remote horizons played a leading part. Despite his success in Florence he preferred to retire to the country, where he became the moving spirit of the so-called Umbrian School.

At the Court of Urbino young Raphael had daily opportunities of feasting his eyes on the most refined achievements of contemporary art. Meanwhile his teacher Perugino instructed him in the expression, on traditional lines, of both physical beauty and a grace instinct with deep religious faith. So well did he assimilate his master's methods that, in his early phase, it is no easy matter distinguishing his work from Perugino's. However, in some of his smaller pictures he brings to Perugino's compositional schemes a beauty so novel and so richly colorful that their forms are changed out of recognition. The themes may be the same, the spirit is quite different. Raphael's beauty is too graceful to be sensual, adapted even to the expression of religious sentiment, and, though containing no radically new elements, diverges from the tradition of the previous century. Thus, out of the blue so to speak, there came into the world a well-nigh peerless painter, dedicated heart and soul to his ideal of beauty, an ideal he kept before him even when his style underwent a change. And Raphael's conception of the *beau idéal* held unchallenged sway throughout Europe for three centuries and more, as being the very acme of perfection.

RAPHAEL (1483-1520). ST MICHAEL, CA. 1502. (12 ⅛ × 10 ½″)
LOUVRE, PARIS.

RAPHAEL (1483-1520). THE THREE GRACES, CA. 1500. ($6\frac{5}{8} \times 6\frac{5}{8}''$)
MUSÉE CONDÉ, CHANTILLY.

The small pictures referred to above are the *Vision of a Knight* (National Gallery, London), the *Three Graces* (Musée Condé, Chantilly) and the *Madonna del Conestabile* (Hermitage, Leningrad). The "Vision of a Knight" is the romantic title which has been foisted on a picture that probably represents Hercules with Virtue and Vice competing for his favors. We may assume this picture to be earlier than the other two, since it shows signs of technical inexperience, indeed a certain awkwardness—qualities which, however, far from impairing it, lend it a special charm. It might well be the fantasy of a precocious child artist who has imparted, by some artifice of innocence, the wistful loveliness of a dream of spring to the figures, landscape and tapering tree, the slender axis of the composition. In the *Three Graces* some have thought to see the reproduction of a sculptured group or an ancient seal. But surely it is clear enough that Raphael was not "reproducing" anything ; on the contrary, he created a rhythmic, very slightly plastic linear composition in which the figures of the three women are outlined, all on the surface, against the sky—three presences of a delicate loveliness miraculously arising, as if conjured out of air, against a distant landscape background. The composition of the *Madonna del Conestabile* is more elaborate, the figure being inscribed within a circle limiting the spatial planes and tightening as it were the affective link between the Mother and the Son, while the distant scene seems like the landscape of a dream.

These three pictures are so unlike anything by Perugino that it has been suggested that, before going to Perugia, Raphael may have studied in the *bottega* of Timoteo Viti, and thus familiarized himself with the glowing color of Ferrarese art. But for one thing, it seems unlikely that Raphael would have found anything to inspire him in the work of that drearily mediocre painter, Viti ; also, we must take into account his boyhood at Urbino and the countless opportunities he there had of seeing some of the best work of the day. One thing is certain : in the subtle difference between the three early works in question and the art of Perugino we can discern the distinctive traits of Raphael's personality : the sweetness and tranquil beauty which were to be the constants of his art.

They were painted, it would seem, around 1500. Three years later came the *Coronation of the Virgin* in the Vatican, where is also the *Madonna enthroned between Saints* painted by Perugino some five years before ; and it is interesting to compare the works of master and pupil. Raphael's picture is all disarming loveliness and smiling grace, and forms are brought out by the brightness of the colors. Perugino's composition has more vigor and formal solidity, while the distribution of bright and dark areas and of the colors is much more carefully contrived. It cannot be denied that beauty alone does not suffice to make a noble work of art ; something more is needed, an ordered coherence between the various elements of which the picture is composed. Viewed from this angle, Raphael's painting is defective. Though the *Coronation of the Virgin* is a relatively small composition, it is none the less too large ; the gemlike colors which were so effective in Raphael's small pictures seem lost in the wider expanse of an altarpiece. Also, the charm of figures devoid of any psychological pretensions ceases to operate when the painter seeks to emphasize the poignant grief of the apostles gazing at the Virgin's empty tomb. Finally, there is no denying a certain awkwardness in the visual relationship between the celestial and terrestrial figures : the problem so ably solved by Perugino in his *Virgin in Glory* (1500, Uffizi). Reasons for the failure of the *Coronation* altarpiece are the painter's inability to mask the contrast between "presentation" and "representation" and, secondly, his use of a technique unsuited to works of large dimensions. We can see the difference in the small paintings of the predella which have a lightness and a spontaneity of movement not merely illustrating action but bringing the scene as a whole to life.

Here, then, we find a distinct advance on Raphael's 'prentice work ; he has mastered a new element of his art, the rendering of movement, and this, too, he attunes to beauty, always his supreme concern. In the predella there is no longer any clash between the dainty elegance of the representation and the dimensions of the picture surface. Raphael, in short, has found himself.

The rapidity with which his art matured is proved by the *Marriage of the Virgin* (Brera, Milan), dated 1504. In this picture Raphael fell back on a lay-out used by Perugino for the same subject in a work commissioned in 1499 and not yet completed in 1503 (Caen Museum). But he excelled his master both in the general effect and in the perfection of the parts. Perugino failed to convey so fully the feeling of apparent space as created not only by perspective projection but also by the grouping of figures and the strictly geometric volumes of the temple. By now Raphael had learnt all he could from his teacher, whose limitations he all too clearly saw. It was time to strike out on a new path, and in 1504 he moved to Florence, "to learn more," as Giovanna Felicia Feltria announced in a letter introducing the young painter to Pier Soderini.

Once in Florence Raphael soon discovered that Perugino was outmoded, a survival from the Quattrocento ; for a young painter, keen-eyed and forward-looking, Florence spelt Leonardo and Michelangelo. What has been called his Florentine style took form between 1504 and 1508. This does not mean that he spent all his time in Florence (actually most of his painting was done at Perugia), but that Florence was for the nonce his "spiritual home." Nevertheless he did not imitate Leonardo or Michelangelo, though he must have watched with excited interest the progress of their work in the Palazzo Pubblico. But he never desisted from his quest of beauty, of perfect craftsmanship and of that *sprezzatura* which was his lifelong ideal. In exploring new fields, he kept for a while to the motifs of his former teacher. But although still appearing in his *Ansidei Madonna* (1505-1506, National Gallery, London), these motifs are recast with an eye to the unity of a composition truly monumental in conception. In the *Marriage of the Virgin* the relationship between figures and background had been more of a narrative than of a visual order, and the former, generally darker than the architectural setting, were out of tone with the ground. But in the *Ansidei Madonna* a color dynamism of a special kind, expressed in terms of masses, is generated by the relationship between the dominant brown of throne and figures, and the blue-grey architecture. Here it is evident that Raphael had grasped Leonardo's synthetic handling of forms, though without as yet employing the *sfumato* which was its corollary. But in the *Madonna del Gran Duca* (Pitti Palace) he has perfectly assimilated it. A uniform dark background enables him to make the figures stand out sharply and they are rendered with a sensitivity lacking in his earlier work, which gives them at once the elusive spirituality of heavenly apparitions and the tactile values of solid bodies. For Raphael does not, like Leonardo, allow his *sfumato* to envelop forms modeled in relief but cuts it short where they begin. Thus he succeeds in investing the object represented with the grace of formal abstraction without sacrificing the actuality of visual experience, while the gleaming colors of his early phase dwindle into monochrome.

RAPHAEL (1483-1520). THE TEMPI MADONNA, CA. 1505. (29 ½ × 20 ½″)
ALTE PINAKOTHEK, MUNICH.

This abandonment of the faintly sensuous beauty of his *Madonna del Conestabile* and the blandishments of color was Raphael's tribute to the spirit of Florentine culture.

The *Madonna del Gran Duca* did much to consolidate his fame. The works he now produced were universally accepted as flawless paradigms of beauty, even in cases where his personality made itself less felt and the results fell short of his highest standard. But into the *Tempi Madonna* (Munich) he put the best of himself. The perfection of the forms somehow heightens our sense of the bond of deep affection between the Mother and Son, while the movement linking them together and the harmony of the dark tones against the sky redeems the conventionality of the pyramidal composition and an over-emphasis on sculpturesque values.

The world-famous prototypes of female beauty Raphael created in this second or Florentine period—the *Madonna del Prato* (Vienna), the *Madonna del Cardellino* (Uffizi) and the *Belle Jardinière* (Louvre)—have very similar settings. The figures are placed in open country against one of those low, remote horizons that Perugino also favored. The Madonna is watching her Son or the child St John at play, sometimes speaking to them. All three Madonnas look like portraits of exceptionally handsome young women, done from the life—so much so that one almost feels the models are posing to display their charms. Raphael had certainly seen Leonardo's *St Anne,* but he deliberately shut his eyes to the spiritual implications of his elder's style and also to the suggestive power of a judicious unfinish. He aspired to something else: a completely realized plastic beauty in which the figures had both material volumes and at the same time a significance more real, more valid than that of their earthly existence. Raphael, in a word, transmuted Leonardo's grace into beauty. The three works named above are perfect of their kind, but when we turn to the *Portrait of Maddalena Doni* (Pitti Palace, Florence) we perceive Raphael's limitations. Patently inspired by the *Monna Lisa,* the figure is too massive, too static, and there is something at once superficial and uninspired about the presentation. What was superficial in Raphael's early work was not his response to beautiful things but his response to life in general. Once he had grasped the principles behind Leonardo's modeling in paint, he made the most of them. But he was careful not to venture outside this field, in which he felt himself secure. Thus it is only natural that those who prefer the perfectly "finished," self-contained work of art to one that opens vistas on infinity should find Raphael more satisfying than Leonardo. Nor need we be surprised if, in his quest of form devoid of any vagueness, he discarded Leonardesque *sfumato* and was, rather, drawn towards the acknowledged master of fully plastic form and sculptural effects: Michelangelo.

When Atalanta Baglioni, "whose eyes had no longer tears enough to weep for her son's crimes and the vengeance of her kinsmen," asked Raphael to paint a *Deposition from the Cross* (1507) in which her own sorrows were reflected in those of the Mother of the Crucified, he began by sketching out a composition in the style of Perugino, full of tragic pathos. But after a while he thought better of it and instead of bearing in mind the grief of the bereaved mother or even his own inclinations, he decided to use this picture as a pretext for displaying his familiarity with classical antiquity and the technique of Michelangelo. Thus he made much of the dramatic elements, stressing the tensions of figures and, preoccupied with the harmony of attitudes and gestures, relegated to the background the group of women beside the swooning Virgin. Also, he lingered too long over details, to the detriment of emotional drive and imaginative freedom. How different were the small pictures of his early youth, all charm and spontaneity ! It now was clear that, if he was to regain that first fine rapture, he must no longer seek his models in antiquity or the grandiose art of Michelangelo, so foreign to his temperament. For his personal vision was entirely different, poetic and inspired by naïvely Christian piety.

The 1507 *Deposition* (Borghese Gallery, Rome) proved that Raphael was no longer a provincial artist, but had thoroughly mastered all the technical accomplishments of Florentine art at its most expert and sophisticated. But three conditions had yet to be fulfilled before he could make good his personality and emancipate himself from the influences of his early training. First, he had to acquire more ease of execution, so that perfection came quite effortlessly ; secondly, to substitute poetic contemplation for dramatic action ; and finally, an occasion had to arise impelling him to get every ounce out of himself. And in the fall of 1508 the Stanze of the Vatican opened their doors to him.

The Stanze where Raphael now was called to work consisted of a series of rooms above the Appartamenti Borgia in the Vatican. In October 1508 a team of painters, amongst them Sodoma, Bramante and Lotto, was still engaged on decorating them and traces of their paintings still survive on the vaults of the Stanza della Segnatura. But they soon ceased working and Raphael undertook to decorate the walls, single-handed—a task on a far larger scale than any of his previous ventures.

The fresco wrongly called the *Disputa* actually depicts the "Triumph of Religion." The cause of the misnomer was the fact that the persons represented, saints and doctors of the church, are involved in a fervent debate—certainly not a "dispute"—concerning the Eucharist. The theme here is theology, while that of the so-called *School of Athens* on the opposite wall is philosophy (in its widest sense, including the sciences of ancient Greece). The frescos on the other walls celebrate poetry (Mount Parnassus) and the rule of justice (Jurisprudence) respectively.

Theology, philosophy, poetry and justice bulked large in Renaissance culture and Raphael was supremely successful in clothing them in pictorial form ; hence, perhaps, the reason of his immediate success. Pope Julius II and all the cultivated members of his entourage saw in these frescos a reflection of their deepest aspirations ; indeed this set of frescos might be described as an apotheosis of the cultural ideal of the Renaissance. In an apotheosis rhetoric is indispensable and one of Raphael's gifts was that of giving rhetorical effects a liveliness and spontaneity—not to say naïvety—that freed them from any trace of the pomposity and stiffness too often found in such works, and of transmuting rhetoric, by means of *sprezzatura*, into poetry. Propounded by Raphael's friend Baldassare Castiglione, *spezzatura* (unconstraint) bore out the dictum *ars est celare artem* since it meant interpreting emotion by way of natural, graceful gestures, without any unseemly emphasis on expressive elements.

RAPHAEL (1483-1520). PORTRAIT OF POPE LEO X, 1517-1518. (60 ½ × 46 ¾″)
UFFIZI, FLORENCE.

RAPHAEL (1483-1520). PORTRAIT OF POPE LEO X (DETAIL), 1517-1518.
UFFIZI, FLORENCE.

The setting Raphael gave this vision of the several aspects of Renaissance culture was of a kind he had not hitherto employed: an ideal architectural complex. When studying under Perugino, he had familiarized himself with the rendering of far horizons and vast open spaces, symbols of the infinite. But in the *School of Athens* space is given a new significance; the architectural elements are no longer mere décor, but functional to the structure of the picture—an innovation which, thanks to Raphael, affected all the subsequent painting of the Italian Renaissance. It is quite otherwise with the *Disputa*. True, we have here a perspective in depth that indicates the relationship between the divine figures and the human elements: popes, cardinals, jurists and poets. But brilliant as is the handling of space, this picture still conformed to the tradition of the many "Coronations of the Virgin" in which the relations between heaven and earth had been conveyed on very similar lines.

RAPHAEL (1483-1520). PORTRAIT OF POPE LEO X (DETAIL), 1517-1518.
UFFIZI, FLORENCE.

The use of this traditional conception of space enabled Raphael to devote his whole attention to figures and their attitudes. As early as the 18th century it was pointed out that Raphael does not represent "completed actions." He recorded movement at the moment of its inception, not when it had been completed and was, therefore, of the past. Obviously an incipient movement conveys the play of feeling far better than would a presentation of the figure in repose; hence the agitation pervading the scene of the *Disputa* and also the dance-like rhythms of the *Parnassus*. In the latter fresco the figures, distributed in groups, are all remarkably beautiful; indeed all of Raphael's figures, even white-bearded patriarchs, seem endowed with eternal youth.

Judiciously restored, the *Disputa* has now regained its pristine brightness and we can admire the delicacy and aptness of the coloring, which at once defines forms and contributes to the organization of space. But here neither the color nor the light is adequate to create, by itself, the illusion of actual three-dimensional space. Light does not absorb the figures; rather, the contrary is true. In the *Disputa* the figures are dark, standing out on a bright ground—which theoretically should ensure the maximum pictorial effect; but Raphael failed in this because he paid too much attention to the local chiaroscuro of each figure. The scene of *Gregory IX presenting the Decretals to St Raymond of Penafort* is the first fresco in which Raphael faced up to this problem unequivocally and stressed the function of color. And in so doing he gave a new development to the technique employed in the *Ansidei Madonna*.

Nevertheless he felt a desire to go still further and to create by means of color-light a more intimate relationship between figures and their setting. This he did in the *Mass of Bolsena* in another of the rooms. Here at first glance we can see that the spatial architecture of the *School of Athens* has given place to construction in terms of color. The lights and shadows of the church build up a setting for the forms which they envelop even in the foreground, beyond the big bench acting as a sort of backdrop, in front of which the altar bathed in light at once spaces out and sets off the dark-toned figures. Saturated with light, the colors acquire a glowing sheen not found in the work of any other painters of Central Italy. But beauty of color and perfect integration of the figures into their setting are not the only virtues of this noble fresco; thanks to Raphael's new vision those slightly rhetorical effects which still obtained in the commemorative decorations of the Segnatura are here eliminated. What gives this picture of a miracle that had taken place at Bolsena in 1264 its lifelikeness is its presentation in "modern" garb, as an incident occurring at the Vatican in the presence of Pope Julius II, his attendants, the Swiss Guards, and some handsome Roman women. Thus his desire to pay homage to the pope, his patron, led to one of Raphael's finest works; moreover in the group of Swiss soldiers we have a wholly admirable synthesis of Florentine and Venetian technique. Perugia, Florence and Rome had played their part in enabling Raphael to realize his dream of an ideal beauty; this new conception of color *in excelsis* was transmitted to him, with Sebastiano del Piombo, Lorenzo Lotto and the Dossi as intermediaries, by Venice, where Giorgione now was pointing the way to a whole new world of art.

The *Mass of Bolsena* figures in the Stanza d'Eliodoro, so named after the fresco representing the *Expulsion of Heliodorus from the Temple.* In the same room are the *Liberation of St Peter* and the *Meeting of Leo I and Attila.* These were executed between 1511 and 1514, and as Julius II died in 1513, the last wall was painted under the auspices of Leo X. This change impaired the unity of the ensemble. Julius II had wished the Stanza della Segnatura to celebrate his civil and religious ideal, and this second room to illustrate his victories. The *Expulsion of Heliodorus from the Temple* commemorates the pope's victory over the Venetians who had occupied a portion of the States of the Church. The *Mass of Bolsena,* in which a miracle convinces a doubting priest of his error, symbolizes the pope's triumph over the cardinals who had proposed to hold a Council at Pisa with a view to deposing him. The *Liberation of St Peter* recalls the incident when the pope was almost taken prisoner at Bologna, while in the *Meeting of Leo I and Attila* Julius II wished to remind beholders that just as Leo I had forced the barbarians to retreat, he, Julius, had averted the risk of a foreign invasion.

Unlike the symbolic decorations of the first Stanza, the subjects Raphael had now to deal with were historical events. In the *Mass of Bolsena* he had succeeded in transmuting an ancient legend into a scene of contemporary life, and had produced a masterpiece. Still he could not always work with the same fervor and in the *Expulsion of Heliodorus,* notwithstanding the beauty of the temple shown in full perspective and the light falling on the pope in prayer, we cannot help being conscious of Raphael's failure to achieve the dramatic effect he was aiming at. The amply molded forms, derived from Michelangelo, and the impetuous movement of the group including Heliodorus do not suffice to create an atmosphere of drama. And despite the balanced presentation of Julius II and his troops, the composition does not hold together. The *Liberation of St Peter* is a technical feat, and its violent contrasts of light and shade anticipate some of the procedures of Baroque art. Raphael had not only an almost uncanny gift of prescience but an equally amazing facility of invention; here he brings off effects of which, only two years earlier, he would never have dreamed. But it is essentially a virtuoso performance, fruit of an imagination more spectacular than creative.

Lastly in the *Meeting of Leo I and Attila* Raphael displays so little interest in the style that he seems to have quite forgotten his discoveries in the field of color and even in the rendering of space. Massed on the surface of the composition, horses and their riders are little more than illustrations of an historical event. Poetry and dramatic action alike are absent, and elegance is the painter's chief concern—Renaissance art is giving place to Mannerism.

Some of Raphael's larger portraits anticipate, or keep closely to, the style given such masterly expression in the *Mass of Bolsena.* Earliest, perhaps, is the portrait of Julius II (Uffizi), in which the artist brings out clearly the character of his model: quick-tempered, bursting with energy, always ready to leap to action and enforce his iron will. Here the painter's easy mastery of his medium is no less striking than his psychological insight. In a sense this portrait is dramatic, but here as always Raphael's sense of the dramatic found expression solely in potential not in overt action.

RAPHAEL (1483-1520). THE DISPUTA, 1509.
FRESCO, STANZA DELLA SEGNATURA, VATICAN.

*Pages 52-53: details.*
*Folding plate: entire fresco.*

Very different is the *Portrait of a Cardinal* (Prado), an essentially poetic study of a face. The beauty Raphael aspired to give it was not merely personal or formal but also in its implications, the sublimity of its patrician refinement, almost the aloofness of a demigod. Even the scarlet of the cardinal's cloak—both intense and restrained in tone—seems invested with an aristocratic elegance exceptional even in Raphael's work. And we are tempted to see in this a spiritual self-portrait, the most authentic image of himself the painter has bequeathed to us. If this be so, it corroborates what Vasari has to tell us about Raphael: "Whenever he went to the court he was escorted by fifty young painters, all highly gifted, a sort of royal retinue. Indeed he lived, not like a painter, but like a prince." This "aristocratic" quality of beauty was not confined in Raphael's art to persons of lofty rank. In his *Baldassare Castiglione* (Louvre), a portrait of the man who was described by the Emperor Charles V as "*uno de los mejores caballeros del mundo*," the color-scheme is black-brown-grey with faint glints of gold, a complex of tonal values rather than rich hues; in fact the subdued harmony of the colors is a reflection, as it were, of the spirit of the true-born gentleman at its noblest.

Quite other is the gaze of Leo X as portrayed with his nephews Giuliano de' Medici and Ludovico de' Rossi. We cannot but be amazed at the rapidity with which Raphael's conception of the portrait had matured in the twelve years between the half-length likeness of Angelo Doni made about 1506 and this group. Pope Leo X has not the tense expression of Julius II, nor the patrician beauty of the *Cardinal*, nor the endearing amiability of Castiglione. This portrait was made to celebrate the social prestige of the pope and his patronage of arts and letters (symbolized by the illuminated book), with a certain emphasis on the fineness of the hands—on which the pope prided himself. Thus the model's strong personality makes itself felt amid a number of extraneous elements—which may imply that the artist was less in sympathy with him. In any case, however, this is plainly an "official" portrait.

But there was no lack of interest on Raphael's part in, for example, his painting of a handsome Roman woman of the lower classes, *La Donna velata* (Pitti). It has been remarked that the sumptuous dress looks rather out of keeping with the woman's personal appearance; it looks as if she had dressed herself up for the sitting. She has a shy, faintly puzzled gaze. "Why," she seems to be thinking, "should I be singled out for so high an honor?" Apparently Raphael found this sitter and her ingenuous air to his liking, for he used her some years later (in an idealized rendering) as his model for the *Sistine Madonna* (Dresden).

In 1511 and 1512 Sigismondo Conti, a friend of Julius II, commissioned Raphael to paint the *Madonna di Foligno* (Vatican) for the high altar of Santa Maria in Aracoeli in Rome. This work is based on the legend of the Ara Coeli, the apparition of the Virgin to Augustus. In Raphael's picture the Roman Emperor is replaced by Sigismondo Conti, who died in February 1512. Though Raphael may have begun work on the picture at the same time as the Stanza della Segnatura, he must have spent some years on it, as it is done in the new technique employed for the *Mass of Bolsena*.

The *Madonna della Seggiola* (Pitti) is one of Raphael's best-loved pictures. Here once again we cannot but appreciate the poetic glamour with which the sacred figure is invested, yet with an uneasy feeling that its spiritual quality suffers a little by the emphasis on physical perfection. None the less the happy disposition of the figure within the circle of the picture space, the plastic vigor of the forms and the color harmony compel our admiration. Red, green and yellow sing out melodiously, but their accord is purely superficial, there is no real relationship of values holding them together.

Very different was the creative inspiration behind the *Sistine Madonna* though it too was "made to order." The curtains drawn back on either side to reveal the Queen of Heaven moving forward over the clouds create a frankly theatrical effect. And equally of the theater is the gesture of Pope Sixtus commending to the Virgin the assembled congregation. St Barbara is too suave, too mannered for her beauty to come to life—but her role is only that of a supernumerary. Two small angels leaning on their elbows lighten the monumental impact of the scene. But though several of its elements may fail to move us, the picture as a whole has a singular appeal. The Virgin's movement is delightfully supple and thanks to a skillful distribution of the figures the surrounding space is at once clearly articulated and infinite in depth. Painted around 1516, this picture marks the close of Raphael's Renaissance period, though so far there is no trace of mannerism.

But, unlike the *Sistine Madonna*, the *Incendio del Borgo* in the third of the Vatican Stanze—it is the only picture in this room on which Raphael himself worked—is definitely mannerist in conception. Here the artist sought to vie with Michelangelo's nudes and stressed the elegance of the figures. Perspective is used to create the illusion of space but there is no longer any real spatial composition and the buildings represented have no constructive values. Looking at this work, which must be written down a failure, we realize that the ideal architecture, the feeling for space and the physical beauty which so delight the eye in Raphael's masterpieces are a sort of happy miracle, based in the last resort on an unstable equilibrium—all the more precarious because it relied entirely on spontaneity and an idealized sensuality. But there came a time when Raphael felt he had mastered his art from A to Z, had nothing more to learn, and when he came to regard even color as no more than an easy means of representing visual data with forcible directness. And now he aimed at imparting a new spirituality to his figures, at making them more mobile and dramatic, and at stressing relief by stronger contrasts between light and dark areas. Unfortunately his genius did not lend itself readily to this new program; what it needed was that subtle balance between the physical and the spiritual, between presentation and representation, which was universally regarded for the next three centuries as art's supreme achievement. By 1514 Raphael had ceased believing in this; what he now sought for was a form of expression less spontaneous, at once more intellectual and more fanciful. It was his vast success that brought him to this pass—and it also prevented him from carrying out his new intention. As chief architect of St Peter's, inspector of excavations and conservator of antiquities, he had hardly time enough even to design cartoons for his pupils and the

Flemish tapestry-weavers who interpreted his work at Brussels. True, he is not the only painter who ended up by letting the desire for a more "intellectual" art cramp his creative inspiration. But in Raphael's case the results were little short of disastrous, as can be seen if we compare his decorations of the third room in the Vatican with that miracle of beauty, the *Mass of Bolsena*.

Death came to Raphael when he was only thirty-seven and at the height of his fame. So potent was the spell his art had cast on his contemporaries that all alike, from the pope to the humblest of his assistants, felt that with his passing something truly divine had left the world. Yet Raphael had already crossed the summit of his art and set foot on the downward slope. He had given of his best and the hour had struck for him to quit the scene if art's impending setbacks, due to the dead hand of academicism, were not to be laid to his account.

RAPHAEL (1483-1520). THE LIBERATION OF ST PETER (FRAGMENT), 1511-1512.
FRESCO, STANZA D'ELIODORO, VATICAN.

Born in 1475, Michelangelo Buonarroti was the son of a Florentine gentleman who held the office of podestà (mayor) in the small Tuscan towns of Caprese and Chiusi. He was educated at Florence and in 1490 admitted to the famous school of art established in the Medici gardens, studying there until the death of Lorenzo the Magnificent in 1492. The social standing of his family and the favor shown him by Lorenzo may account to some extent for the overweening pride so characteristic of the man and of his art.

Twenty-three years younger than Leonardo, Michelangelo reached maturity in the early years of the century when the older artist, whose rival he soon became, stood at the height of his fame. He won the confidence of Pope Julius II and was employed on large-scale works in Rome before the coming of Raphael whom, despite the influence he exercised on the younger man, eight years his junior, he came to regard as a dangerous, too successful rival. Comparing the dates of their deaths—Leonardo's in 1519, Raphael's in 1520, and Michelangelo's in 1564—we can see why their paths diverged so widely. All three had shared in the same artistic climate, that of the first two decades of the 16th century, but after the deaths of Raphael and Leonardo, Michelangelo had many long years before him for building up a body of work stamped with his unique personality and a style that was to condition European art for half a century. He lived long enough to see the end of an era, the Renaissance, and the beginning of another, that of Mannerism. When we recall the course of history in 16th-century Italy, we can imagine what it must have meant to start out as Michelangelo did in the cultured atmosphere of Lorenzo's court and, after enjoying the patronage of Julius II, to have to carve out a new career after the fall of the Florentine republic and to bow to the dictates of the then all-powerful Counter-Reformation.

Fundamental to Michelangelo's whole conception of art was the fact that he was born to be a sculptor. Yet his fame rests largely on his frescos and a *magnum opus* in the field of architecture: the paintings in the Sistine Chapel and the dome of St Peter's. When in 1508 he set to work on the Sistine ceiling, he voiced his dissatisfaction in a letter to his father: "Painting is not my profession... I am wasting my time." And in 1547, when appointed chief architect of St Peter's Church, he complained that "architecture was not his trade."

It is noteworthy that, unlike his paintings, a great many of his sculptures were left unfinished. This suggests that he painted because he was compelled to, whereas he did his sculpture to please himself; and, actually, it is in the latter that his highly individual genius reveals itself most fully.

An old tradition has it that he studied in the school of Domenico Ghirlandaio but nothing in his work bears this out. It was from ancient statuary that he derived his ideal of the nude body as a symbol of the perfection of the universe and the harmony of natural forms; from Leonardo that he learnt the significance of movement as at once a force of nature and a law of life. But it was within himself he found that impulse to colossalize all he touched which dominates his art.

In a well-known passage Michelangelo set forth his views on the role of plasticity in art. "I say that painting seems to me all the better, the more it tends towards relief, and relief all the worse the more it tends to the condition of painting." His paintings are the logical outcome of these views. In the *Holy Family* (Uffizi), a tondo painted for Angelo Doni, the sinuous line of the figures is doubtless inspired by Leonardo; yet the rendering of them in illusionist relief, like forms carved in the round, is incompatible with Leonardo's aesthetic. Though the picture deals with a sacred theme, Michelangelo placed two nudes in the background, simply because they satisfied his conception of an harmonious arrangement of the picture surface. Little is known about the *Battle of Cascina* that Michelangelo was commissioned to paint in 1504 on a wall of the great hall of the Municipal Council of Florence, except that he refused to represent a scene of actual fighting. He opted for a group of nude figures in strenuous movement, a pretext for which was furnished by an incident of the battle when the Florentine soldiery was surprised by the enemy in the act of bathing. This work was not carried out and even the preliminary cartoon has disappeared; but we are told that along with Leonardo's *Battle of Anghiari* it constituted, as Vasari puts it, "a lesson for the world." And the scene gave him a welcome opportunity for expressing movement by the tensions of nude forms. Similarly he included nudes in the monument of Julius II (amongst others those wonderful *Slaves* now in the Louvre); in the Sistine ceiling (the *Creation* and the *Drunkenness of Noah*) and, to startling effect, in the *Last Judgment*, where all the figures were naked until the ecclesiastical authorities insisted on having clothes painted on them.

To Michelangelo's thinking, tension and movement were basic to pictorial art, no matter what the subject. This can be seen in his paintings of architectural elements, where the accents are so placed that their presentation has no relation to any system of static weights and thrusts, but is dynamic through and through. And the movement in his painted or sculptured figures is no less forceful; confined within rigorously fixed limits, it is permeated by a sense of terrific strain, an endless struggle to break free. Michelangelo's isolation of the human figure—a sculptural procedure—was diametrically opposed to Leonardo's practice of blending forms into the surrounding atmosphere. In Leonardo's paintings solid objects tend to become atmospheric, whereas in Michelangelo's sky and water harden into stone. Associated with this conception is his rejection of the perspective representation of space. Not that his forms exist *in vacuo*; but the idea of space is conveyed solely by images whose swelling masses presuppose the third dimension. In this respect he cuts the figure of a revolutionary, since one of the 15th-century artists' chief concerns was the rendering of space. Moreover, since space was then regarded as a prerequisite of the delineation of "the real"—indeed as a symbol of the artists' conquest of it—Michelangelo gave the impression of turning his back on reality as well. In any case his cult of the gigantic and his heaven-scaling ambition took the form of a constant, irrepressible urge to transcend reality. This was why he found no satisfaction in the ideal of beauty cherished by the Italians of the Renaissance. Raphael's notion of the beautiful, for example, was based on the art of concealing art, on *sprezzatura*, and could only be realized by an artist at peace with himself, dwelling in an ivory tower. But Michelangelo's ideal was too much bound up with his moral convictions, too passionate, too closely involved in the tragic history of his times, for his art to have an air of effortless ease and not to reflect his spiritual unrest and the catastrophic changes in the world around him.

This will to discover a form of expression superseding both reality and beauty had its roots in a new attitude to art, the total confidence Michelangelo felt in the style he had worked out and his immense pride and faith in his abilities. Similar traits we have already found in Leonardo and Raphael, but in neither case carried to such lengths. For a century the beautiful and the real had engendered masterpieces, but once movement became the artist's chief preoccupation, they were relegated to the lumber-room of dead ideals. Thus Michelangelo paved the way to mannerism.

One of his statues may be regarded as a complete embodiment of his aspirations: his *David*. With this youthful feat he became famous overnight and it is still one of his most popular works. His *David* is a gigantic lad, instinct with energy, poised on the brink of his heroic exploit. We feel that every nerve is on the stretch and the figure of this strapping youth is human power personified. It breathes at once the joyous paganism of Lorenzo's "Garden School," the serene confidence of the Renaissance, its emancipation from medievalism, and the civic pride of the Florentine republic. Yet on its purely artistic merits this statue is inferior to many of Michelangelo's later works.

Basic to the life and art of Michelangelo is an inner conflict, the disquiet of a soul perpetually at odds with itself. True, he sometimes got the better of his divided impulses, but the triumph was short-lived; far from arriving at a definitive solution of his problems, he found them recurring with ever-increasing vehemence. Trained as he had been in Lorenzo's entourage and never weary of declaring his allegiance to the sculpture of antiquity, he was marked out to be a frankly pagan artist—but Michelangelo had an *anima naturaliter christiana*. Moreover he was doubtless greatly exercised by the preaching of Savonarola and that great reformer's prophecies of calamities to come; forebodings that seemed to be confirmed by the advance into Italy of King Charles VIII and his armies. On that occasion he fled to Venice and then to Bologna, where he stayed until the end of 1495.

Michelangelo's successive "escapes" have much to tell us about his strangely complex personality. The first was certainly due to fear. But when in 1506, feeling that Julius II was seeking to humiliate him, he abruptly left Rome, the motive was indignation at such treatment. In 1529, after he had been appointed engineer-in-chief of the fortifications of Florence, foreseeing Malatesta Baglioni's treachery' he fled to Ferrara and thence to Venice; but once the siege had started, he returned to Florence and displayed great courage in the death-struggle that ended in the capitulation of the city. Heroism played an important part in his art and these "flights" may be regarded as sudden breaks in a tension under which his nerves occasionally gave way, though his spirit and morale remained unbroken.

When as a young man he was living in Florence, then by general consent the leading intellectual and cultural center of all Italy, he must have had high hopes for the future. But his rise to fame brought with it new anxieties, intensified when he was called to work at Rome for Julius II, a man as passionate and headstrong as himself, and for Leo X, who had not the faintest inkling of the great artist's spiritual anguish. And how profound must have been his mortification when, after the fall of Florence, he had to work again for the Medici, whose arbitrary rule he had so bitterly resented!

After the Sistine ceiling Michelangelo's life became still more agitated and arduous, despite the vast success of these paintings. Thanks to Raphael's intervention the Pope allowed him to leave Rome. Between 1513 and 1516 he made the *Slaves* for the colossal tomb that Julius intended to have erected for himself; also the *Moses*. After being given a commission for the façade of San Lorenzo he wasted much time collecting the necessary marbles in the quarries, only to find on his return that the project had been abandoned as being too costly. Next he agreed to execute the Medici tombs in the sacristy. Meanwhile there had been the sack of Rome (1527), the restoration of the Florentine republic (1527), and the siege and fall of Florence (1530). Michelangelo, whom Pope Clement VII had taken back into favor, was compelled to work for the very men who had been his enemies of yesterday. Within the seventeen years between the death of Julius II in 1513 and the collapse of the Republic in 1530 fell the most critical phase of Michelangelo's life and art. For Italy, too, these were tragic years, involving as they did the loss of the country's independence, in whose defense Michelangelo had played a valiant part. Then there had come the cleavage between the Catholic Church and Luther's party of Reform. Though the Reformation was suppressed in Italy, the movement, spreading over Europe, fired the enthusiasm of many of the greatest Italian thinkers, amongst them Michelangelo, rebellious as ever. He had a deep affection for Vittoria Colonna, whose spiritual father Bernardino Ochino was, by way of Giulia Gonzaga, in touch with the Spanish reform-minded religious writer Juan de Valdes. But in the event neither Vittoria Colonna nor Michelangelo dared go as far as heresy and with the coming of the Counter-Reformation both acquiesced in it. All the same they were in sympathy with the views of the Italian reformers, views somewhat different from those prevailing in other countries where the Reformation had gained ground. Going back to Savonarola, the Italians declared that Man and God were, spiritually, in direct communion with each other. But they also had a humanist background, which led them to differentiate moral conduct from mystic fervor. The result was that when Calvin sought to organize Protestantism on political lines, he encountered the hostility of the Italian heretics who had taken refuge in Switzerland. For though they had rejected the dogmas of the Roman Catholic Church, they had no wish to adhere to any other form of dogma. Moreover, as Anabaptists, they claimed to sense the presence of God directly as an inner light, and rebelled against all authority, even that of Holy Scripture. Thus they sowed the seeds of the moralistic deism and the "enlightenment" which came to fruition in the 18th century.

It is easy to imagine Michelangelo's spiritual anguish, compelled as he was to serve the Counter-Reformation whose aims were at variance both with his own mystical faith and with that spirit of the Renaissance which had meant all to him in his youth and his distress found poignant expression in his poems of this period.

MICHELANGELO (1475-1564). THE PROPHET JEREMIAH, 1508-1511.
FRESCO, CEILING OF THE SISTINE CHAPEL, VATICAN.

Comparisons have been often, perhaps too often, made with Dante. But the Sistine ceiling does not depict a journey to Hell or to Paradise. Between Dante and Michelangelo humanism had intervened, and what the latter depicted was, rather, a journey into the past, to the origins of the human race. Michelangelo's conception of this journey was strictly ordered; the architectural elements which form its framework underlie the images, acting like the pedestal of some gigantic monument, and it is this that gives the ensemble an atmosphere of repose, even a somewhat abstract quality.

MICHELANGELO (1475-1564). CEILING OF THE SISTINE CHAPEL, 1508-1511. OVEI

He labored on the Sistine Ceiling, his most "finished" work, without a break from 1508 to 1511, and it is not going too far to say that many Italian artists, Raphael to begin with, and many foreign artists too, regarded it as a heaven-sent revelation. When we enter the huge chapel by the door facing the altar we are immediately conscious of a world of difference between the paintings on the ceiling and those on the side walls. Yet barely thirty years had elapsed since the best painters of Central Italy had made the latter. Their works reveal both the artists' scrupulous deference to Holy Writ and a desire to depict biblical episodes realistically and in spatial settings bringing out the perspective relations of objects in a graceful and convincing manner.

But Michelangelo cared nothing for decoration, for the perspective representation of space, for the chapel whose ceiling he was painting, or for traditional interpretations of the Old Testament stories. He subordinated everything—even the wishes of his patron,

-ALL VIEW OF THE FRESCOS. (CA. 45 FT. × 134 FT.) (PHOTO ANDERSON)

the pope—to his insatiable pride and his determination to create a world exclusively his own, a world in which he mingled superhuman figures with architecture of his own devising and arranged them in an order at once symmetrical and more intricate than that in any previous picture. Such was his mastery of the human form and architectural elements that he now could give free expression to his genius, conjuring up a world quite other than the world we know; in no wise mystical, but supremely grandiose, built to an heroic scale. It is sublime in the way that a frenzied uprush of natural forces, a cataclysm can be sublime. Yet this sublimity was, rather, inherent in the mind of Michelangelo, who stamped with his personality every figure, every detail. The biblical allusions are no more than adjuncts to the painter's vision of a grandeur never seen on earth. The Sistine ceiling is of the nature of an epic poem, but its epic quality derives not from the story that is told but from the artist's supercharged imagination.

MICHELANGELO (1475-1564). THE TEMPTATION, 1508-1511.
FRESCO, CEILING OF THE SISTINE CHAPEL, VATICAN.

*Folding plate: General view of the Sistine ceiling.*

The *Prophets* and *Sibyls* are in a class apart. Michelangelo's original intention had been to paint in the center only some architectural elements shored up laterally by figures of apostles seated on thrones, and even in the final version the *Prophets* and *Sibyls* uphold the central panels in which are the historical scenes and the *ignudi*. As a result of this Caryatid-like function they are given proportions that seem gigantic relatively to those of the other figures. All are leaning forward from their thrones; some of them—Zachariah, Joel, Isaiah, the Delphic, Erythrean, Persian and Libyan Sibyls—are so placed that they seem like architectural units. On the other hand, Ezekiel is making a gesture of surprise and Daniel's head, thanks to an opportune patch of shadow, seems to jut forward outside the framework of the picture, while a bold foreshortening separates Jonah from the architectural context.

MICHELANGELO (1475-1564). ESTHER AND AHASUERUS, 1508-1511.
FRESCO, CEILING OF THE SISTINE CHAPEL, VATICAN.

MICHELANGELO (1475-1564). THE LAST JUDGMENT (DETAIL), 1536-1541.
FRESCO, SISTINE CHAPEL, VATICAN.

MICHELANGELO (1475-1564). THE CONVERSION OF ST PAUL (DETAIL), 1542-1545.
FRESCO, CAPPELLA PAOLINA, VATICAN.

To link up the *Prophets* and *Sibyls* with the central zone Michelangelo had to invent a plastic motif corresponding to the projections of the thrones. This is the function assigned to the *ignudi*. Like that of the nudes in the background of the *Holy Family*, their only *raison d'être* is one of illustrating Michelangelo's cherished ideal of the perfection of the nude human body. But they also play a leading part in the pictorial architecture of the whole and Vasari may well have had them in mind when he observed that "Michelangelo was more successful in subordinating the lay-out to the figures than the figures to the lay-out."

The first historical scene Michelangelo painted on the ceiling was the *Deluge*. Here he had not yet settled down into his style; there are frankly realistic elements in the landscape and indications of planes echeloned in depth. Some of the figures, for example the mother and two children on the mountain top and others of the same group, are admirable, but the general effect is unsatisfactory. Michelangelo could conjure up filled but not empty spaces and, above all, he had not the knack of "representation." None the less we owe to him some of the most stupendous plastic creations the world has ever seen, those which made contemporaries speak of the *terribilità* of his art. The plane he worked on was not that of illustration, but an ideal plane of pure forms. Thus while eschewing empty spaces, he had also to avoid the counter-risk of over-crowded compositions. *Noah's Sacrifice* is not one of his most successful works. First of his masterpieces (taken in their chronological order) are the *Temptation* and the *Expulsion of Adam and Eve from Paradise*. The tree which overhangs both scenes, at once dividing them and binding them together in a single decorative rhythm, is a skillfully devised structural element, while the figures have a rare grace, even a touch of femininity seldom found in Michelangelo's work, though it is also present in the *Creation of Eve*. In depicting Eve's sensual beauty, her panic fear when driven from Eden and her poignant invocation of the Father she has offended, Michelangelo reveals the depth and warmth of his human feeling. Most famous of the scenes on the Sistine ceiling is the *Creation of Adam*. Despite the angelic host surrounding God the Father, the two leading figures seem alone. The rising ground behind Adam and the flowing drapery behind his Creator build up zones of darkness stressing the modeling of the figures. The overwhelming tension we sense in them might have been "discharged" in close proximity, but by a brilliant stroke of the creative imagination Michelangelo has limited their contact to the touch of finger on finger. By this rhythmic approach of the two fingers, giving and receiving life, these mighty forms are imbued with a supremely poetic quality, the spiritual significance of the scene takes precedence of its material side, and the fully plastic volumes acquire a purely ideal import. In the *Creation of the Animals*, *God creating the Luminaries*, and the *Division of Light and Darkness*, we have almost an impression that the huge form of God the Father hovering in the upper air is laboring against the pull of gravity; but there is superb power and grandeur in the gesture of the Creator of the Sun, Moon and Stars. In the scene that is a pendant to this, the *Creation of the Plants*, the Creator's muscular body, shown in back view and in strong foreshortening, with willfully exaggerated stresses, brings out the essentially decorative function of Michelangelo's figures. Thus the *Creation of Adam* remains the high point of Michelangelo's art prior to 1511. But the paintings in the lunettes are rich in intimations of the future; sculpturesque effects are subordinated to a wholly pictorial beauty, and we find a variety of colors conspicuously absent in the rest of the ceiling, which seen from a distance seems almost monochrome. Here the elongation of forms foreshadows mannerism, figures melt into the atmosphere and are here and there accented with dramatic *élans* (in the case of Jehovah, for example). All of which suggests that Michelangelo was moving towards "true" painting, even towards Baroque—but this tendency was cut short by his return to sculpture.

In this connection we may recall an observation made not long ago by Clements on the relationship between the art of Michelangelo and the notion of *sprezzatura* formulated by Castiglione and put into practice by Raphael. Unlike the latter Michelangelo had no desire to paint his figures with apparent ease; on the contrary, he wished them to demonstrate that much hard work and mental effort had gone to their making. Disdaining natural facility, he even went out of his way to pile up difficulties, so as to enjoy triumphing over them in the end.

When from the ceiling painted between 1508 and 1511 we turn to the *Last Judgment*, painted between 1536 and 1541 on the wall behind the altar in the Sistine Chapel, we cannot fail to be struck by the many differences between the two works. Here there is no architectural framework binding the scene together; Michelangelo seems to have deliberately discarded everything in the nature of a setting so as to concentrate on the human figure, which under such conditions could enjoy greater freedom of movement and be presented with the maximum dramatic force. Instead of architecture there is an empty expanse of blue-black sky: space without depth or infinite according to the painter's wish. All the figures except that of Christ are arranged in groups articulated in relation to the empty space surrounding them. From the horizontal ledge on which Christ stands, stream down two long clusters of bodies: the Blessed moving towards God and the Wicked hurtling down to hell. These two streams of humanity are linked together by the angels of the Last Judgment.

We must remember that this fresco has reached us in very poor condition and that all the figures, originally nudes, were repainted by the order of Pope Paul IV, between 1555 and 1559, after the Inquisition had accused Michelangelo of leanings towards Lutheranism. So when we seek to understand the part played by the figures in the general effect the artist was aiming at, we have to picture to ourselves how they originally appeared. For by so strongly centralizing and compressing the dramatic elements Michelangelo stepped up the emotive tension of the ensemble; there is none of that sense of relative calm implicit in the figures of the ceiling, due there to the structural lay-out which precluded any extreme displays of feeling. But in the *Last Judgment* he calls on individual gestures to evoke a frenzy of despair. The expressive power of this amazing scene does not derive from an arrangement of pictorial masses; on the contrary, we see an array of separate forms moving like painted statues within the composition. Each gesture expresses the torment of the Damned; this is the end of the world, not Resurrection Day; Christ does not judge but execrates, while the terror-stricken Virgin crouches at His side. This is an apocalypse of universal anguish rather than a Last Judgment. God is pouring the vials of His wrath on all alike and Michelangelo himself, like a fallen Titan rejoicing in the world's catastrophe as a compensation for his own predicament, seems to join forces with this God of vengeance.

In his frescos in the Cappella Paolina, the *Conversion of St Paul* and the *Crucifixion of St Peter*, painted between 1542 and 1550, there is none of this titanic passion. Here all is resignation, even at times indifference. True, the gestures in the *Crucifixion of St Peter* are diversified and balanced in *contrapposto*, but they are, after all, irrelevant. The only stylistic innovation is the use of colors more varied and lustrous than before. Thus towards the close of his career he came to discern the possibilities of Venetian art and what he might have learnt from it.

We can follow the changes coming over his style in the series of superb drawings made for the *Crucifixion*; in them he uses *sfumato* as if he were painting in colors, softening outlines and creating delicate transitions. Here it is almost as if he were talking to himself, expressing his love and compassion for suffering humanity. Michelangelo's insistence on plastic values, his arrogance and paganism, his passionate cult of the grandiose have yielded to the tranquillity of a soul already touched by divine grace. These drawings foreshadow the *Rondanini Pietà* whose sublime immateriality and rejection of plasticity reflect the mood of melancholy acceptance of the human lot that had now descended on this once rebellious soul. Thus in his old age Michelangelo paid heavily for the pride and Promethean fervor of his youth, for the heroic part he played in the great adventure of the Renaissance. But it was for this very reason, the disillusionment that came to him towards the close of his career, that he broke with the Renaissance and became the first modern artist.

Michelangelo's statues are a visual transcription of his changing moods. After the *David* (1501-1504) embodying the pride of youth rejoicing in its strength, he made about eleven years later the *Slaves*, victims of circumstance whose life force has not been extinguished by suffering and bondage. The rebellious young *Slave* in the Louvre might be an avatar of Prometheus Bound. The allegorical figures of the Medici tomb demonstrate the soul's release from its earthly prison. Like the rivers of Hades, *Dawn* and *Twilight*, *Night* and *Day* symbolize man's unescapable destiny, while, beyond the pale of this earthbound life, the image of the Madonna watches over the mortal remains of Giuliano and Lorenzo de' Medici. The allegorical motif derives, apparently, from Plato's *Phaedo*, while the statues were inspired by works of classical antiquity, if at a far remove. The movement vitalizing the nude figures, a tendency to expand forms and that elongation of proportions, with a view to stressing poses which makes the figures so grandly dominate their architectural setting, reveal the artist's dissatisfaction with his earlier achievements. What we have here is not a struggle against rigorously fixed outlines, but a step towards an art set wholly free from linear contours—a tendency that finds its climax in the Madonna, a frozen effigy of grief, yet given a form so sinuous that there is no longer any question of clearly defined circumscribing lines.

MICHELANGELO (1475-1564). THE RONDANINI PIETÀ, 1555-1564. SCULPTURE.
(HEIGHT: 6 FT. 1½ INCHES) CASTELLO SFORZESCO, MILAN.

The major works of sculpture of the final period are a series of Pietàs. In the last of these, the *Rondanini Pietà*, we see all that Michelangelo had now eliminated in his own art and all that he bequeathed to the art of the future. From the *David* to this last *Pietà* he followed a path leading away from the physical to the spiritual, from appearances to the secret workings of the heart, from paganism to Christianity, from representation to expression. And we have a feeling that all the calamities that had befallen Italy were synthesized in this *Pietà*, whose very formlessness is a paradigm, as it were, of that elusive entity, the human soul.

CORREGGIO

The small town of Correggio, from which the painter Antonio Allegri (ca. 1489-1534) took the name by which he is always known, lies in the fertile, climatically favored plain of Emilia. At that time it was under the sway of the Da Correggio family who had had their hour of glory in the 13th and 14th centuries, but by now were little more than country squires who, under unrelenting pressure from the Pope, the Emperor and the great houses of Este and Gonzaga, were hard put to it to retain some semblance of their former power and prestige. During the artist's lifetime the castellan of Correggio was Veronica Gambara (1485-1550), a lady of much intelligence and a poetess highly esteemed by Aretino, Ariosto, Francis I and the Emperor Charles V. However, Correggio never actually worked for the ruling family, though he kept in touch with them and Veronica Gambara made no secret of her admiration for one of his pictures, a *Magdalen*.

Thus like Raphael Correggio came of provincial extraction, but the court of his hometown was far less important and less culturally developed than that of Urbino. No one ever thought of sending the young artist to Rome or Florence; indeed it is doubtful if he ever visited either of these cities. He worked for the churches of the towns of Correggio and Reggio and other places in the neighborhood, but it was in Parma that he created the works which placed him in the front rank of the artists of the day. In 1510 Reggio had been wrested from the Este family, lords of Ferrara, by the Pope, and the same fate befell Parma, which was incorporated in the States of the Church from 1512 to 1531. This being so, Correggio could not benefit by commissions from the Este court, whose protégés, in any case, were Giovanni and Battista Dossi. And it was only relatively late in Correggio's career that Federigo Gonzaga of Mantua became alive to his exceptional gifts and commissioned him to paint a series of mythological scenes depicting the Loves of Jupiter, for presentation to the Emperor Charles V.

Despite the remarkable qualities of these frankly pagan pictures, we must not forget that Correggio spent most of his life painting for convents and provincial churches pictures and frescos with a popular appeal, and that it was to these alone that he owed a worldwide renown that lasted for the next three centuries.

Correggio was shaped by the best artists of the region where he lived. In his youthful works we find echoes of the art of Francesco Bianchi Ferrari (said to have been his

CORREGGIO (CA. 1489-1534). THE ASCENSION (DETAIL), 1520-1524.
FRESCO, CHURCH OF SAN GIOVANNI EVANGELISTA, PARMA. ►

teacher), Lorenzo Costa and Francesco Francia who familiarized him with the glowing colors of 15th-century Ferrarese painting. From the days of Vasari to the present time all writers on Correggio's art have dwelt on the superb quality of his color and there can be no question of the importance of these early contacts with Ferrarese tradition. Nevertheless a young, forward-looking artist can hardly have failed to find Ferrarese draftsmanship outmoded and it is not surprising that Correggio decided to go to Mantua to study Mantegna, then regarded as the best humanist painter of all North Italy and famed for the vigor of his drawing, his knowledge of anatomy and scientific perspective.

All the same the style of his maturity clearly owed more to Leonardo than to the Ferrarese or to Mantegna. Even in the earliest works we can see that his creative imagination led him to aim at effects of light and shade akin to Leonardo's *sfumato*, though treated in a quite personal manner. Did Correggio meet Leonardo and did he have an opportunity of seeing his pictures in Milan and Florence? Though it is still impossible to answer these questions, we need only look at his paintings to see that none understood better than he the lesson of the master, and none so greatly profited by it. For what Correggio took over from Leonardo was not only his *sfumato* but also his feeling for compositional unity, directness of expression, and rapidity of movement —thereby effecting the transition from the 15th to the 16th century.

There is an interesting parallel between the early phases of Correggio's career and Raphael's. Both moved away from provincialism towards the art of the capital, from Quattrocento to Cinquecento style, under Leonardo's guidance. But, after that, their paths diverged since, though starting out from the innovations of Raphael, and above all Michelangelo's, Correggio developed a sweep and a new breadth of treatment in his handling of figures so personal that in his later phase we are hardly conscious of any debt to previous masters. Perhaps the most that can be said is that Correggio's art brings to mind a free interpretation of the color and light of the Sistine ceiling, without the formal and moral rigor or the dramatic complexity of Michelangelo's imagery. Also, while responsive to Raphael's aesthetic harmony and transcendent beauty, he was at a loss when it came to integrating them into his art. For there is no denying that he lacked the noble spirituality of Michelangelo and Raphael; this perhaps is one of the reasons why it has always seemed so difficult to account for the indisputable excellence and attractiveness of his work.

If Correggio's contemporaries praised him to the skies, they often found his work "surprising." Shocked by his technical audacities, one of them went so far as to describe the groups in the dome of Parma Cathedral as "a hash of frogs"! Vasari, a discerning critic, though biased in favor of the mannerism initiated by Michelangelo, was clearly baffled by him. "No one," he writes, "excels him in the handling of colors," and he goes on to extol the sweetness, the *morbidezza* and grace of Correggio's art, his elegant renderings of women's hair, the smiling charm of his angels, the beauty of his landscapes. But he points out and even stresses shortcomings in his drawing, due, he suggests, to the fact that Correggio had the misfortune to be out of touch with Rome and knew nothing of Michelangelo and the art of antiquity.

Thanks, however, to the Carracci's vigorous championship of his work and the high value then attached to their opinion, Correggio's position was unassailable throughout the 17th century. And when the spiritual ferment of that century gave place to the bland, lighthearted skepticism of the 18th, Correggio became the most adulated of all painters—so much so that, writing in 1760, Daniel Webb remarked that he had "put his critics to the blush," and he was hailed, not without reason, as a precursor and a master of rococo.

But time took its revenge in the 19th century, when Correggio was berated by several eminent authorities, amongst them Kluger, Burckhardt and Ruskin. He was accused of wanton sensuality, of failing to achieve "absolute form" and architecturally ordered composition. But against these quite unjustified strictures we may set off the views of the more clear-sighted critics who drew attention to the very real charm of his artistic personality: his humanistic Epicureanism, his touches of whimsy, the suavity of his forms and his gift for expressing the subtlest shades of feeling. Better perhaps than any other writer Riegl has shown a true appreciation of his art when he sees in it a symbol of modern taste reacting against the past, and in the painter a precursor of Baroque. For ancient art depicted *will* that isolates the individual, whereas Correggio depicts *feeling*, which brings him into harmony with his environment and becomes *desire*, which in its turn gives rise to *ecstasy* (religious or erotic).

Correggio painted some small religious pictures before 1514, the year in which he was given the order for a large altarpiece, the *Madonna and St Francis* (Dresden), for the Franciscan church at Correggio. Best of the small pictures is the *Nativity* (Brera, Milan). Here glowing Ferrarese color and clean-cut drawing in the Mantegna manner are merged into a soft penumbra glimmering with the first rays of daybreak, while forms are rendered with an extreme lightness of touch, as though not to ruffle the silence enveloping the Child. In the far distance the sky is beginning to brighten. This subordination of the figures to an over-all play of light and shade certainly derives from Leonardo, but in Correggio's case it does not serve any "scientific" purpose. What, on the contrary, he is aiming at is the expression of quite homely feelings, too spontaneous to be sentimental, too everyday to be religious. Nor do the angels fluttering in the air, an alcove reminiscent of a Roman edifice and a pillar serve to give this placidly domestic scene the air of a sublime event. Perhaps it was because he wished to transpose the sacred narrative on to the level of a folktale that Correggio linked together—for the first time, as Emile Mâle has pointed out—the "Nativity" and the "Adoration of the Magi," a juxtaposition of popular iconographic themes often resorted to by later painters. In the *Madonna and St Francis*, one can feel that this was the artist's first venture into the field of large-scale composition; the parts tend to break away from the whole, to the detriment of the over-all unity of the scene. Some traits of 15th-century art persist, but there is a keener feeling for the monumental and for movement, and space is more freely rendered. This is very different from Mantegna's representations of the Madonna and Saints, and there is no trace of his architectonic order in the lay-out. Nor do we find as yet the well-knit unity of expression that Correggio

CORREGGIO (CA. 1489-1534).
MADONNA WITH THE MAGDALEN AND ST JEROME, CA. 1527-1528. (80 ½ × 55 ½″) PINACOTECA, PARMA.

was later to attain. But the Virgin and Child are wonderfully graceful figures, while the throbbing colors have a new intensity.

Some years later Correggio decorated the Camera di San Paolo (the Abbess's room) in the Convent of St Paul at Parma. In it he depicted a sort of pergola hung with garlands, a motif taken from Leonardo's decorations in the Sala delle Asse of the Castello Sforzesco in Milan, but treated here more fancifully, with small oval windows through which cupids are peeping. These tiny figures play much the same part as Michelangelo's *ignudi*. But unlike the latter, they are mere whimsies, though such is their verve and playful grace that we forget they serve no functional purpose. Similarly the trellis of the pergola is upheld by shell-shaped lunettes containing allegorical fantasies. Their subjects are culled from mythology, but interpreted so freely as to seem mere *jeux d'esprit*. Some female nudes, draperies and tracts of exquisitely suave color are other engaging features of this mythological extravaganza. Above the fireplace is a picture of Diana paying homage to the chastity of the Abbess —clearly, if humanism was in favor at the Convent of St Paul, it was not taken overseriously but romantically, not to say light-heartedly, and it was in this spirit that Correggio chose to interpret it.

The cupola fresco in the Benedictine church of San Giovanni at Parma, made between 1520 and 1524, shows a distinct advance. The style is broader, even monumental, though without any diminution of the liveliness and gaiety distinctive of Correggio's art. Here he realized his conception of the *beau idéal*, a conception less exalted than Raphael's owing to his undisguised delight in sensual appeal. The figure of James the Less may be regarded as one of the first embodiments of this ideal. In a small lunette painted in foreshortening he portrayed St John the Evangelist in Patmos; owing to the position and dimensions of the lunette the figure seems to be lunging forward out of its architectural setting and the driving force behind this movement produces a strange impression of spiritual power. Illusionism, perhaps, but illusionism of a kind that justifies itself triumphantly. It is certain that the Cinquecento painters had no trouble in painting certain objects with a verisimilitude that deceived the eye—a case in point is the painted tapestry in the Vatican which visitors regularly took for real tapestry—but Correggio employed no purely material *trompe-l'œil* devices of this kind. Though his religious feelings went no deeper than a superficial, unthinking acquiescence in the Christian verities and legendry, these feelings were sufficiently active and vital to hoodwink beholders into thinking that the bodies he so lovingly painted in his religious scenes were endowed with lofty spiritual significance. The subject treated in the cupola of San Giovanni is the *Ascension*. A highly skillful foreshortening of Christ's body brings out the infinite blue void above the clouds, while the glorious nature of the event, the triumph of their Master, is reflected in the happy faces of the apostles young and old. There are few figures and each is strongly individualized. Here, too, Correggio has solved the problem of giving the illusion of boundless space solely by his handling of figures, but it must be admitted that he lacks Mantegna's constructive sense, as revealed in the Bridal Chamber of the Ducal Palace at Mantua.

So much admired was the *Ascension*, both for its novelty and its beauty, that the Chapter of Parma Cathedral invited the artist to paint the dome of the Cathedral. The subject set was the *Assumption of the Virgin*, and the work took him four years (1526-1530). The dome being much larger, the painter realized that he could better convey the impression of infinite space by refraining from defining the plastic qualities of individual bodies and by merging figures into a swirling throng levitated in a vast ascending movement. This movement is suggested by different zones of light superimposed one upon the other up to the open sky, and seconded by color gradations. Correggio subordinated the human figure to pictorial construction in terms of light, starting out from the apostles nearest to the earth, pouring up through the clouds and glancing across the angels and the soaring

CORREGGIO (CA. 1489-1534). ANTIOPE, CA. 1531. (74¾×38¾") LOUVRE, PARIS.

CORREGGIO (CA. 1489-1534). MADONNA WITH THE MAGDALEN AND ST JEROME (DETAIL),
CA. 1527-1528. PINACOTECA, PARMA.

CORREGGIO (CA. 1489-1534). DANAË (DETAIL), CA. 1531.
GALLERIA BORGHESE, ROME.

figure of the Virgin, towards the Light supreme of Godhead. Here he gave expression to an ecclesiastical ideal and this may explain why the Parma dome was adopted as the model of all Baroque decoration.

The early *Nativity* and the dome of Parma Cathedral represent the two extremes of Correggio's approach to religious art; the former is like a simple melody, the latter like the finale of a symphony scored for full orchestra. Between these limits are several Madonnas, all grace and suavity: the *Campori Madonna* (Modena), the *Madonna of the Basket* (National Gallery, London), the *Virgin and Child* (Uffizi), and the *Mystical Marriage of St Catherine* (Louvre). One of the best altarpieces is the *Madonna with the Magdalen and St Jerome* (Parma) where the transversal composition links up the figures as in a *sacra conversazione*. The Magdalen's gesture as she bends her cheek towards the Child is a delightful touch, poetic and tinged with sensuous appeal. The *Madonna della Scodella* (Parma) and *Night* (Dresden) are charming interpretations of sacred scenes treated in a pleasantly homely way. But Correggio was less successful in altarpieces whose themes lent themselves to decoration only; in such cases—in, for example, the *Madonna and St Sebastian* and the *Madonna and St George* (Dresden)—all seems artificial and contrived. Nor was he capable of representing a dramatic scene, as is quite plain in the *Deposition*. In it he drew inspiration from some earlier work, perhaps a Gothic prototype, that seemed to offer possibilities for a "modern" re-interpretation; unfortunately his attempt to combine the physical signs of mental anguish with the gracious charm that is the keynote of his art led to untoward results, a sort of parody of grief.

Federigo Gonzaga, or his mother Isabella d'Este, was happily inspired when he or she gave Correggio an order for a series of pictures on mythological themes. *Antiope* (Louvre), *Danaë* (Rome), *Leda* (Berlin) and *Io* (Vienna) are perfect of their kind; in them the artist had themes exactly suited to his temperament. In Parma Cathedral he achieved an ecstatic vision sublime in its own right and not as a religious revelation. The same is true of *Io*. *Danaë* and *Leda* are pagan through and through, yet there is something more, something not due exclusively to lovely colors and enchanting landscapes. In no scene of antiquity do we find this special grace, a recall or an echo as it were of the divine grace latent in this fine artist's soul. Thus even the frankly pagan pictures have a Christian undertone. In *Io* the milky white of the nude blends into the cooler grey of the clouds, while a smoothly flowing arabesque and highlights on the body give the composition an harmonious unity. In *Danaë* the whiteness of the body, welling up from a dark background, seems gradually to overflow the picture surface, giving the figure the soft translucence of an ivory bas-relief. In *Leda* the tale of Leda and the swan is presented as a holiday outing in the country, organized by some attractive maidens. Delightfully natural, it illustrates one of the lighter sides of Renaissance life.

For three centuries art lovers admired and enjoyed the paintings in the Parma dome. Meanwhile, however, the picture sequence of the *Loves of Jupiter*, secluded from the public eye in palaces, seems to have been ignored, one of the reasons being the alleged "impropriety" of these enchanting scenes—scenes in which, for once, Correggio felt free to indulge, without constraint or qualms of conscience, his natural instincts.

# THE RENAISSANCE IN GERMANY

ALBRECHT DÜRER (1471-1528). PORTRAIT OF A YOUNG MAN, 1500. (11 × 8 ¼″)
ALTE PINAKOTHEK, MUNICH.

# 2

## FROM DÜRER TO HOLBEIN

By the time Leonardo, Raphael and Michelangelo had embarked on their careers, they had behind them a full century of humanism; and not only had the works of classical antiquity come under careful observation, but (what was even more important) a mathematical theory of art practice had been drawn up. By an intensive study of what then were called "measurements" (i.e. geometry and perspective), the humanists had placed art on a scientific basis, and stressed the superiority of the mental equipment essential to the artist as against the mere craftsman or artisan.

In the preface to his book published in Nuremberg in 1525 and entitled *Underweysung der Messung* (Instruction in Measurement), Albrecht Dürer wrote: "Until now many gifted young painters have been shaped in Germany without any theory of art and guided solely by the light of daily experience. They have sprouted up like wild plants, untouched by the gardener's hand. Though some by constant practice have acquired facility and produced works that, if arbitrary and irrational, possess a certain power, all understanding painters have deplored their blindness. It is clear that with their deftness of hand and great experience in handling color our German painters have developed remarkable proficiency, but they lack the science of measurements." This, according to Dürer, had been discovered by the Italians, in the light of the art of antiquity, two centuries before; in point of fact, Brunelleschi had worked out the laws of pictorial perspective about a century before Dürer wrote these words.

But, needless to say, there is far more to art than "measurements." Grünewald, who knew nothing of them, was a superb painter and if Dürer achieved greatness, this was not because he had studied geometry and perspective at Bologna (relatively late in life, as it so happened). Despite his enthusiasm for the discoveries of the Italian Renaissance, Dürer still belonged temperamentally to the Middle Ages, to which even more conspicuously Grünewald also belonged. Indeed it has recently been suggested that the latter deliberately reverted to the idealistic art of an earlier age; an hypothesis perhaps uncalled for, since in the Low Countries, where under the lead of Van Eyck and his disciples a great art had developed at the beginning of the 15th century, life still went to a medieval rhythm for the next hundred years and more.

In any case there was so prodigious a flowering of art in Germany during the early 16th century that this country vied with Italy for supremacy in Europe. A great religious revival had taken place a century earlier and, with it, despite political dissensions, had come a new, if ill-defined, awareness of man's moral and intellectual possibilities. Whereas in the 14th there had been few German universities, many were founded in the following century—at Leipzig, Greifswald, Freiburg, Ingolstadt, Tübingen and elsewhere—and some of these displayed a lively interest in the humanistic conceptions that were making good in Italy. Nevertheless the German people was still at the mercy of provincial overlords and the Empire still too weak to protect its liberties. Thus, from the end of the 15th century on, there were frequent revolts against the authority of the local princes, while the harshness of ecclesiastical taxation fomented religious unrest. The result was that when in 1517 Martin Luther nailed his famous Theses to the door of the Castle Church at Wittenberg, while the élite saw in this no more than an incident in some sectarian dispute, the populace at large knew better, as did the shopkeepers and artisans.

When we study the artistic climate of Germany during this period, we find that, after the definitive establishment of Lutheranism in several parts of the country, aesthetic activity soon declined. But there were good reasons why, in the years when Luther was in active conflict with the Empire and the Papal See, German art rose to heights it had never previously attained.

From the viewpoint of the modern historian and in time's perspective, Luther's protestantism is seen to be no more than a return to the theological conceptions of the Middle Ages; there was little really new in his doctrines. But the German artists did not trouble their heads with theology. It was Luther's driving force, his popular appeal, his revolt against the malpractices and highhandedness of the civil and ecclesiastical powers that fired the enthusiasm of both populace and artists. None the less, once protestantism had crystallized into a system of dogmas, bigoted for all their novelty, the artists' inspiration seemed to dry up at the source.

During the 14th century mysticism had swept over Germany, especially in the days of Johann Eckhart (ca. 1260-1327) whose writings were condemned by the authorities because they advocated direct communion with God, independently of the Church. All the same Eckhart exercised considerable influence not only on heretical sects but also on orthodox believers, while by way of that profound thinker Nicholas of Cusa (1401-1464) humanist culture gave a philosophical turn to the mystical aspirations of the age. Nicholas held that God can be apprehended by intuition, an exalted state of the intellect in which all earthly limitations cease to function. He extolled the "simpleton," that is to say the unschooled layman who does not read or write but, like the first fathers of the race, studies the works of nature, God's book, with an understanding eye. Thus he heralded the transition from medieval mysticism to modern empiricism, and he is known to have influenced Leonardo's thought.

We find a similar attitude in Albrecht Dürer and this explains both his predilection for the imagery of medieval tradition and his feverish quest, in drawing after drawing, of an ever fuller understanding of the natural world. His leanings towards mysticism and his strong moral sense led him to approve of Luther. In 1520 he wrote: "If some day God vouchsafes me to meet Doctor Martin Luther, I shall make his portrait from the life with the utmost care and engrave it on copper, so as to perpetuate the memory of the Christian man who did so much to deliver me from a great affliction of the soul." And when a report went round that Luther had been imprisoned, Dürer, not knowing that this rumor was a feint, voiced his grief with passionate sincerity. "O God in heaven, have mercy on us; Lord Jesus, pray for thy people and succor us in our hour of need. I beg you, all good Christians, to join with me in pitying this man inspired by God and praying Him to send us another man enlightened as he was. O Erasmus of Rotterdam... mark how the foul tyranny of worldly might and the powers of darkness prevail in the land. Listen, O Knight of Christ, take horse and ride at our Lord's side, defend the truth and win the martyr's crown." It may seem strange that Dürer should couple Erasmus and Luther in this way, but this confusion of ideas reflects the state of mind of many Germans at the time. They resented the authority of the Church of Rome because it was something alien and incomprehensible, and also because of a conviction —not altogether unfounded—that it was corrupt. But what they wanted was a reform of the Church, not open war with it, and highly as they thought of Luther, his intransigence dismayed them. Hence the popularity of the great humanist Philip Melanchthon (1497-1560) who, while alive to the moral justifications of Luther's crusade, hoped to effect a compromise with the Catholic Church on the basis of humanism—which of course meant nothing to Luther. To Melanchthon's thinking, as Panofsky has pointed out, Dürer's style bore the marks of the *genus grande* (of the art of Rhetoric), Grünewald's of the *genus mediocre*, and Cranach's of the *genus humile*. This classification obviously derives from Aristotle's *Poetics* in which poets and painters are divided into three categories according as they "imitate" men superior to ourselves, inferior to ourselves or similar to ourselves.

Today, no doubt, many see in Grünewald a far greater artist than Dürer. But, as a good humanist, Melanchthon regarded as the "grand manner" that which approximated most closely to the classical; and this, as was only to be expected, he discerned in the art of Dürer, who sought to interpret even the protestant revolution in terms of humanism. But every revolution ends by going to extremes, and when, to safeguard protestantism, Luther allied himself with the temporal powers, the Anabaptists stirred up the nation to revolt. They advocated a way of life in strict accordance with the Gospels, a sort of Utopian communism, and total submission to that inner voice which kept the individual in constant touch with God. Such was the origin of the Peasants' War in South Germany.

In 1526 Dürer completed the *Four Apostles*, which he dedicated to the Town Council of Nuremberg, his native town. On these panels he inscribed extracts from the Gospels and a brief homily bearing on the political and religious crisis of the day. "In these perilous times it behoves all civil authorities to be mindful of their duty of withstanding human temptations and hearkening to the voice of God alone. God forbids that anything should be added to or substracted from His Word." This was a warning against the Anabaptists. For though Dürer was ready to give the religious revival his moral support, he refused to follow the zealots when it came to destroying humanist culture.

With Grünewald it was quite otherwise. After the Anabaptists had been expelled from Seligenstadt where he lived, he was deprived of his office of Court Painter—which suggests that he had been involved with the extremists. He now took refuge with the protestant community at Halle, then at daggers drawn with the archbishopric, and it was there he died in 1528, the same year as Dürer. In the inventory of his estate mention is made of a "seditious document," which was in fact a declaration in favor of certain citizens accused of fraternizing with the rebels. And the difference between the attitudes of Grünewald and Dürer towards the Reformation throws light on the part played by humanism in Germany.

GRÜNEWALD

The artist's first biographer, Joachim von Sandrart, writing in 1675, describes him as "Matthaeus Grünewald, commonly known as Matthaeus von Aschaffenburg." While stressing the painter's vast renown, he admitted that, to his regret, only the scantiest information about him was available. Since then, however, documents have been unearthed showing that his real name was Mathis Neithardt-Gothardt. The name "Grünewald" never appears, but in view of its general acceptance, it has always been retained. Sandrart seems equally unreliable as regards the birthplace he assigns to Grünewald. Probably he was born at Würzburg somewhere between 1455 and 1460. According to some authorities his earliest extant work is the portrait of a young man, to all appearance an art student, engaged in drawing; this bears the monogram M N, suggesting that it may be a self-portrait. However, its ascription to Grünewald is hazardous. In 1485 Mathis Neithardt was living in the Bishop's Palace at Aschaffenburg (this shows that he was older than Dürer), where he had Canon Heinrich Reitzmann for his friend and patron. In 1490 he left Aschaffenburg and went to work as a sculptor at Worms. In 1501 he was enrolled as a citizen and master artist at Seligenstadt near Aschaffenburg, where in 1510 he supervised the rebuilding of the castle, his official designation being "Master of Works and Painter in Ordinary to the Prince Elector" (Archbishop Uriel von Gemmingen). Before this he had painted, about 1503, the *Christ Scorned* at Munich and, about 1505, the Basel *Crucifixion*. Records show that a son, Andreas, was born to him in 1512. About this time he was commissioned by Guido Guersi, Superior of the Antonian convent church at Isenheim, to paint the polyptych at present in the Musée d'Unterlinden at Colmar. Begun about 1512, this gigantic work was completed three years later. Meanwhile Grünewald also worked at Seligenstadt where (according to Reitzmann) he was in 1514 and again in 1516. A year later and again in 1519 he was employed as Superintendent of Works at Aschaffenburg, and in 1520 he entered the service of Archbishop Albrecht of Mainz who had formed a humanist center there. In that year he attended the coronation of Charles V at Aachen, where he met Dürer.

Led by Goetz von Berlichingen (immortalized by Goethe in his play of the same name) the peasants occupied Aschaffenburg and Seligenstadt, but in 1525 Albrecht of Mainz expelled them. His recovery of power was followed by savage reprisals and Grünewald had to leave. He moved to Frankfort in 1526 and found employment there

MATTHIAS GRÜNEWALD (BEFORE 1460-1528). CRUCIFIXION, 1512-1515. (105 ¾ × 120 ¾″)
CENTRAL PANEL OF THE ISENHEIM ALTARPIECE. MUSÉE D'UNTERLINDEN, COLMAR.

MATTHIAS GRÜNEWALD (BEFORE 1460-1528). CRUCIFIXION, DETAIL: ST JOHN THE EVANGELIST, THE VIRGIN AND MARY MAGDALEN, 1512-1515. ISENHEIM ALTARPIECE. MUSÉE D'UNTERLINDEN, COLMAR.

as an hydraulic engineer; next year, perhaps because he felt unsafe in the atmosphere of persecution then prevailing in that city, he moved to Halle where he had trusted friends. He died in 1528.

This outline of the facts of Grünewald's life, brief and perhaps over-simplified though it is, illustrates one of the facets of his curious personality. Much esteemed as a fine craftsman, as an hydraulic engineer and as one of the leading German painters, he nevertheless failed, or declined, to win a high place in the social order of the day, the reason being his intense religious zeal and his devotion to his divine Master. To his mind, the revolting peasants were the true successors of the ancient martyrs—and such a view was bound to tell against his worldly success. He died a poor man, leaving to his heirs only a few "banned" books and his paint brushes.

The origin of his mystical preoccupations has been traced to the "Revelations" of the 14th-century saint, Bridget of Sweden, whose works had a great vogue in Germany

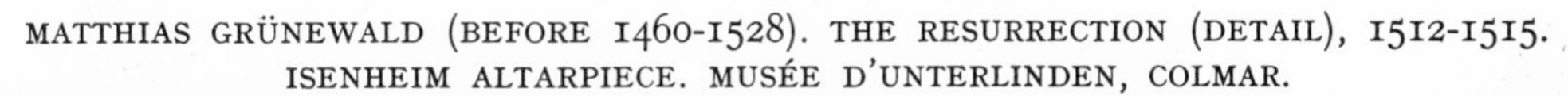

MATTHIAS GRÜNEWALD (BEFORE 1460-1528). THE RESURRECTION (DETAIL), 1512-1515.
ISENHEIM ALTARPIECE. MUSÉE D'UNTERLINDEN, COLMAR.

at the beginning of the 16th century. Her poetic images have sometimes an expressive power approximating them to Grünewald's creations. St Bridget's invocation of Christ on the Cross is a case in point. "The hair and beard were steeped in the blood flowing from the wounds inflicted on the Sacred Head. The bones, hands and feet of the most precious Body were cruelly cleft asunder. So brutally wast Thou scourged and scored with agonizing wounds that Thy innocent flesh and skin were torn and lacerated till the agony was past enduring. Thus didst Thou suffer for us, O Man of Sorrows!"

And no less impassioned is her invocation of the Virgin: "Thy brows and eyelids excel in splendor the sun's rays... Let the beauty of thy thrice-holy cheeks be lauded more than the roseate effulgence of the dawn. Praised be the sacred mouth and soft lips fairer than the beauty of roses and all flowers. Let thy sacred arms and hands and fingers be blessed and revered eternally, more than the costliest gems... Let thy most precious breast be lauded more than the purest gold; when the hammer strokes echoed in thy bosom and thy heart was wrung as though clenched in a vice, how cruel was thy agony!"

Such is the realism, such the instancy of her visions, that the saint does not scruple to dwell on all the parts of the body with a view to glorifying their several functions and redemptive virtues. And so as to transcend the material and attain a realm of spiritual values, she never specifies the *form* of what she is describing, but pictures it in terms of color and radiant light. To ascend from the world of matter to the celestial plane—that was the Swedish mystic's aspiration, and Grünewald's too.

So preponderant is the part played by the Isenheim Altarpiece (1512-1515) in Grünewald's œuvre that we have thought it best to devote our attention chiefly to this masterwork of 16th-century art. It is divided into three independent parts. (1) *The Crucifixion,* flanked by *St Anthony* and *St Sebastian,* with *The Entombment* on the predella. (2) *The Virgin adored by Angels,* flanked by *The Annunciation* and *The Resurrection.* (3) *The Apotheosis of St Anthony* (sculpture) with *The Hermits Anthony and Paul in Converse* and *The Temptation of St Anthony* on the side-panels.

One of the first things that strike us in this altarpiece as a whole is the artist's obvious disregard for architectonic lay-out and uniformity in the representation of the various scenes. In the first part, for instance, though the two saints on the lateral panels are depicted symmetrically and each is posted on a marble pedestal, one is placed higher than the other and only one of the wings has a landscape background. In the second group there is a still greater discrepancy, the rendering of space in the *Annunciation* being entirely different from that in the *Resurrection* where the scene is depicted wholly on the surface—or, what comes to much the same thing, in undefined or infinite depth. In the *Virgin adored by Angels,* the central picture of the second triad, no visual relationship exists between the figure of the Virgin on the one hand and the group of angels and the building on the other.

The images, then, do not compose a "represented" scene; rather, they are "presented" independently. This lack of visual unification and ordered structure brings the time factor into prominence. For Grünewald gave little thought to that spatial unity which, created by the Florentines in the early 15th century, conditioned all Italian art. True, Grünewald was not ignorant of linear perspective, but we have only to look at the *Annunciation* to realize that his way of seeing was still essentially Gothic, though associated, in his case, with humanism. For the figures are by no means Gothic; they have the immediacy, the forcibleness, the anatomical expressionism, the factual reality characteristic of Renaissance art; and, in particular, its light effects.

Thus there is a disharmony between the general conception of this altarpiece and the painter's handling of its diverse elements. Yet so powerful is Grünewald's creative genius that he turns what might have proved a handicap or blemish into a constructive factor and to deplore the lack of co-ordination would be idle pedantry. The *raison d'être* of this unorthodox composition is the state of high emotional pressure at which Grünewald worked; he put himself, heart and soul, into every figure he portrayed with an intensity unparalleled in the history of art.

Bürger has rightly pointed out that in Grünewald's painting bodies *per se* play a secondary role; gestures count for more. This is also true of Gothic painting and sculpture, but though here the expressive quality of gestures is no less intense than in the work of the great Gothic artists, bodies are far more in evidence. In other words the conflicting claims of the spiritual and the material are reconciled in a continuous dramatic tension implicit in the artist's style, not an extraneous factor deriving from the subject, and that "cosmic" smile we glimpse now and again in the *Virgin adored by Angels* signifies for Grünewald something no less poignant than the grief of the mourners over the dead Christ.

The dramatic tension mentioned above is particularly apparent in the drawings. In a study for *Peter the Apostle* (Dresden), Peter sinks to the ground praying for mercy, dazed by an unseen light—unseen because it shines within the soul alone. In the *Kneeling Virgin* (Berlin) where, probably owing to the apparition of the archangel bringing the glad tidings, the Virgin has abruptly stopped reading, the figure seems to have no body; all we see is a complex of sinuous lines purporting to render hair and garments but actually expressing Mary's awed amaze. And in the *St Dorothy* (Berlin), a study for the lost altarpiece of Mainz Cathedral, the linear rhythms giving movement to the figure build up an effulgence so intense as to translate it into the "world of light" glimpsed by the mystics of all ages.

Again, in the Isenheim *Crucifixion*, it is the figures alone that hold our gaze and we hardly notice the landscape dwindling into darkness like a vision of infinite space from which emerge the figures, grandiose presences suddenly materialized out of the ambient air. Christ's body is heavy and, though nailed to the Cross, seems to be sagging earthwards. His flesh a mass of hideous wounds. As against this macabre scene, the Magdalen cuts an almost childish figure with her hair streaming over her pink dress, as she invokes the dead Savior. No bigger than a little girl's, her stature is out of scale with that of the other figures, and the color of the dress is almost gay, yet proportions and colors alike combine to give the maximum emotional intensity to her cry of lamentation. Still more impressive are the juxtaposed figures of the Virgin and St John.

The Virgin's white dress billows out unconfined by contour-lines, and contrasting with the Evangelist's red robe, this patch of white shines forth, fluid, impalpable, almost weightless. Here we have a visual "effect" defying analysis but singularly impressive.

In the *Virgin adored by Angels*, the Virgin is the focal point of a whole cataract of wonderfully luminous colors. The angels are singing and the light, too, sings. The colors do not harmonize with the light and this is as it should be; a concord would bring peace, and here everything is rushing heavenward, straining towards an ecstasy transcending earthly joy. Grünewald has given loving care to the decoration of the chapel; he has included an (unaccountable) crowned saint in the scene and even inserted a bed, a vase—and a bucket! Perhaps these touches of homely realism were meant to counterbalance the almost overpowering joy of the celestial hosts.

The *Annunciation* is the most "rational" panel of the altarpiece. Here colors and light harmonize, space is well defined, the figures behave in a reasonable way—and by the same token Grünewald's peculiar charm is missing. But in the *Resurrection* he once more let his teeming imagination have its way. At the bottom of the picture sleeping soldiers sprawl, bathed in an unearthly light, while vividly colored draperies stream up above the tomb, following and covering the body of the ascending Lord. In *The Hermits Anthony and Paul in Converse* the figures of the saints are beautifully done; Anthony radiant with light and joy, full of vitality, and Paul the Hermit old, decrepit, his bony fingers withered by long privations. The landscape is all in jagged spikes, a scene of ghoul-haunted desolation like that which shows St Anthony assailed by a horde of hideous monsters, so grotesque as to be unconvincing.

But this indifference to plausibility was Grünewald's way; as early as 1503 or thereabouts in the *Christ Scorned* (Munich), he had shown that the spiritual significance of his subject was his chief concern. Here the cruelty depicted is on the moral rather than the physical plane. Though there are traces of inexperience in this picture, his style has already taken form. Nearly two decades later, in the Munich *Sts Maurice and Erasmus* (1520-1522), we find a new feeling for the monumental, while the wealth of colors and brilliant highlights create the atmosphere of a scene in some old legend. Here Grünewald gave free rein to his amazing virtuosity in his rendering of the light reflected on Saint Maurice's armor, while no less striking is his portrayal of the brown, negroid face. And in the harrowing *Crucifixion* (Washington), the face of the Evangelist is truly unforgettable.

In the church of Stuppach near Mergentheim (Württemberg) is a *Virgin* dated 1519, in every way worthy of the *Virgin* of the Isenheim Altarpiece. She is smiling and a rainbow replaces the conventional aureole. It was St Bridget who had put into the Virgin's mouth the words: "Prayers hover above the world like the rainbow in the clouds," and as Benesch has pointed out, this many-colored radiance linking up the Virgin with the sky is an emblem of the union of the earthly paradise and heaven.

These pictures may perhaps be described as "commentaries" on Grünewald's supreme achievement, the Isenheim Altarpiece. They go to prove that his power lay above all in that sense of a world beyond reality which enabled him to spiritualize all he touched and to imbue even a smiling sky with strangely dramatic tension.

MATTHIAS GRÜNEWALD (BEFORE 1460-1528). THE VIRGIN ADORED BY ANGELS, 1512-1515.
(105¾ × 120¾″) ISENHEIM ALTARPIECE. MUSÉE D'UNTERLINDEN, COLMAR.

**DÜRER** Albrecht Dürer was born at Nuremberg in 1471. Son of a goldsmith, he began by following his father's profession; next, he studied painting under Michael Wolgemut, from 1486 to 1490. At the end of his apprenticeship he started on the usual *Wanderjahre* of the German student. His original plan was to go to Colmar to complete his studies under Martin Schongauer, but he spent a year and a half traveling about Germany (where exactly is not known) and when early in 1492 he reached his destination, it was to learn that the Colmar master had died shortly before. After making a name for himself as a wood-engraver at Basel, then a leading center for the publication of books illustrated with woodcuts, he moved to Strasbourg. In 1494 he went back to Nuremberg and soon after his return got married. The marriage was not a success, as his wife, who was both strait-laced and parsimonious, objected to her husband's devoting so much time to mathematics and humanistic studies (his closest friend was the local humanist Willibald Pirckheimer) instead of attending to his "trade." Their difference of opinion illustrates in a homely way the contrast between the medieval tradition of the artisan and Dürer's determination, by dint of sheer hard work, to attain the status of a Renaissance artist.

Soon after his marriage he went to Venice where he stayed until the spring of 1495, visiting meanwhile other North Italian cities. A remark made by him at this time shows how much store he set on Italian art and how keen was his desire to participate in the Renaissance movement: "In the last century and a half the Italians have uncovered and exploited what had been hidden for a thousand years." He went to Venice a second time in 1505, staying there until 1507. By then he was no longer the unknown painter of his first sojourn but acclaimed as a great master. The German community in Venice gave him a commission for an altarpiece; he was made much of by the nobility and struck up a friendship with Giovanni Bellini whom of all the Venetian painters he most admired. Dürer spent some time in other towns, and at Bologna he gave careful study to the Italian methods of rendering perspective and proportions.

When in Nuremberg, between these two stays in Italy, he devoted all his time and energy to engraving. On his return from his second journey he studied foreign languages as well as mathematics, preparatory to the writing of his big treatise on the theory of art (published in 1525). In 1512 he was given commissions for various kinds of work by the Emperor Maximilian who until his death (in 1519) continued to patronize him. Between 1520 and 1521 Dürer made his last long journey, this time to Aachen, its object being to secure from the new Emperor, Charles V, a continuance of his pension. He was handsomely received and his request was granted. After his return to Nuremberg, his health began to fail, and he died in 1528.

It was thanks to Dürer that first the tastes and then the theories of the Italians became acclimatized in the German-speaking lands and it was he who familiarized his fellow countrymen with the new conception of art as a means to knowledge. For aside from his creative impulse, Dürer had an insatiable interest in natural phenomena of all kinds, in scientific and religious problems, and he was the first and perhaps the only German who was something of a "universal genius" of the type exemplified by Leonardo.

Though Dürer's art is essentially Germanic, Vasari was convinced of his Flemish origin, the reason being that he could not bring himself to believe that any great nordic painters existed outside Flanders. "If," he wrote, "this singular and universal artist had been a native of Tuscany instead of Flanders and could he have studied as we have the treasures of Rome, he would have excelled us all, as he is now the finest and most esteemed of all the Flemings."

We have already spoken of Dürer's feelings about Luther, and it should here be pointed out that it was thanks to the climate of the early Reformation that the artist was able to voice his most profound convictions. Believing as he did in an "illumination from within," his aspiration to an absolute was a necessary consequence of his religious faith. Yet this conflicted with a no less imperative will to the expression of form, linking up with the desire for an objective understanding of reality that was the result of his Italian sojourn. Hence that inner conflict which persisted throughout his career and which accounts for his hostility to the real, his intolerance of those canons of "measurement" or proportion to which nevertheless he had vowed allegiance. Sometimes, in his most successful works, he succeeded in reconciling these anomalies. But these favored moments were sporadic; usually he was dissatisfied with his productions, and his temperamental restlessness, his eagerness to explore all that differed from himself and his environment led him to strike out continually in new directions. As already mentioned, there was a strain of the fantastic in his make-up, and though what won him Europe-wide fame in his own time was the technical perfection of his means, it is his indefatigable spirit of enquiry that makes him seem so near to us today.

Doubtless one of the reasons why Dürer wrote his treatises was a desire to clarify his views on art, but we must not forget that such yearnings for an absolute and a taste for pedagogy are innate in the German temperament. His *Underweysung der Messung* (Instruction in Measurement) is dated 1525, his "Treatise on the Fortifications of Cities, Towns and Castles" was published in 1527 and his "Treatise on Human Proportions" (posthumously) a year later. When he made his second journey to Venice, Dürer, like other northern painters, was already acquainted with the rules of perspective. But none of the northerners had as yet any notion of what Dürer himself styled *Kunst*, art *qua* art, as distinct from questions of technique. The novelty of this conception, sponsored by the Italians, lay in the fact that it was more concerned with painting itself than with the observation of nature. It stood for the *perspectiva artificialis* as against *perspectiva naturalis*, while enjoining what was called the "correct construction" of all three-dimensional objects, including the human body. Thus, for him, the theory of proportions depended on that of perspective also. When Dürer returned from his second stay in Italy he had learnt at Bologna the methods of "correct construction"; his instructor, whoever he was, was obviously someone familiar with Piero della Francesca's writings and his purely geometric analysis of painting. Dürer restated the Italian theories, merely adding some technical demonstrations. And he agreed with the Renaissance Italians in regarding perspective as not only a means of representing actual space but also as an ideal norm of order and harmonious design.

In his engraving *Adam and Eve* he set out to demonstrate his mastery of the classical conception of beauty, but as time went on, and under Leonardo's influence, he came to realize that beauty assumes many forms and that proportions change in accordance with the structure and movements of the figures represented. Moreover, as a result of studying Leonardo's so-called caricatures, he went into the question of the total or partial distortion of bodies, with a view to showing (as a warning to painters) how easy it is to lapse into the monstrous.

Dürer's own aesthetic is set forth in Book III of his *Human Proportions.* Though some of the ideas derive from Italian writers on art theory, he does not share their views regarding the nature of "pure beauty" and goes so far as to attack those who think that beauty can be achieved by measure and proportion alone. Pursuing his researches on a deeper level, he investigates the "mystery of Nature" from the angle of the artist, coming to the conclusion that a work of art can be truly great even though the subjects

ALBRECHT DÜRER (1471-1528). SELF-PORTRAIT, 1493. (22 ¼ × 17 ½″)
LOUVRE, PARIS.

ALBRECHT DÜRER (1471-1528). ALPINE LANDSCAPE, CA. 1495. (8 ¼ × 12 ¼")
WATERCOLOR DRAWING. ASHMOLEAN MUSEUM, OXFORD.

depicted be of a mean or uncouth kind. And in any case the artist was constrained to make do with relative beauty since absolute beauty was perforce an unattainable ideal.

What Dürer aimed at above all was a coherency between the parts and the whole, an appropriate, all-embracing symmetry and harmony. Geometric rules-of-thumb cannot tell us what we should select in the appearances of nature; that is a matter for the artist's intuition and his sense of pictorial construction. "No man can create a beautiful picture merely by the exercise of his imagination unless he has a mind equipped by the observation of reality. That is why a great painter need not wholly copy nature; he can exteriorize what he has stored up within himself for years, his accumulated visual experience." Thus an inner synthesis is effected enabling the artist to body forth the real and the imaginary at one and the same time. This theory was quite a new one, unknown to the Italian Renaissance, which was already moving towards the conception of art as pure creation.

Dürer's conception of the artist's vocation is set forth in another passage. "Only great artists will be able to understand the strange view I now put forward, out of deference to the truth. In one day a man may sketch something with his pen on a sheet of paper or limn it with his graver on a little block of wood, and what he thus devises in a single day may be far better and more artistic than a big work over which he has toiled assiduously for a whole year. This is a heaven-sent gift. God often bestows the possibility of discovery and the intuition of making something excellent on a man whom none other equals in his age and the like of whom has not been seen before and will not be seen again for many, many years." This view of the artist is one that appeals to the modern mind, despite the efforts of a certain school of criticism to question the existence of great art geniuses endowed with "a heaven-sent gift."

In the lands north of the Alps there had developed during the 15th century a tendency to break with Gothic tradition and to devote more attention to the faithful representation of reality and improvements in technique. Following Jan van Eyck, the northern painters made use of breaks in the line, more and more frequent, and graduated colors in relation to the ebb and flow of light. At that time line bulked large in the art speech of the day (notably in that of Rogier van der Weyden) and Dürer too, who had been trained as a goldsmith before he took to painting, proved his extreme interest in design by his lifelong activity as an engraver on wood and copper. Indeed, when we remember that he was first and foremost an engraver, we cannot but be amazed at the driving force of that creative instinct which enabled him triumphantly to cross the frontier from the purely linear to the pictorial, and after being an alumnus of Medievalism to become a great Renaissance master.

From Martin Schongauer Dürer learnt the virtues of precision, a strictly ordered interpretation of visual data controlled by a well-marked style. As against this, an anonymous painter, the so-called Housebook Master of Amsterdam, showed him that touches of improvisation did not come amiss and that by a dexterous handling of light, line could be reduced to a minimum. However, his early training was that of an illustrator and it was to his virtuosity as a draftsman in the medieval tradition that, in his lifetime, he owed his vast prestige. But in order to achieve an art in which form *qua* form was paramount he inclined towards a classical style enabling him to range beyond mere illustration, which, calling for meticulous craftsmanship and extreme attention to details, however trivial, involved all too often a sacrifice of the general effect.

If Dürer showed so much interest in those "specialities" of his Italian contemporaries, perspective, proportions and the nude, this was because he wished to find a means of integrating the human body into its spatial environment. He copied—or freely interpreted—one of Mantegna's prints, another by an anonymous Ferrarese painter, and Pollaiuolo's *Battle of Nudes*. During and after his visits to Venice and North Italy he turned to good account his studies of the work of Gentile and Giovanni Bellini, Leonardo and several other Italian masters. Jacopo de' Barbari's art revealed to him the perfection of classical form and the virtues of *contrapposto*. He was also interested in the works of classical antiquity, though he may have become acquainted

ALBRECHT DÜRER (1471-1528). THE ADORATION OF THE MAGI, 1504. (39 ¼ × 44 ⅞") UFFIZI, FLORENCE.

with them only through Italian drawings. These explorations of a realm of art so foreign to that of late medieval Germany led him away from the time-hallowed religious themes towards secular subjects.

Always inclined to go to extremes, he was in a sense the most aggressive of all the painters of his time. But he was a many-sided man, so vain of his good looks as to portray himself as a new "Nazarene" (Munich, 1500), intensely serious, yet capable on occasion of displaying a sprightly wit, even in his homilies.

When crossing the Brenner Pass in 1495 he made three watercolor sketches of Trento and the environs; delightfully spontaneous works, painted as personal *souvenirs de voyage,* not for others' eyes. Here there is no lingering over details, these pictures are completely natural, not to say unstudied, and the touch has an airy lightness—they are in fact "impressions," lively, colorful and charming to the eye.

His first large-scale work was the *Apocalypse* series of fifteen woodcuts, completed in 1498, which created something of a sensation and enjoyed immediate success. In these the real and the impossible are so closely intermixed that it is difficult to distinguish between them. In the *Vision of the Seven Candlesticks* St John the Evangelist is shown kneeling not as a mere spectator but as a participant in the scene. The candelabra are in finely wrought gold and though the scene is set in the clouds, so realistic is it that we forget the fantastic nature of the vision. When the subject is more dramatic this transposition on to the plane of the real is even more complete. The woodcut of the *Four Horsemen of the Apocalypse,* for example, is a scene of violence, charged with terror and strewn with bodies of the dead and dying; but for the presence of a few symbolic accessories it might be the picture of a medieval battle. In *St John devouring the Book,* the angel who according to the Revelation had "feet as pillars of fire" is given a head encircled with rays and instead of legs two little columns ending in flames. Dürer takes such pains to make the unreal realistic that we forget this is the stuff of dreams. Yet, though some details in these woodcuts are perfect of their kind, we cannot help feeling that the artist overstressed the horrific elements in the sacred text. The same might be said about the earlier series of seven woodcuts known as the *Large Passion.* Several German and foreign painters drew inspiration from these woodcuts, notably from the *Ecce Homo, Bearing of the Cross* and *Lamentation of Christ.*

Between 1495 and 1500 Dürer's output was prodigious. For one thing, he now started engraving on copper, better suited than wood for the realistic rendering of details. But we can see that he was aiming at a style more flexible than that of Schongauer, whose engravings were miracles of exactitude. At this time Dürer's vision approximated more nearly to that of a painter, and it was the period of some of his most successful prints. *St Eustace and the Stag* (1501) has the quality of a folk tale and in it figures and animals are set out in depth as well as in the foreground, without any logical links between them. And it is due to this "irrational" arrangement that the forms, though rendered wholly in the Renaissance manner, do not clash with the fairytale atmosphere of the little scene. In *Nemesis* (1501-1502), inspired by a Latin poem by Politian, Dürer demonstrates his entire mastery of the proportions of the female nude standing and shown in profile. Still we cannot help feeling that he tends to overemphasize realistic details such as the woman's bulging muscles and obesity and that the powerful effect of this figure is due chiefly to its finely balanced poise. The *Temptation* (1504) demonstrates his skill in bringing out the tactile values of different substances with his graving tool. The two nude figures have a classical beauty and thanks to a well-devised *contrapposto,* in pursuance of which the weight of each body bears on one limb only, the scene, though static, is charged with potential movement.

ALBRECHT DÜRER (1471-1528). THE ADORATION OF THE TRINITY, 1511. (56¾ × 51½")
KUNSTHISTORISCHES MUSEUM, VIENNA.

Between 1502 and 1504 Dürer painted two of his finest pictures: the Munich *Nativity* and the *Adoration of the Magi* (Uffizi). In the former the scene is laid amid ruins set out in full perspective so that the spatial relations between the figures are clearly indicated, while thanks to a diagonal lay-out, they are integrated into the surrounding space. The ruined buildings of various shapes and sizes, the angels and the groups of people around the Holy Family make this picture seem frankly anecdotal, like an illustration, but this seemingly random assemblage of pictorial elements and their very quaintness endow the scene with a poetic, legendary glamour. Still more remarkable is the *Adoration of the Magi* which Dürer painted with especial care, for Frederick the Wise. Space is presented in depth and the eye is led to a faraway horizon by the positions of the figures, grouped in a roughly pyramidal schema. Spaced out both on the surface and in depth, these figures have a monumental quality, though still invested with that air of spontaneity and simplicity which is one of the charms of Dürer's art. Unlike the *Apocalypse* in which the emphasis on the horrific has something rather childish about it, this *Adoration* is human through and through, all grace and suavity. Though line is given the major role, the colors too play an important part—colors not only rich and brilliant, but exquisitely harmonizing with the over-all distribution of light and shade.

During his second visit to Venice, in 1505, Dürer, now one of the foremost artists of the day, was given a commission by the Fondaco de' Tedeschi (the local German colony) for a picture of the *Feast of the Rose Garlands* for the church of San Bartolomeo (now in Prague Museum). It shows, against a landscape background, the Confraternity of the Rosary, priests and laymen crowned with white roses (symbols of joy) and red roses (symbols of the Passion), gathered together to combat the heretics and do homage to the Virgin. In the foreground are Pope Julius II and the Emperor Maximilian I, and behind them an array of portrait figures reminiscent, like the composition, of Giovanni Bellini. But while keeping to the tradition and technique of the Venetians in a general way, Dürer has a vivacity of line distinctively his own.

Some of the portraits of his Venice period suggest that the painter had made a careful study of the art of Giovanni Bellini, who thirty years before had renounced the linear style and taken to representing form by arrangements of light and shade. Dürer, too, in his *Portrait of a Young Woman* (Berlin), dissolves line into form and, by the use of zones of light and shade, gives the image a plasticity more fully rendered than in his linear representations and reinforced by a dexterous handling of color. The *Portrait of a Young Man* (Hampton Court) also recalls Bellini (and Catena too), but with a more forcible directness in the style.

It was also in Venice that Dürer painted *Christ among the Doctors* (Thyssen Collection, Lugano). Some have thought to see in a portrait by Luini the Leonardesque prototype used by Dürer as his model. In any case the contrast struck here between beauty and ugliness is in keeping with a principle laid down by Leonardo, one of whose "caricatures" certainly suggested to our artist the figure of one of the Doctors. Indeed some have thought this to be a Gothic version of an original by Leonardo.

Two panels dated 1507 (both in the Prado), representing *Adam* and *Eve* respectively, were originally intended to illustrate the *Temptation*; actually they are, rather, two studies of the nude. Here the style is more Gothic than that of the *Temptation* engraved in 1504, where the artist was seeking to achieve classical form by means of relief, anatomical precision and an heroic-monumental treatment of the figures. But when in Venice, chiefly as a result of his contacts with Bellini, he realized that, when all was said and done, this sort of classicism did not come naturally to him—it was something imposed from without—and that he would do better to impart a hint of movement to his figures so as to make them less statuesque and more alive. In *Eve* the sinuous arabesque of the body, which seems to be faintly spinning on itself, is a distinctly Gothic touch, but modified by Italian influences and, like much post-Renaissance Gothic, tinged with Mannerism.

In 1511 Dürer completed the *Adoration of the Trinity* (Vienna), depicting the Trinity encircled by Saints and, below, the multitude of persons not admitted to God's presence. As the artist explains in an inscription on the decorated frame made by himself (Nuremberg Museum), this scene represents the aftermath of the Last Judgment. It is a vision of heaven with two distinct horizons: one extending behind the company of the Blessed and the other, lower down, on earth, stretching out into infinite distance. The visionary effect of this remarkable work, due to the "double horizon," is enhanced, paradoxically enough, by the realism of the perspective and the figures. For though the latter are portraits and space is normally presented, one has a feeling of being transported into a world far removed from earthly things. Hence, no doubt, the immediate success of this picture and its influence on later art. Moreover, its spirit was in keeping with certain aspects of the Counter-Reformation. Just as survivals from the Gothic had helped to modify the style of the Renaissance and point the way towards Mannerism and the Baroque, so medieval tradition, but for the obstacle of humanism, would certainly have been enlisted in the service of Counter-Reformation art.

Wholly taken up by this work, Dürer neglected color far more than he would have done in Venice. Indeed it seems that after painting it he temporarily abandoned painting in favor of engraving and his discoveries in the former art led him to make changes in his treatment of chiaroscuro with a view to securing more elaborate effects. Noteworthy among the engravings of this period is the *Trinity* (1511), a woodcut which by some optical illusion seems permeated with Titian's color-light. The same synthesis of light and shade is also realized with brilliant success in a dry-point engraving, *St Jerome by a Pollard Willow* (1512).

By dint of seeking to obtain more varied massings of light and shade in his engravings, Dürer came to appreciate better Grünewald's achievement and, like him, to stress emotive values, to tend towards mystical effusion and a more expressive luminism. But his fiery temperament led him towards a mysticism that was something other than religious ecstasy; rather, a Faustian vision of the world. It was perhaps this new insight into Grünewald's work that gave rise to his three most famous engravings: *Knight, Death and Devil* (1513), *St Jerome in his Study* (1514) and *Melencolia I* (1514).

ALBRECHT DÜRER (1471-1528). THE FOUR APOSTLES, DETAIL: ST JOHN, 1526.
ALTE PINAKOTHEK, MUNICH.

ALBRECHT DÜRER (1471-1528). THE FOUR APOSTLES, DETAIL: ST PAUL, 1526.
ALTE PINAKOTHEK, MUNICH.

ALBRECHT DÜRER (1471-1528). THE FOUR APOSTLES, 1526. ALTE PINAKOTHEK, MUNICH.
ST JOHN AND ST PETER (84¾ × 29⅞″). ST MARK AND ST PAUL (84¼ × 29⅞″).

Dürer, it will be remembered, had been moved by a false report of Luther's murder to bid Erasmus (who in 1501 had written his *Handbook of the Christian Soldier*) to become "the Knight of Christ," to defend the Truth and win the martyr's crown. In the engraving he shows the "Christian Soldier" marching boldly forward, giving no heed to the devil who dogs his steps. While the armor, Death and the devil conform to the time-honored German tradition, the posture of the Knight reminds us of Donatello's monument at Padua, while the horse derives from a Leonardesque model. Though these anomalies weaken the unity of the composition, the contrast between medieval and Renaissance elements heightens its spiritual significance. Dürer has here personified so to speak the new religious aspirations of his epoch, and this work is far more than a picturesque illustration of a typically medieval theme.

*St Jerome in his Study*, on the other hand, is a masterpiece of scientific perspective and every object is assigned its geometrically correct place. Nevertheless the ebb and flow of light and shade playing across the neatly ordered, schematic lay-out brings the whole scene to vibrant life. When painted by an Italian artist—the picture in the National Gallery, London, probably by Antonello da Messina, is a case in point—the same subject had perhaps more spontaneity and certainly was less elaborately worked out. But this very elaboration led Dürer to give the well-worn theme an unconventional turn. Other artists had used it to celebrate the life of contemplation, whereas the scene that Dürer conjures up is pervaded with a rankling unrest that once again is Faustian in mood. So much so that we are reminded not of Antonello but, rather, of Rembrandt.

Nor is there any trace of contemplation, of spiritual self-communing or ordered thought in the *Melencolia I*, so much admired by Melanchthon. This woman is the effigy of despair, the compass she is holding rests inactive, everything around her is lying in disorder, the building behind her is unfinished, even the dog seems *in extremis*. As Panofsky has observed, this scene links up with the ancient idea of the four "humors" or "temperaments" of man, most unfortunate of which was melancholia since it came from Saturn. In Dürer's plate the melancholic humor is associated with a litter of scientific instruments as if to emphasize the plight of the artist or intellectual, a misfit in the social system. Since melancholy arises from the predominance of the imagination over the reasoning faculty, it ranks first in the scale of values—hence the number added to the inscription: *Melencolia I*. It expresses the artist's profound conviction of the futility of all human effort, the bankruptcy of "science."

From 1512 to 1519 he was in the employ of Maximilian I. For him he designed the large, composite woodcuts known as *Triumphal Arch* and *Triumphal Procession*. Besides a host of Gothic reminiscences, the patterning of the arch contains hermetic allusions in the form of emblems culled from the *Hieroglyphica*, a treatise on Egyptian hieroglyphs by Horus Apollo (2nd or 3rd century A.D.) which, when published in 1505, had a great vogue in humanist circles. Dürer's previous work had made it clear that decoration was not his forte and since his aim here was essentially decorative, these woodcuts must be written down as failures, while the plethora of details effectively prevents their being assimilated to Baroque.

According to some accounts, Dürer underwent a long period of depression towards the close of his life. This was due to the bitter religious conflict then raging in Germany and his uncertainties about the path to choose as a good Christian. In 1519, however, he definitely espoused the cause of Luther who, he said, "had delivered him from so great an anguish of mind." He now gave up painting non-religious subjects and sought to purge his mind of the humanism he had so laboriously imbibed.

In 1520 Dürer traveled to the Low Countries and made a stay at Antwerp. During this journey he painted several very fine portraits. *A Gentleman* (Prado) and *Bernhart von Resten* (Dresden) have quite exceptional vivacity and forcefulness, while certain characteristic accents—in the hair for example—show that he was moving away from the Venetians and towards the contemporary Flemish masters. From this trip Dürer returned a sick man (he never shook off the effects of a fever contracted in Holland), more and more distressed by the turn of events in the religious life of his country. This distress is reflected in a drawing of himself made at Basel in 1522, which shows him, in an *Ecce Homo*, as a desolate, defeated aging man with nothing left of the "Nazarene" of an earlier day, with flowing locks, rejoicing in his beauty.

He had intended to return to Antwerp to paint two altarpieces, a *Crucifixion* and a *Virgin with the Ancestors and Parents of Christ and Angel Musicians*, but though he spent infinite pains on the preparatory work, neither altarpiece ever saw the day. Only two panels of the second, depicting four saints intended to stand on either side of the Virgin, were completed. Wrongly named the *Four Apostles*, these four figures represent Sts John the Evangelist and Peter, Sts Paul and Mark. Dürer donated them to the City of Nuremberg, writing on the frame a warning against heresies and false prophets. For Nuremberg, now Lutheran, had to struggle against the fanatics and *illuminati* preaching a social as well as a religious revolution. Under the circumstances a "Virgin attended by Saints" would have seemed too Catholic in spirit, so he painted the saints only, giving prominence to Paul and John, saints particularly esteemed by Lutherans. In this, his last big work, we find Dürer's creative power and technical proficiency at their highest. Never before had he painted figures so grandly conceived, comparable with those of the greatest Renaissance artists. But there is nothing Italian in the expressions of the faces, which have a typically Germanic, Lutheran grimness. Here the divided purposes we sense in Dürer's personality from the very start commingle, but, far from being reconciled, make no secret of their antagonism. In these majestic figures we have both a final manifestation of Dürer's unquiet spirit and an epitome of his art.

**HOLBEIN**

Hans Holbein the Younger is undoubtedly one of the most popular 16th-century German artists. Though Dürer is universally acclaimed as a great master, he is somewhat inaccessible, at times recondite, and while we cannot fail to recognize the power of his creations, they are apt to disconcert us. As for Grünewald, his art is profoundly disturbing, instinct with an exalted spirituality, yet it can hardly be said he is a popular artist in the general acceptation of the term. But everybody can enjoy a Holbein portrait, such is its union of fine craftsmanship and subtle characterization, of elegance and dignity, and such its atmosphere of assured well-being, whether the sitter is the Burgomaster of Basel, Erasmus of Rotterdam, or Henry VIII and his ill-starred wives. But these portraits tell nothing or next to nothing about Holbein himself and his reactions to his models. Nor can we learn anything about the man he was from his religious scenes or from his many decorative works (only the preliminary drawings for which have survived), or from his innumerable woodcuts and copper-plate engravings—all of them completely impersonal, non-committal. What they have in common is a technical perfection that the artist seems to have achieved quite effortlessly, almost without giving thought to it. Holbein, too, was schooled in the Gothic tradition (inculcated by his father), but he assimilated the lessons of Italian art far more readily and thoroughly than Dürer and had no trouble or qualms about solving a problem which presented itself to some of his contemporaries as a well-nigh insoluble dilemma. No other German painter had an apprehension so instinctive and complete of the Italian ideal of the beautiful. He possessed what Vasari, speaking of Raphael, called "an amazing natural facility," but while Raphael makes us feel the love he brought to the creation of a beauty all his own, Holbein shows no trace

HANS HOLBEIN (1497/98-1543). THE ARTIST'S FAMILY, 1528-1529. (30¼ × 25⅛")
KUNSTMUSEUM, BASEL.

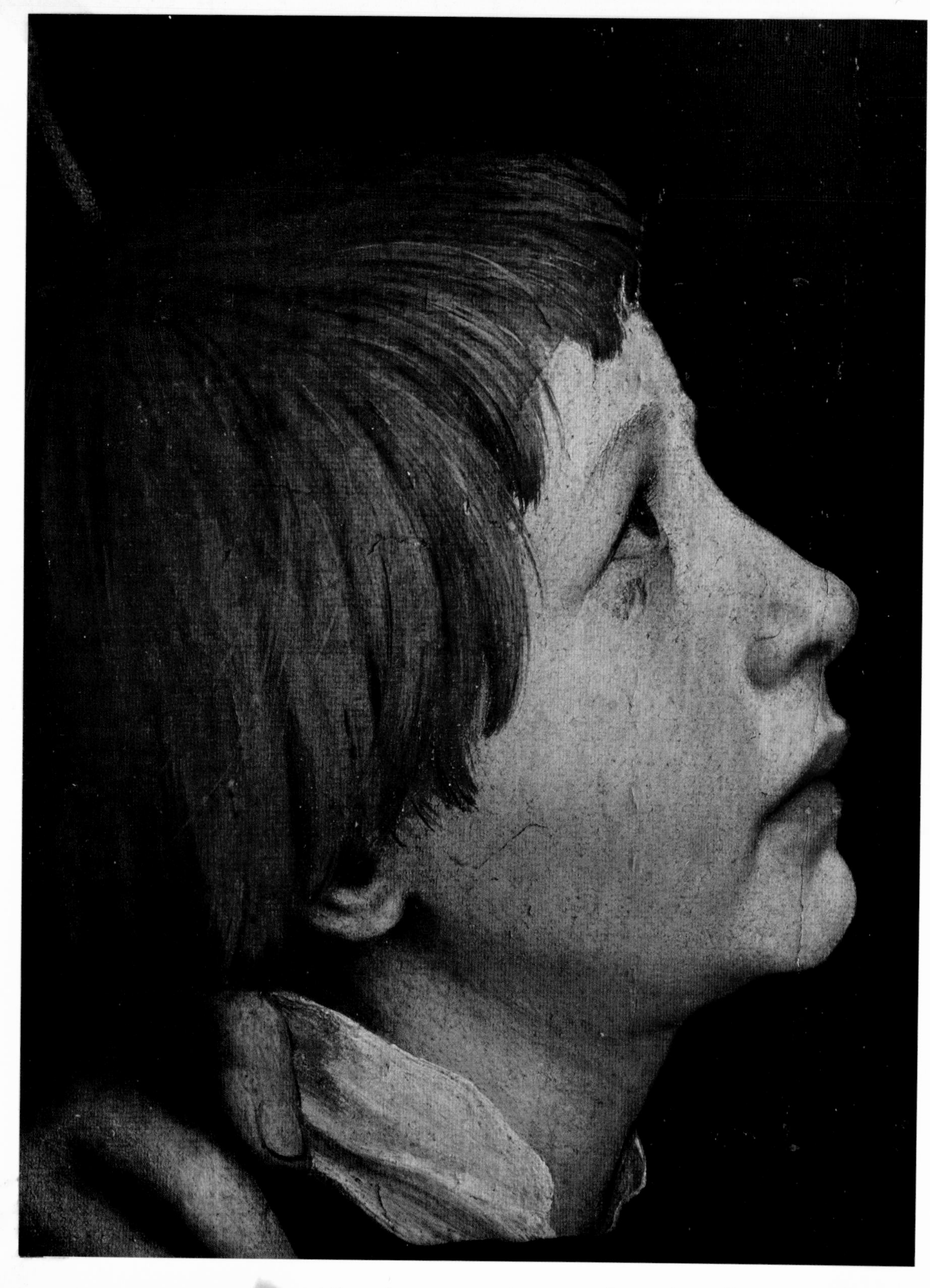

HANS HOLBEIN (1497/98-1543). THE ARTIST'S FAMILY (DETAIL), 1528-1529.
KUNSTMUSEUM, BASEL.

of any such emotion. That, in fact, is one of his limitations. Holbein was a superb technician and gifted with a natural taste superior to that of his contemporaries which enabled him, while bringing out the characters of his sitters with power and subtlety, to give them a distinctive elegance. But we can never tell how he felt towards them; whether he liked or disliked them; even if they interested him at all. Though perhaps one of the finest portrait painters of all time, he falls short of real greatness as an artist.

To this general rule there is one exception: the family portrait of his wife and his two children. When after a two years' stay in London he returned to Basel in 1528, he found his wife ill and depressed by his long absence. Departing for once from the objectivity of the professional portraitist, Holbein here reveals both his emotions as a father and husband and a sympathetic understanding of his models' inner life. Though the figures do not, perhaps, tell out so strongly as in his other portraits and lack their sumptuous embellishments, such is the spiritual insight here revealed that this picture takes a very high place in Holbein's œuvre.

Grünewald had fraternized with the revolutionary zealots; Dürer was an ardent partisan of Luther; Holbein, on the other hand, was a friend of Erasmus and Sir Thomas More, both of them advocates of an enlightened Catholicism. Familiar with Italian art theory and practice, he painted scenes of ancient history. His way of living, his choice of friends and his works prove him to have been a cultured man, and it was probably his humanistic outlook that prevented him from collaborating with the zealots when in 1529 they got the upper hand in Basel.

Born at Augsburg in 1497 or 1498, Holbein went to Basel in 1515 in the capacity of assistant to Hans Herbst. A year later, however, when he was only eighteen or nineteen, he painted the portrait of the Burgomaster and his wife—which shows that he had set up as an artist on his own account. Next year he traveled to Lucerne to make some decorations, then to Milan where, under the influence of Italian art, he modified his style. In 1519 he returned to Basel, where, having acquired the rights of citizenship in the following year, he built up an extensive practice, painting several portraits, religious pictures and decorations in the Town Hall. In 1524 he journeyed to France, and put in a stay at Lyons where he saw Clouet's work and was commissioned by local printing-houses to make two sequences of woodcuts, the *Dance of Death* and *Icones Veteris Testamenti*. But since as a result of the Reformation there now was less demand for works of art, Holbein decided to try his luck in London where, thanks to a letter of introduction from Erasmus, he secured the patronage of Sir Thomas More, who was loud in praises of his abilities. On his way to England he had stopped at Antwerp where he called on Quentin Massys. After making several portraits in London he returned to Basel in 1528. The Protestants were now in the saddle and busily engaged in "purifying" churches and palaces by the wholesale destruction of the works of art adorning them. Though Holbein did not ally himself with the Reformers, he was careful, when decorating the Town Hall, to illustrate biblical themes instead of the subjects from Roman history he had used in previous decorations. In 1532 he migrated for the second time to London, where there was a great demand for his portraits, and he was now appointed Court Painter to Henry VIII. On several occasions he was sent to the Continent to make portraits of ladies whom the king proposed to marry. He remained in London until his death in 1543.

His first large portrait was that of Jacob Meyer, Burgomaster of Basel, and his wife. Although containing reminiscences of his father's style, the technique is crisper, more precise; in the background are two triumphal arches inspired by one of Hans Burgkmair's prints. The *Bonifacius Amerbach,* painted in 1519, has all the forceful realism we associate with Holbein's portraits, but he had not yet attained the objectivity and detachment distinctive of his later art. It is in the portraits of Erasmus made in 1523, when Holbein was only twenty-six, that these appear for the first time.

Under Grünewald's influence he painted the macabre *Dead Christ* in Basel Museum and drew a very striking *Ecce Homo* (Berlin). The *Lais Corinthiaca* of 1526 (Basel), an eye-pleasing portrait of a courtesan, shows the direct influence of Leonardo. Seemingly attaching little importance to the difference one would expect to find between a depiction of the Virgin and that of a young woman of easy virtue, he used the same type of figure in the painting of the Burgomaster's family in prayer before the Virgin, made for the palace of Prince William of Hesse at Darmstadt: a work effective in its way, if too blatantly materialistic. The eight scenes of the *Passion* (Basel) show that Holbein had fully mastered the perspective representation of space and Leonardesque *sfumato.* Still, this is not one of his best works; in it his employment of *sfumato,* a technique calling for extreme discretion and apt to decline to sentimental prettiness, led Holbein towards a sort of mannerist artificiality. More spontaneous and pictorially far more rewarding was his use of *sfumato* as a means of realizing effects of light and shade that linked up with Flemish tradition, as in the *Adoration of the Shepherds* (Freiburg-im-Breisgau). The shutters painted for the organ in Basel Cathedral, now in Basel Museum, are the sole surviving examples of Holbein's decorative ensembles (others being known only by drawings or copies). Despite the skill displayed, the figures are hardly a success and there is an even greater over-crowding of natural elements —trees and plants—than in similar Italian works. Holbein had not much imagination, as can be seen from his engravings, which are weak in the illustrative details. Even the fifty-eight woodcuts in the picture sequence of the *Dance of Death* and the ninety-one in *Icones Veteris Testamenti* (Old Testament scenes), world-famous though they are, have little real artistic value.

To see Holbein at his best we must turn to the portraits made in London. They are more broadly treated than his earlier portraits and show that he was breaking new ground. The figure, for example, is given an appropriate setting, with accessories of various kinds. Holbein, in fact, was seeking to transform the portrait pure and simple into a "picture"—one in which everything was calculated to bring out the wealth and elegance of the person or persons represented. This method, however, tended to enhance the sociological rather than the artistic significance of the paintings. In point of fact his most completely successful portraits, those which today we can admire without reserve, are the lightly tinted drawings most of which are now in Windsor Castle.

HANS HOLBEIN (1497/98-1543). THE AMBASSADORS, 1533. (82 × 82 ¼″)
REPRODUCED BY COURTESY OF THE TRUSTEES, NATIONAL GALLERY, LONDON.

In these the artist did not linger over rendering form in detail; on the contrary, he reduced linework to a minimum, merely hinting at the presence of the body—and thereby created drawings which, for purity of line, have never been excelled.

Some of Holbein's large-scale portraits are unique of their kind, nothing short of miracles of craftsmanship. Particularly noteworthy are the *Portrait of Georg Gisze* (Berlin)—Gisze was a wealthy German merchant settled in London—*Derich Born* (Windsor), *Robert Cheseman, the King's Falconer* (The Hague) and, last but not least, *The Ambassadors* (National Gallery, London). The two figures in the last-named picture

HANS HOLBEIN (1497/98-1543). THE AMBASSADORS (DETAIL), 1533.
REPRODUCED BY COURTESY OF THE TRUSTEES, NATIONAL GALLERY, LONDON.

are the ambassador Jean de Dinteville and Georges de Selve, Bishop of Lavaur. Both are shown almost full face and there is no visual link between the figures except the setting in which they are placed: a room full of books and precious objets. The musical, astronomical and mathematical instruments are rendered with illusionist realism; yet something in their disposition creates a vaguely "surrealist" atmosphere, intensified by the queerly elongated representation of a skull lying across the carpet. This effect is heightened by the trance-like rigidity of the figures and the preternaturally sharp definition given the various objects in the room.

On the other hand the portraits of *King Henry VIII* (Rome), *Edward, Prince of Wales* (Washington), *The Duke of Norfolk* (Windsor) and *Anne of Cleves* (Louvre) are typical show-pieces; sumptuous, lavishly ornate, self-consciously elegant—a far cry indeed from that happy ease which, according to Castiglione, should be the ideal of the perfect

HANS HOLBEIN (1497/98-1543). THE AMBASSADORS (DETAIL), 1533.
REPRODUCED BY COURTESY OF THE TRUSTEES, NATIONAL GALLERY, LONDON.

HANS HOLBEIN (1497/98-1543). PORTRAIT OF KING HENRY VIII, 1540. (34¾ × 29½″)
GALLERIA NAZIONALE, ROME.

courtier and the master artist. Nevertheless the *Portrait of a Young Man* (Vienna) and the *Self-Portrait* (Uffizi) reveal both a profound psychological insight and Holbein's amazing power of making a painted likeness seem a living presence.

CRANACH THE ELDER

Like Holbein, Lucas Cranach the Elder owes his fame chiefly to his portraits. Though these speak for an artistic personality remarkable in many ways, they lack the elegance and grace—typically Italian qualities—that we find in Holbein's work. For Cranach was out of sympathy with the spirit of the Renaissance, and devoted heart and soul to the Gothic art, realistic in trend, that was its avowed antagonist. For this reason his work was much to the taste of his fellow Germans.

Cranach was born in 1472 at Cronach (whence he derived his name) in Upper Franconia. After studying under his father he came under Dürer's influence. In 1502 he went to Vienna where there was then a vogue for landscape painting, a genre in which he was destined to excel. In 1505 he was appointed Court Painter to Frederick the Wise of Wittenberg, Prince Elector of Saxony. In 1508 he was sent to the Netherlands to paint the portrait of the boy who afterwards became the Emperor Charles V. Then, having struck up a friendship with Luther, he joined the Reformation movement and began to take part in the public life of Wittenberg, being elected a town councillor in 1519 and holding the office of Burgomaster twice (in 1537 and 1540). On his return from the Diet of Worms (1521), Luther wrote him an affectionate letter and Cranach made a portrait of his friend disguised as a friar in order to escape arrest on his way back from Worms. In 1526 he painted the wedding portrait of Luther and Catherine von Bora. At the age of eighty (in 1552) he moved to Weimar, where he died in 1553.

The portraits of his early years, notably that of Johannes Cuspinian and his wife (Winterthur), display remarkable energy and vivacity. Still quite a young man, Cuspinian held the post of Rector at Vienna University, was an accomplished humanist and a much esteemed poet. Cranach portrays him in rich attire against a landscape background that at once sets off and complements the figure. Several of his other Viennese portraits have no less dignity and expressive power, but one hesitates to describe them as truly humanistic in conception. For here and there we can discern glints of irony, much more in the spirit of Late Gothic than in that of the humanist artists whose work has, uniformly, a stately, monumental quality.

LUCAS CRANACH (1472-1553). PORTRAIT OF MARTIN LUTHER, 1529. (14⅜ × 9″) UFFIZI, FLORENCE.

LUCAS CRANACH (1472-1553). DAVID AND BATHSHEBA, 1526. (14 1/8 × 9 3/8″)
NEUES MUSEUM, WIESBADEN (PROPERTY OF THE KAISER FRIEDRICH MUSEUM, BERLIN).

LUCAS CRANACH (1472-1553). THE JUDGMENT OF PARIS, 1529. (40 1/8 × 28″)
BY COURTESY OF THE METROPOLITAN MUSEUM OF ART, NEW YORK.

The *Portrait of Martin Luther* (Uffizi), made in 1529, is at once a wonderfully expressive character study and a model of pictorial construction. Here, keeping to the traditional Gothic style, the artist has not overstressed realistic details, whereas in his portrait of Luther's parents he falls into this error, with the result that the spiritual significance of the work is blurred.

The distaste that Cranach felt for humanism and the art theories stemming from it is illustrated by the contrast between two pictures of the same model, Cardinal Albrecht of Brandenburg. The first (Darmstadt), painted in 1525, might almost have been titled "St Jerome in his Cell"; the second (Berlin), painted in 1527, "St Jerome in the Wilderness." In the Darmstadt picture the painter's inspiration seems to have failed him in his attempt to solve the problem of representing the interior of a room in scientifically exact perspective by an interplay of zones of light and shade; in the Berlin picture, on the other hand, he has given free rein to his creative imagination, since, being less realistic, the subject permitted him to introduce an element of fantasy and charge the scene with magic overtones.

The *Portrait of Doctor Johannes Scheyring* (Brussels), painted in 1529, has intense vitality, though it must be admitted that Cranach has made his sitter look more like an ape than an esteemed physician. On the other hand his likenesses of children, such as the *Prince Moritz von Sachsen*, show him in a gentler mood and the figures have all the fragile charm of early youth. In his *Ideal Portrait* (1526) of Sibyl of Cleves, it seems that what he aimed at was to sublimate the model into a vision of more than human splendor by clothing her in fantastically rich apparel. This portrait illustrates one of Cranach's outstanding qualities, which, however, is seen to best advantage in his nudes: his flair for decorative effects. He clearly took a particular delight in painting the nude figure, as we can see in his *Adam and Eve* and his mythological scenes such as the *Judgment of Paris, Venus and Cupid, Diana and Apollo*. But what gives these figures their singular appeal is not their plastic values or their harmonious proportions; still less the painter's knowledge of anatomy. Cranach uses them as pretexts for flowing surface decoration in which Gothic line is given an ingenious twist to stress the presence of some unlooked-for detail or unwonted object, as when some of the nudes are shown wearing enormous hats. We find touches of erotic suggestiveness which seem hardly in keeping with Lutheran austerity or what was to be expected of a worthy Burgomaster of Wittenberg; they probably derive from the "courtly" style of Late Gothic, and also from a feeling of the need for an occasional respite from puritanism.

Cranach's landscapes are particularly attractive; a good example is the *Stag Hunt* (ca. 1529) in Vienna. Here the composition is spangled with a host of tiny specks of light, bringing the entire scene forward on to the picture surface, and the perspective projection is of a purely fantastic order. Spatial arrangement is governed by the Gothic arabesque, reinforced by a color-scheme in which green predominates. Color plays an important part in Cranach's art; it is wedded to form with the happiest results in *Judith and Holofernes* (Vienna), whose reds and yellows sing out on a dark ground, each zone of color containing tracts of chiaroscuro that take the place of light.

LUCAS CRANACH (1472-1553). VENUS, 1532. (14½×9¾")
STÄDELSCHES KUNSTINSTITUT, FRANKFORT.

The *Earthly Paradise* (1530, Vienna) is a green landscape sprinkled with minute touches of light, against which the figures stand out, clearly defined by bold, emphatic coloring. In sum, Cranach's color orchestration might be described as a luminist interpretation, on the boldest, most fanciful lines, of the Gothic miniature.

There is nothing of Dürer's or Grünewald's high morality, and equally nothing of Holbein's elegant humanism and smooth technical perfection in Cranach's work. Indeed he seems to take neither life nor art quite seriously. But he had an original personality and employed Gothic line and the colors of the illuminators to fine effect in those delightful pictures, whimsical, with a discreetly sensual appeal, which in his day were so greatly to the liking of the German princes and still mean much to all who can enjoy the divagations of an artist's fancy at its freest.

**HANS BALDUNG GRIEN**

Hans Baldung Grien (or Grün) was born at Gmünd (Swabia) in 1484 or 1485. Nothing is known about his early training but traces of the art forms of Alsace, where the school of Schongauer was flourishing at the time, can be detected in the drawings and engravings of his youth. At Nuremberg he worked as Dürer's assistant and the affectionate relations between the two men persisted after Baldung left that town in 1505. He stayed four years (1512-1516) at Freiburg-im-Breisgau, but most of his life was spent in Strasbourg, where he held the post of Town Councillor and official painter to the Bishop's Court. He died in 1545.

His paintings prior to 1520 show a sense of plastic values not found in any other German artist of the time, while his delicate, jewel-like colors are reminiscent of 15th-century art. After 1520 he took to what might be described as plastic mannerism, making lavish use of lights and vivid colors; next, some five years later, in 1525, he adopted Cranach's Gothic line, while also showing signs of Italian influences, amongst others Marcantonio's. His major work is the altarpiece of Freiburg-im-Breisgau, in which his considerable gifts are seen at their best. The scene of the *Flight into Egypt* has the charm of an old-world folktale, while the *Nativity*, with its subtle effects of nocturnal light, is equally delightful in a different way. But of mystical emotion he had none, his feet were solidly planted on the earth and his *Crucifixion* fails to move us—evidently he knew nothing of Grünewald's art. He was, however, a very adroit draftsman, with a fine feeling for elegance of line; his drawings in white touches on dark paper are not only delicately perceptive but also reveal a familiarity with Renaissance techniques —foreshortening, for example—though without detriment to his highly personal style. He has a predilection for such subjects as Witches' Sabbaths and death under its grim or grotesque aspects, and strikes a note of healthy, robust sensuality even in works of a would-be edifying order. His skill in rendering volumes and his feeling for graceful form can be seen in *Venus* (1525, The Hague) and *Vanitas* (1529, Munich). Of all the German painters of the early 16th century none had a surer sense of style and by the same token none was nearer in spirit to the Renaissance.

◄ HANS BALDUNG GRIEN (1484/85-1545). VANITAS, 1529. (32⅝ × 14⅛″) ALTE PINAKOTHEK, MUNICH.

NICOLAS MANUEL DEUTSCH
HANS LEU

Linking up with the German tradition was a whole group of Swiss painters, one of them being Nicolas Manuel Deutsch. "Deutsch" was a translation of "De Alemanis," the Italianate name assumed by his family when they settled at Chieri, a small town near Turin. His grandfather returned to Bern where, about 1484, Nicolas was born.

NICOLAS MANUEL DEUTSCH (CA. 1484-1530). PYRAMUS AND THISBE. (59 ½ × 63 ¼″) KUNSTMUSEUM, BASEL.

HANS LEU (CA. 1490-1531). ORPHEUS AND THE ANIMALS, 1519. (22¾ × 20″)
KUNSTMUSEUM, BASEL.

HANS BALDUNG GRIEN (1484/85-1545). THE NATIVITY, 1520. (41¾ × 28″)
ALTE PINAKOTHEK, MUNICH.

ALBRECHT ALTDORFER (BEFORE 1480-1538). ST FLORIAN TAKING LEAVE OF HIS COMPANIONS, CA. 1518. ($31\frac{7}{8} \times 26\frac{3}{8}''$) THE ST FLORIAN ALTARPIECE. UFFIZI, FLORENCE.

After studying under Hans Fries, he traveled to Basel and South Germany, where he came under the influence of Dürer, Baldung Grien and the Italian engravers, though without breaking with Gothic tradition. Besides being a painter, he was a writer, a poet and, above all, a man of action. He fought in the Italian campaign in 1516 under Von Stein, and took an active part in the struggle with the Papacy. The work by which he made his name as an artist, his *Dance of Death* (1517-1520), has disappeared and is known only by a copy. He wrote two farces satirizing the Pope and clergy, which were performed during the 1522 carnival while he was at the wars in Italy. His political activities procured him a seat in the Council of Bern and in 1528-1529 he was sent on diplomatic missions to Zurich, St Gall and Baden. He died in 1530.

Deutsch was less a painter than a draftsman with a very lively imagination who put an immense vitality into his line. True, there were lapses in his taste; in the *Ten Thousand Martyrs*, for example, one of the panels of the Grandson altarpiece, he overdoes the hideousness of the wounds, while in his *St Anthony* he fails to make the monsters really terrifying. Nevertheless in some non-religious works, such as *Pyramus and Thisbe* and the *Judgment of Paris* (both in Basel) we cannot but admire the wit and fantasy with which he interprets the ancient myths, whose *dramatis personae* he boldly clothes in 16th-century costumes. No less attractive is the booklet dated 1520, now in Basel Museum, containing a series of vignettes of women and German foot-soldiers, in which an amazing delicacy and elegance of line is allied with fanciful decorative motifs; these little scenes might be described as guide-posts along the path of Gothic style towards an exuberant mannerism.

Another interesting Swiss painter was Hans Leu the Younger, born at Zurich about 1490 and trained by his painter father in the Late Gothic tradition. Between 1507 and 1513 he traveled in Germany, where he came in contact with Baldung Grien, Deutsch and also Dürer, with whom he started up a lifelong friendship. His most successful works are landscapes in which the Swiss Alps make what is perhaps their first appearance in painting. Hans Leu died in 1531.

ALBRECHT ALTDORFER

One of the things that strikes us most in the German painting of the first half of the 16th century is the new prominence given to scenes of nature. Grünewald's landscapes bear the imprint of his unquiet spirit; Dürer, in his watercolors, was the first to treat landscape as an end in itself. But it was left to Altdorfer to exploit the utmost possibilities of the landscape of fantasy.

Altdorfer was born at Amberg (Bavaria) a little before 1480; his father, Ulrich, was a painter, as was his brother Erhard Altdorfer. He was enrolled a citizen of Regensburg (Ratisbon) in 1505 and in 1509 the City Council paid him a large fee for a picture, thus testifying to their high opinion of his work. In 1513 he bought a house and in 1519, in his capacity as a member of the City Council, published the edict expelling the Jews from Regensburg; then he took part in building the Schöne Maria church on the site of the former synagogue. From 1526 until his death in 1538 he was City Architect and a member of the Council.

ALBRECHT ALTDORFER (BEFORE 1480-1538). DANUBE LANDSCAPE NEAR REGENSBURG, 1520-1525.
(11¾ × 8⅝″) ALTE PINAKOTHEK, MUNICH.

ALBRECHT ALTDORFER (BEFORE 1480-1538). THE BATTLE OF ALEXANDER (DETAIL), 1529.
ALTE PINAKOTHEK, MUNICH.

By general consent Altdorfer is one of the most typical artists of the Danubian School which, amongst other painters, included Wolf Huber. He was influenced by Dürer and Cranach and, at one stage of his career, by Grünewald. Also he profited by the lessons of Italian art. But so strong was his personality that he not merely assimilated but transformed all he took from others.

Friedländer distinguishes three phases in his artistic evolution. First, from 1507 to around 1520, when he painted small light-keyed pictures in which there is still some indecision in the drawing, though the colors are altogether delightful. Next, towards 1520, he took to stronger colors and sensational effects, as in the St Florian altarpiece (1518). Finally, in his last period, he calmed down, giving forms normal proportions and dappling the picture surface with sudden gleams of light. It was in rendering the

ALBRECHT ALTDORFER (BEFORE 1480-1538). THE BATTLE OF ALEXANDER (DETAIL), 1529.
ALTE PINAKOTHEK, MUNICH.

ALBRECHT ALTDORFER (BEFORE 1480-1538). THE BATTLE OF ALEXANDER, 1529. (62 × 47 ¼″)
ALTE PINAKOTHEK, MUNICH.

mystic life of the forest that he excelled and there are reasons for believing him the first artist to make landscape the sole theme of a picture (Munich), to the exclusion of figures, and he thus may be regarded as a pioneer in this genre.

In an interesting article in the *Gazette des Beaux-Arts* (May-June 1953) Georg Gombrich points out that Leonardo and the Venetians were the first to recognize the intrinsic value of landscape, brought it into fashion and created a public for it. From humanism they had learnt that what counted most of all in a work of art was its aesthetic quality, not its "message," moral or anecdotal. Thus the landscape painters of the North found in Italy a ready market for their productions; Federigo Gonzaga, for example, bought (in 1535) no less than a hundred and twenty Flemish paintings, twenty of which were "fire pictures." In 1548 Vasari, writing to Benedetto Varchi, observed that "every cobbler had a German landscape in his home." In 1548, too, Paolo Pino explained why the Germans excelled in the art of landscape painting. Italy, he pointed out, being "the garden of the world," was more pleasing to the eye than any painting could possibly be. On the other hand, the artists of the North lived amid untamed forests which supplied them with excellent and exciting motifs. Pino was, in fact, describing what came to be known in the 18th century as the picturesque, and had in mind the peculiar appeal of "wild nature" to certain temperaments.

It was Altdorfer who made the happiest use of this new freedom, in those (to use André Gide's epithet) "gratuitous" landscapes, whose sole but signal merit consists in the prodigious scope he gave to his creative fancy. In his famous *St George and the Dragon* (Munich), the actors in the drama are hardly visible, what holds our gaze is the densely surging mass of the forest, with a narrow vista opening on a dim horizon. Painted on the surface, the tangled leafage is interspersed with flakes and shimmering lines of light; light, indeed, is the animating principle, seeping into the green luxuriance of the foliage or flashing forth from it in a haze of broken gleams. The raw material is real enough, the German *Urwald*, but by the magic of these light-rhythms the painter has imbued it with the glamour of an enchanted forest in some ancient legend. In the *Satyr Family* (1507) in Berlin the painter has thought up a weirdly primitive setting in keeping with the theme, and given free play to his imagination, the result being a landscape almost unique of its kind—Pino's "wild nature" transposed into the prehistoric age.

In the third book of his *Chirurgia* Paracelsus traced a resemblance between vegetable life and the human organism. "Plants grow in the same way as men, they have their skins and limbs, heads and hair. They have bodies and a nervous system; so sensitive is the stem that if you strike it the plant dies. They are bedecked with flowers and fruit, as man is gifted with the faculties of hearing, seeing and speaking." Elsewhere he says: "The body is a tree and life a flame consuming it." And it is in this spirit that Altdorfer tells us, so to speak, the life story of a landscape, in one of the pictures now in Munich. Man's presence is needless since, as he pictures it, the landscape itself is human. Framed between two great trees, peopled with wisps of dancing light streaming in glittering recession up the mountains, cliffs and clouds, the whole scene comes to life because it is a vivid reflection of the artist's inmost being.

In the *Battle of Alexander* (Munich) the landscape is charged with awe-inspiring, tragic grandeur. The commission for this picture was given by William IV of Bavaria, who presumably wished it to be an historical battlepiece of the normal kind. But the forms of the soldiers are so completely swallowed up by the landscape that they dwindle into leaflike streaks of living light. What gives the scene its compelling power is not the battle itself but its aspect of some cosmic cataclysm, in which everything is in commotion and the sky mottled with an unearthly, lurid glow. Leonardo endowed a scene of battle with a like cosmic significance; but Altdorfer gets his effect by the use of thrilling color. He is not out to enlarge our knowledge of the world, nor does he, like Leonardo, aim at any scientific validity; with an amazing sense of purely pictorial values, he builds up a world of sheer imagination.

# PAINTING IN THE NETHERLANDS

HIERONYMUS BOSCH (CA. 1450-1516). THE GARDEN OF EARTHLY DELIGHTS, CA. 1485. (86½×76½″)
CENTRAL PANEL OF A TRIPTYCH. PRADO, MADRID.

# 3

## FROM BOSCH TO BRUEGHEL

On the threshold of the 16th century Flanders, unlike Germany, had behind it a great art tradition: that of Van Eyck and his successors. And though there had been frequent exchanges of ideas between the Flemings and the Florentines throughout the 15th century, the two art streams had never converged; there was still a basic incompatibility between the Northern artists' outlook on the world and that of the Italians. Florentine painting stood for the humanist ideal and the aesthetic of the Renaissance, whereas Flemish artists remained faithful to the religious tradition of the past, while carrying to its extreme limit the realism that had characterized late medieval art. But at the close of the 15th century the traditional art of the Low Countries underwent a radical change, particularly conspicuous in the work of Bosch.

The mood of Van Eyck's art was one of total serenity, of a profoundly pious mind at peace with itself and with the world at large. One feels that no shadow of doubt ever crossed his mind; assured of knowing all that needed to be known about man and nature, he depicted them with loving care, down to the least detail, and with a craftsmanly skill that has never been excelled. Looking at his paintings, we have a momentary conviction that the world is indeed just as he shows it, an earthly paradise beatified by the divine light of God and by that of its visible counterpart, the sun.

Around 1480 the most highly esteemed painter at Bruges was Hans Memling, a man as little troubled as Van Eyck by any doubts as to the perfection of the natural world. He had a delicate sense of human beauty but, as compared with the art of his immediate predecessors, both the aesthetic quality of his work and its spiritual message seem superficial. In that same year, 1480, Bosch was producing work utterly unlike Memling's; most pessimist of painters, he saw the devil rather than the God in man and was more concerned with giving unfettered expression to his nightmare visions than with celebrating the beauty of the Madonna.

The contrast between Memling and Bosch reflects the conditions of life in the Low Countries at the end of the 15th century. Commerce and industry were thriving and the cities rapidly acquiring great wealth. The court of the Dukes of Burgundy at Brussels was one of the most sumptuous in Europe and the Church had successfully adjusted mystical effusion to a well-ordered pattern of dogmas, symbols and sacred images controlled by a rigid iconography. But there was also much poverty and the country was so full of tramps and beggars that it was found necessary to organize a system of relief. Though frowned on by the Church, the mystical tradition still held its own; it was a tradition stemming from Jan van Ruysbroeck (1293-1381), the "Ecstatic Teacher," and from Geert Grote (1340-1384) who censured the misdeeds of the clergy and called for a moral and religious revival among the laity.

The religious conflicts of the Late Middle Ages made themselves felt with extreme virulence in Flanders. As Huizinga has pointed out, "the 15th century was a period of terrible depression and a life-sickness that boded ill for the future... Gloomy forebodings haunted the mind of 15th-century man: a constant fear of oppression and deeds of violence, obsessive thoughts of hell and the Last Judgment, of the perils of fire, famine and plague, of the nefarious doings of witches and evil spirits." But there was no hint of these apprehensions in the art of Van Eyck's disciples; whereas they loom large in that of Bosch.

**HIERONYMUS BOSCH**

Hieronymus Bosch (ca. 1450-1516) was born at Bois-le-Duc, called 's-Hertogenbosch in Dutch. Former capital of North Brabant, 's-Hertogenbosch was far removed from the great centers of Flemish art and strongly traditionalist in spirit. Bosch's father and grandfather were painters, and the family hailed from Aachen in Germany; hence the family name "Van Aken." But Hieronymus preferred to be known as "Bosch," last syllable of the name of his birthplace. There are frequent references to him in the records of the Brotherhood of Our Lady at Bois-le-Duc between 1480 and 1512; from them we learn that he was a member of the orchestra and regularly took part in the mystery plays—which goes to show that he spent all or most of his life in his hometown.

Temperamentally independent as a man and as an artist, he stood outside the art currents then developing in his native land and kept nearer to the tradition of the illuminators than to that of Flemish painting. But so adventurous was his genius that, with his eyes fixed on the past, he glimpsed what was to be the art of the future. Except in a few works dated after 1500, he shows no sign of any knowledge of humanism or of the Renaissance. He was a wholly medieval painter who, unwittingly bypassing the Renaissance, anticipated modern art.

The *Hay Wagon*, the *Garden of Earthly Delights* in the Prado and the Lisbon *Temptation of St Anthony* are works in which both subject and motifs were entirely original creations of the artist's imagination. The theme of the *Hay Wagon* comes from an old Flemish proverb: "The world is a heap of hay and everyone takes from it whatever he can grab." On the left wing are *The Fall of the Rebel Angels, The Creation of Eve, The Temptation* and *Adam and Eve expelled from Paradise.* This last scene acts as a prelude to the vision of moral degradation symbolized by the people crowding round the wagon, while on the right wing is a vision of Hell, lit by the glare of leaping flames —the destination of the persons represented on the central panel, the *Hay Wagon.* The latter contains a great number of small figures, amongst them the Pope, the Emperor and princes following the cart. A crowd is scrambling on to it, trying to snatch a wisp of the delectable fodder; some are falling under the wheels, others are eating and drinking or making music. On the side panels, when closed, is the *Prodigal Son.*

The Lisbon *Temptation of St Anthony* represents a fantastic Witches' Sabbath, in which fish, pigs and all kinds of animals assume more or less human forms. It is one of those weird "caprices" to which Bosch owes his fame and in which he conjures up from his prolific imagination unheard-of tortures and indulges in preposterous distortions.

In the *Garden of Earthly Delights* we are shown a seething mass of tiny figures acting out their vices in accordance with an elaborate symbolism like that set forth in the medieval dream-books. "The cherries, raspberries, strawberries and grapes they are being given and eating with such gusto are symbols of sexual pleasure. The apple-boat sheltering the lovers recalls a woman's breast, the birds symbolize lust and shame, and the fishes the thrills of sensual delight or secret fears, while the mold is a female emblem. Here Bosch has represented in telling form the repressed desires haunting the subconscious" (Charles de Tolnay). The wings, left and right, when open represent the Earthly Paradise and Hell respectively; when closed, a large, transparent sphere, the earth enveloped in water before the creation of man.

Thus the three pictures are allegories with a moral purpose, depicting the punishments in hell awaiting those who yield to the triple lure of the world, the flesh and the devil. They embody three commandments in pictorial form: Be chaste, Love poverty, Shun temptation. But though the painter was careful to include all the symbols of his message and took infinite pains over rendering each exactly, we may question if, being what they are, these extraordinary pictures really served a moral purpose.

At first sight one wonders why Bosch peopled these scenes with such tiny figures. But we have only to imagine the effect they would have produced had they been of normal size—in which case their lewd or uncouth postures would certainly have shocked the beholder. As it is, their smallness makes each scene look like a Lilliputian carnival or a puppet play. True, there are allusions to unnatural vices in the *Garden of Earthly Delights*, but these take the form of symbols; the manikins themselves are as chaste as anyone could wish. What is more, their facial expressions are childishly naïve. Far from "representing," Bosch merely "presents" these figures along with their symbols.

These observations are all the more pertinent when we remember that, anyhow in the *Hay Wagon* and the *Temptation of St Anthony*, the scenes purported to be dramatic. But Bosch was incapable of dramatic effects, even where these were called for and one cannot help feeling that those who read into his work an image of the degradation and anguish of the age he lived in tend to overvalue the moralist as against the artist.

The mainspring of his art is a prodigiously fertile and uninhibited imagination which, striking down to the subconscious, probes the depths of mind and heart, though without taking any of its finds too seriously, and on its return from these subliminal adventures tells the tale of them with cheerful gusto. For the world Bosch evokes is an imaginary one whose denizens are of the stuff that dreams are made of and no more tragical than Prospero's familiars. His lightness of touch and airy freedom enable him to create exquisitely lovely figures—pure despite the symbols—clad in the most delicate of colors. In short we cannot agree with those modern art critics who see in Bosch an expressionist or surrealist born before his time.

To appreciate Bosch's originality as a colorist, we must recall the use of color in the works of Van Eyck's school, for example in the *Portinari Altarpiece* (Uffizi), masterpiece of Hugo van der Goes. In it every color is given a jewel-like luster and we can see the artist's sensitivity of vision in his handling of the lights and shades flickering across each detail. Nevertheless the colors are everywhere conditioned by the images, and are not in any sense autonomous.

HIERONYMUS BOSCH (CA. 1450-1516). THE GARDEN OF EARTHLY DELIGHTS (DETAIL), CA. 1485.
CENTRAL PANEL OF A TRIPTYCH. PRADO, MADRID.

HIERONYMUS BOSCH (CA. 1450-1516). THE GARDEN OF EARTHLY DELIGHTS (DETAIL), CA. 1485.
CENTRAL PANEL OF A TRIPTYCH. PRADO, MADRID.

HIERONYMUS BOSCH (CA. 1450-1516). THE PRODIGAL SON. (53 1/8 × 39 1/4")
CLOSED WINGS OF THE "HAY WAGON" TRIPTYCH. PRADO, MADRID.

HIERONYMUS BOSCH (CA. 1450-1516). THE HAY WAGON. (53 ⅛ × 39 ¼″)
CENTRAL PANEL OF A TRIPTYCH. PRADO, MADRID.

Bosch was the first Nordic painter to achieve the color-light synthesis and keep in mind the tonal unity of the composition as a whole. In the fire in the background of the *St Anthony*, in the town on the right wing of the picture and, generally speaking in all his landscapes, color is used in a manner that was at the time entirely new.

In connection with the three major works discussed above, mention may here be made of some smaller ones which throw light on them from various angles. There is, for example, a series of pictures which, despite their religious subjects, are essentially genre scenes; also some illustrations of proverbs and texts. Though the theme of *The Miser's Death* (Private Collection, New York) derives from the *Ars Moriendi*, its tenor is far from being religious. In it Bosch expounds the vanity of human life with withering irony. The miser is reaching for a bag of gold while an angel bids him turn towards the crucifix and, in the foreground, a thief, holding a rosary in his left hand, stretches out his right towards the money a small devil is offering to him. Standing on the threshold, Death is letting fly an arrow at his victim, the arrow painted with extreme delicacy and precision, as though the artist, with cynical intent, wished to rivet our attention on it. Here, again, there is nothing dramatic in the scene. The light hues of the dying man, telling out in the middle distance against the red and green of the setting as a whole, draw our gaze towards him but, like Death and the thief, he does not seem really concerned with what is happening. What Bosch pictures here is not a conflict of angels and devils over a Christian deathbed; with elegance and feeling, he illustrates the ruthlessness of destiny and the predicament of a soul wavering between vice and virtue.

When painting the *Seven Deadly Sins* (Prado) to decorate a tray, Bosch felt free to introduce motifs culled from popular farces. In *Gluttony* the table manners of the two men eating and drinking are so gross as to be frankly comic and no less ludicrous in *Anger* is the contrast between the would-be ferocity of the gesticulations and their complete innocuousness. Presumably Bosch (anticipating Bergson) saw in ridicule an instrument for curing humanity of its vices, and felt no need to dramatize them.

The *Ship of Fools* in the Louvre (illustrating Sebastian Brant's satirical poem *Das Narrenschiff*, published at Basel in 1494) is full of whimsical inventions, though the formal structure, built up by images in profile painted flat on a background of leafage, is rigorously synthetic. We find similar forms in the mystical scenes of the Berlin *St John in Patmos*, whose themes may have derived from engravings of the "Master E. S." and Schongauer; if so, Bosch thoroughly transformed them and in so doing produced a singularly fine seascape worthy of the greatest Dutch landscape painters of the 17th century. But what strikes one most in this work is its visionary power, sublimating every detail on to a mystical plane; it contains no action, no expression of any definable sentiment, but by his very fidelity to the sacred text the artist brings before us the world of strange enchantments glimpsed by the seer of the Apocalypse.

In the *Altarpiece of the Hermits* (Ducal Palace, Venice), depicting St Anthony, St Jerome and St Giles, though the forms of the devils trying to distract the saints from their prayers are grotesque to a degree, the figures of St Jerome and particularly St Giles

HIERONYMUS BOSCH (CA. 1450-1516). THE PRODIGAL SON (DETAIL).
CLOSED WINGS OF THE "HAY WAGON" TRIPTYCH. PRADO, MADRID.

are invested with a wonderful spiritual purity, attesting the artist's deep religious sensibility. Less successful to our thinking are the *Ecce Homo* (Philadelphia) and the various versions of the *Bearing of the Cross* in which the artist's lack of a dramatic sense weakens the general effect. Thus he fails to bring out the vulgarity and bestiality of Christ's tormentors, and he similarly fails to spiritualize the face of Christ. Though forms and colors are handled with consummate elegance, the subject was manifestly unsuited to his peculiar genius.

As with many painters, it is the drawings that reveal his style at its clearest, most spontaneous. The figure studies for the *Conjuror* (Louvre), with their light touches and breaks in the line, are wonderfully vivacious. True, the Gothic elements in his art are more prominent in his drawings than in his paintings, yet in *Forest that listens and Field that sees* (Kupferstich Kabinett, Berlin) and *Owl's Nest on a Branch* (Rotterdam) medieval symbolism and Gothic whimsy do not detract from the pictorial values of the composition as a whole; such indeed is the freedom and broadness of the execution that they rank beside the finest Venetian drawings of the 16th century.

In the artist's last works (i.e. those thought to be subsequent to 1500) a great change has come over his style. To begin with, the human figure is treated on a larger scale and for this reason greater stress is laid on plastic values. Also, there are signs of a new, more responsible moral attitude towards the persons represented. This becomes evident when we compare the Prado *Adoration of the Magi*, a work of Bosch's last phase, with the Philadelphia version of the same theme, made in his youth. The latter is a medieval story-teller's picture, naïve, fanciful and daintily executed without any great concern for composition; in the Prado version, on the other hand, the figures are grandiose, wholly subordinated to their religious function, and instinct with dignity. The same is true of the personages in the side panels: donors and their sponsors watching the sacred scene. Here all the qualities of the artist's early style are present but, with them, a new feeling for architecturally ordered composition. The background consists of an exquisitely rendered landscape, endowed with a poetic glamour singularly "modern" in tone. Also in the Prado is a *Temptation of St Anthony* belonging to the last period. Demons and their retinue of hybrid monsters still are present but the figure of the saint dominates the scene, its volumes stressed by strong foreshortenings; while the face expresses a serene, unwavering faith and an invincible determination to withstand the tempter's wiles.

Greatest perhaps of the works of Bosch's last period is the *Prodigal Son* (Boymans Museum, Rotterdam). When we compare this with his rendering of the same theme on the side panels of the *Hay Wagon* (Prado) we see that in the latter it is treated anecdotally, like an incident of village life. But in the Rotterdam version the prodigal son is shown as the protagonist, a commanding figure skillfully adapted to the octagonal shape of the panel. Vigorous modeling and bold design, combined with more closely knit composition, enable the artist to bring out more clearly the affective values of the scene. The returning prodigal bears the marks of his privations, has realized the folly of his ways and timidly pleads to be taken back into the home he has forsaken.

There is a haunting pathos in his gaze as he craves forgiveness, and his somber mood is mirrored in the uniform greyness of the countryside and sky, against which the softest, tenderest colors of Bosch's palette shine out gently, like a promise of compassion.

For towards the close of his life Bosch abandoned that mood of savage irony which gives his early work its piquancy, and developed a new sense of moral responsibility, reflected in a tightening-up of his composition and a greater concern with modeling. What, we may wonder, were the reasons for these changes? Was it that on the threshold of old age he gave more thought to the serious side of life? Or was it that he then had come, if by indirect channels, under the influence of Italian art, as is suggested by the *sfumato* in the Ghent *Bearing of the Cross*?

All the same his creative powers are seen at their best when he is in his satirical vein, so well seconded by his broken line and softly luminous colors. It was this that led him to react against the dogmatism of the medieval Church and to champion the cause of the common people, helpless victims of ecclesiastical oppression and social prejudice. To start with, Bosch applied himself to scourging the follies of his time but he gradually moved towards a purer mode of expression, imbuing even the vulgarest images with the sensitivity that had come to him in his middle years. Little by little he achieved a serener vision, putting fantasy to the service of that which is inexplicable in terms of reason. And in the end he gives a glimpse of his true feelings, a vast pity for mankind and a truly Christian charity, in the gaze of the *Prodigal Son* whose folly has brought him to perdition.

**QUENTIN MASSYS**

Bosch was too isolated a figure to be the founder of a school, though many artists (even in Italy) borrowed or adapted some of his motifs without, however, troubling to integrate them in a coherent whole. The only artist who followed in his steps and infused new life into his discoveries was Pieter Brueghel.

Not that there was any dearth of able artists in the Low Countries at the time, one such being Gerard David, who still kept to the traditions of the 15th century. The first to try to graft the art of Leonardo on to the Eyckian tradition (as represented by Dirk Bouts) was Quentin Massys, born in 1466 at Louvain. The earliest mention of him is an entry, dated 1493, in the records of the Guild of St Luke at Antwerp naming him a member. Though resident in that city till his death in 1530, he never lost touch with his hometown and in 1507 was commissioned to paint a triptych for the Confraternity of St Anne at Louvain; this work was completed two years later. In 1508 the Antwerp Carpenters' Guild ordered from him a *Pietà* (finished in 1511) for their chapel in the local cathedral. By this time Massys evidently enjoyed an international reputation, since in 1509 he got an order from Lisbon. He was on friendly terms with some of the most enlightened men of the age, amongst others Thomas More and Erasmus. During his visit to the Netherlands, Dürer called on him, but the two artists do not seem to have taken to each other.

The Brussels *St Anne* triptych (1507-1509) best illustrates the rather special nature of his art. In the central panel are the Virgin, the Child and St Anne, and in the

QUENTIN MASSYS (1466-1530). THE BANKER AND HIS WIFE, 1514. (29 × 26¾")
LOUVRE, PARIS.

foreground, seated beside their children, the Marys of Scripture with four men a little behind them, and some Italianate architecture in the background. This might well be a domestic picture of the household of some opulent, complacent burgher; the men are properly sedate while the women are all grace and smiles. These people seem to belong to the class of the new-rich then coming to the fore in Antwerp. Similarly the scene of the *Death of St Anne* on a side panel is represented with a dainty elegance better suited to some ceremonious occasion than to the tragic event it purports to depict. The composition of the Antwerp *Pietà* (1508-1511) is inspired by Rogier van der Weyden's masterpiece of the same name, but it lacks the spirituality of its prototype, failing to convey any real sense of grief. The people painted by this artist belong to an élite preening itself on its refinement, and though their nerves are always on the stretch they seem incapable of genuine passion.

But Massys has a keen feeling for beauty, if a somewhat formal beauty, fined down to its purest elements. This can be seen in the group formed by Mary, wife of Zebedaeus, with her two sons, James the Greater and John the Evangelist (central panel of the *St Anne* triptych) and in the *Three Marys at the Tomb* (formerly in Berlin), where the smiling grace of the figures is hardly ruffled at all by any outward sign of grief. In his pictures of the Virgin, Massys kept to the Eyckian tradition, while stressing volumes in the Renaissance manner (e.g. the superb *Virgin* in Brussels and that in the Dyson-Perrins Collection, London). On the other hand, when he lets himself be influenced too strongly by Leonardo, he makes blunders, as proved by the Poznan *Virgin*, obviously copied from Leonardo's *St Anne*. Sometimes, apparently conscious of his shortcomings, he sets out to emphasize expressive and emotive values, as in the Berlin *Virgin Enthroned*, where he represents the Mother kissing her Son—with ludicrous results.

His feeling for Renaissance art led him to invest his figures with dignity, but dignity of a social rather than a moral order. Thus he was poles apart from Bosch and when he tried to emulate him lost his bearings. The *Ecce Homo* at Madrid looks like a self-caricature, and the *Temptation of St Anthony* (whose landscape setting was done by Patinir) like a garden party that has taken an erotic turn. The women's figures, and even the saint's, are gracious, winsome—and suggestive.

By far the most popular of Massys' pictures is the *Banker and his Wife* (Louvre), painted in 1514, which shows the couple seated side by side at a table on which are gold coins, a mirror and other tokens of their wealth. Behind them are two shelves strewn with books and miscellaneous objects, rendered with much accuracy and skillfully disposed. The man, who is weighing coins, seems to have fallen into a brown study while his wife who has been perusing an illuminated book turns towards him, a pensive look on her face. They are represented as thoughtful, amiable people, curiously indifferent to worldly concerns, despite the husband's occupation. (In this connection we must remember that to the medieval mind anyone whose business involved dealing in money was usually styled a "usurer.") Seemingly what Massys was aiming at here was to achieve a purely formal beauty by excluding all expressive elements; if so, he failed in his attempt, and this indeed is what makes this little genre piece so delightful.

Given Massys' temperament as set forth above, it was only to be expected that he would excel as a portrait painter. And in fact he had a gift for seizing on the decisive moment when a character betrays itself in a casual gesture or fugitive expression. Typical examples of this can be seen in the diptych, dated 1517, containing portraits of Erasmus (now in the Galleria Nazionale, Rome) and Petrus Aegidius (Longford Castle, Salisbury), in which the figures, done from the life at a revealing moment, bring the very men before our eyes.

There are, however, other portraits of a different nature, those which are built to an architectonic plan, deriving perhaps from Giovanni Bellini. Typical of these is the *Ecclesiastic* (Liechtenstein Collection, Vaduz), whose pyramidal structure standing up against a landscape background gives an impression of massive power, like that of a monument built to last forever.

JOACHIM PATINIR

Born at Bouvignes (near Namur, in present-day Belgium) some time between 1475 and 1480, Joachim Patinir is first mentioned in 1515 as a painter at Antwerp, where he died in 1524. He may have studied with Gerard David at Bruges and certainly collaborated with Quentin Massys at Antwerp. Inspired by Bosch, he specialized in panoramic landscapes which, such is their topographical precision, might almost be described as pictorial maps. These earned him an international reputation. Dürer spoke highly of his landscapes and the Spanish connoisseur Felipe de Guevara, writing about 1540, ranked him with Van Eyck and Rogier van der Weyden among the leading Flemish masters.

While it is true that none of the works unquestionably his are ever without figures, these figures, notably in his religious scenes, are extremely small, dwarfed by the vast expanse of countryside that fills the picture. Patinir in fact, as all contemporary observers noted, was essentially a landscape painter and it was as such that he made his name. As we have seen, the figures in his *Temptation of St Anthony* (Prado) were painted in by Quentin Massys. Here we have an example of that collaboration between artists which,

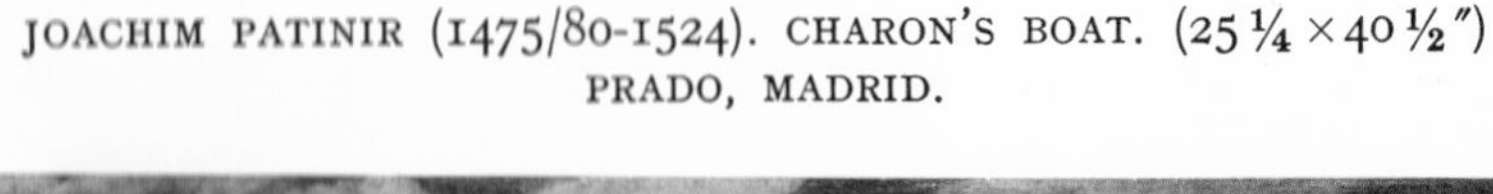

JOACHIM PATINIR (1475/80-1524). CHARON'S BOAT. (25 ¼ × 40 ½″)
PRADO, MADRID.

JOACHIM PATINIR (1475/80-1524). THE REST ON THE FLIGHT INTO EGYPT (DETAIL). PRADO, MADRID.

while very rare in the early 16th century, became a common practice in the next, when each painter tended to confine himself to a specific genre: landscape, still life and so forth. Patinir's specialization in landscape led him to devote much interest to the technical problems peculiar to this form of art. For example he raised his horizon so as to embrace as wide a stretch of country as possible, using three basic tones: brown for the foreground, green for the middle distance, blue for the mountains spanning a remote horizon. Friedländer attributes the popularity of Patinir's landscapes—proved by their many imitations—to the new conditions under which works of art were then being bought and sold. Up to the end of the 15th century artists painted what local authorities and influential private patrons commissioned them to paint, and little else. But in the prosperous city of Antwerp in the early 16th century—as also in Venice—painters were beginning to cater for the hypothetical buyer, for the art lover who visited artists' studios, inspected the finished works and bought the ones that caught his fancy. Conditions, of course, were not everywhere favorable to artists; in Basel, for example, Holbein was hard put to it to find customers. Then, too, with Protestantism sweeping over the North (with iconoclasm in its wake), the private buyer may have shied away from religious scenes; to him a landscape, pleasing to the eye and non-committal, must have seemed the safest picture to acquire.

In such a work as Patinir's *Flight into Egypt* (Antwerp) we notice that the tiny group of figures representing the Holy Family actually counts for very little in the picture. Most prominent are a strange rock formation, a clump of trees and three or four houses; beyond these are woodlands and fields forming a wide circle around a land-locked bay; in the background are mountains and a wide stretch of sky dappled with drifting clouds. This type of landscape differs greatly from that of Altdorfer; its far-flung vistas lure the eye to explore the distant scene and linger on a gay profusion of colors before coming to rest on a far horizon. But a vision of this kind was not self-sufficing, it had to "tell a story." The landscape became a work of art in its own right only when the panoramic view dissolved into a general effect of light and shade, as was the case with the great Dutch landscapes of the 17th century. Still, as a representation of nature the *Flight into Egypt* is a good specimen of the genre to which it belongs, fascinating in its variety of motifs and for the finesse of the execution. This type of landscape became so popular that it persisted until the end of the century.

Similar to it, but more broadly treated, is the *St Jerome* in the Duensing Collection (at Boizenburg, near Hamburg); here the rocks are even more contorted and fantastic. No less strange are the arbitrary shapes of the mountains, tooth-like projections interspersed with castles and caves, in the two versions of the *Assumption of St Mary of Egypt* (Duensing Collection and Crespi Collection, Milan); these scenes also include some animistic motifs borrowed from Bosch. In the Prado *St Jerome* the contrasts of light and shade in the landscape are given an independent pictorial value above and beyond mere panoramic effect. The bright sky overhung with lowering clouds is reflected in the clear waters of the river bordered by dark woodlands. Nowhere in Patinir's work are such light effects better realized than in the Prado *Charon's Boat,* where running up perpendicularly to the horizon the sluggish river mirrors the brightness of the sky with an intensity enhanced by the black trees on the bank. A pallid figure paddling a white boat, Charon is ferrying a lost soul to the Underworld whose leaping flames we glimpse on the far right. Despite the nature of the theme, the mood of the landscape is one of fine serenity, an idyll in Patinir's best vein.

JAN VAN SCOREL

Jan van Scorel was born at Schoorl, near Alkmaar, in 1495 and died in 1562. A product of the 15th-century realist tradition in the Netherlands but shaped by a diversity of later influences, his art evolved first in the direction of Gossaert, then in that of Dürer. After a long journey through Germany and Austria to Venice, and a voyage to Palestine, he settled in 1521 in Rome, where he studied ancient art and the works of Raphael and Michelangelo. In 1522 Adrian VI, a Dutchman, was elected pope and he appointed Scorel, then aged twenty-seven, to succeed Raphael (who had died in 1520) as keeper of the art collections at the Vatican. But the pope died in 1523, and next year Scorel returned to Holland, working for a time in Haarlem, then settling in Utrecht. This was a considerable fund of experience for an artist not yet thirty years old and it fully accounts for his abrupt change of style. That he was able to veer from northern realism to Italian mannerism without losing his balance says much for the versatility of his talent.

The *Portrait of Agatha van Schoonhoven* (Galleria Doria, Rome), being dated 1529, was painted after his return to Holland. It is one of his masterpieces, firmly rooted in the Dutch portrait tradition, yet embellished by that Italian grace and suavity whose secrets he had learnt in Rome. These combine to make it a typical work of the northern Renaissance. In other pictures, however, Scorel drew heavily on mannerism; in *Bathsheba* (Amsterdam), for example. Here there is no action and the nudes are considerably elongated—one in fact is copied from a sculpture by Michelangelo—while the landscape, on the other hand, still keeps to the Flemish tradition.

By and large, Scorel exerted a marked influence on mannerism in the Netherlands, an influence that will be discussed in our last chapter, dealing with the spread of mannerism throughout Europe.

LUCAS VAN LEYDEN

The importance of Lucas van Leyden lies in the fact that his style is markedly different from the traditional Flemish style and has many features in common with that of the great Dutch artists of a later generation. In his lifetime he was famous as an engraver rather than as a painter; the same is true of Dürer, whose influence on him, in all respects, was far stronger than that of the Flemings. Lucas might be described as one of the many painter-storytellers of the Middle Ages; he drew and painted, however, with an uncompromising sincerity and bluntness of statement worthy of a protestant reformer, though he never actually renounced the catholic faith. What interested him most was the correct delineation of the human figure, his interest in it being essentially technical, not aesthetic. Throughout the 16th century his name was a household word amongst artists all over Europe, even in Italy, stress being laid on his complete originality.

Born at Leyden in 1494, he was trained first by his father Hugo Jacobsz, then by Cornelis Engelbrechtsz. The boy proved to be something of a child prodigy and rapidly made a name for himself. In 1517 he married into one of Leyden's leading patrician families. In 1521 we find him at Antwerp where he met Dürer; the two became fast friends and each presented the other with a set of his prints. In 1527 Lucas made a tour of the Netherlands, junketing and reveling all the way and, as contemporary observers noted, "living like a lord"; he returned to Leyden a sick man. Thereafter his health steadily declined and he died in 1533, not yet forty. A tissue of legends quickly grew up around his name, which, though doing much to spread his renown, tended to obscure the true facts of his life.

In Brunswick Museum is a *Self-Portrait* painted by Lucas at the age of fifteen. Brutally forthright, dashed off with a turbulent vitality reminding us of Frans Hals, this is not only the work of a strong personality, but contains in embryo much that was to characterize Dutch painting a century later. Both in his prints and paintings, Lucas proved himself an unflinching realist, though mannerist elements usually make their presence felt beneath his realism.

LUCAS VAN LEYDEN (1494-1533). CARD-PLAYERS, CA. 1514. (14 × 18 5/8")
COLLECTION OF THE EARL OF PEMBROKE, WILTON HOUSE.

JAN VAN SCOREL (1495-1562). PORTRAIT OF AGATHA VAN SCHOONHOVEN, 1529. (14½ × 11″)
GALLERIA DORIA-PAMPHILI, ROME.

The *Healing of the Blind Man of Jericho* (Leningrad), dated 1531, is remarkable for the capable marshaling of figures, the fine sweep of the landscape and the skillful oppositions of lights and darks. The style in the main is that of the Renaissance, though in the two standard-bearers on the side panels we see traces of the transition from Gothic to Mannerism. This mannerist trend is also evident in his *Last Judgment* altarpiece (Leyden), painted in 1526. Here he obviously started with Italian models in mind, but successfully recast the formal, classical conception of the nude by the impetuous vigor of his brushwork. The side panels represent Paradise and Hell when open, and St Peter and St Paul when closed. But the culminating point of Lucas's mannerist phase was probably the Berlin *St Jerome*, generally assigned to 1516. Granted that the dating of these pictures is accurate, they illustrate a stylistic development ranging from Mannerism to Renaissance realism—which goes to prove once again that Mannerism could be arrived at by way of Late Gothic.

PIETER BRUEGHEL (CA. 1525/30-1569). HEAD OF AN OLD PEASANT WOMAN, CA. 1568. (8⅝ × 7⅛″)
ALTE PINAKOTHEK, MUNICH.

PIETER BRUEGHEL

Our knowledge of Brueghel's life is very meager. We know for certain neither the date—some time between 1525 and 1530—nor the place of his birth; probably he came from North Brabant, which forms part of present-day Holland. The earliest mention of him is an entry in the membership rolls of the Antwerp Painters' Guild for the year 1551. In 1552, going by way of Lyons, he traveled to Italy where he is known to have resided in 1552-1553. Back in the Netherlands, he went into partnership with Hieronymus Cock in 1555, producing landscape drawings which the latter engraved. Brueghel's interest seems to have centered for years on engraving, the bulk of his paintings dating from after 1562.

He made a trip to Amsterdam in 1562 and the following year married the daughter of Pieter Coeck, under whom, according to Van Mander, he had studied painting. From now on he made his home in Brussels, where in 1565 the City Council ordered a painting from him to commemorate the opening of the Brussels-Antwerp canal, but he died in 1569 without having filled the commission.

Success came quickly to Brueghel and his work was much sought after by contemporaries. The most influential Catholic dignitary in the Netherlands, Cardinal Antoine Perrenot de Granvella, eagerly collected his pictures. Niclaes Jonghelinck, a wealthy Antwerp burgher, bought sixteen of his canvases and in 1565 commissioned the series of *Months*, one of Brueghel's finest achievements.

He had many friends in intellectual circles. One of his intimates was the famous geographer and humanist Abraham Ortelius, and in Rome the miniature-painter Giulio Clovio, then at the height of his fame, welcomed Brueghel's collaboration. In his *Descrittione di tutti i Paesi Bassi* written in 1567, two years before Brueghel's death, Ludovico Guicciardini refers to him with much respect. Vasari gives a detailed account of several prints made after Brueghel's designs and Dominicus Lampsonius (1572) voiced his admiration of his work. His friend Ortelius, hailing him as the greatest artist of his age, contrasted his bold originality with the stylizations of the mannerists. In 1604 Carel van Mander, in his *Schilderboek*, published the first biography of Brueghel. By the 18th century, however, his reputation was at its lowest ebb; the great French connoisseur Pierre-Jean Mariette was alone in appreciating his genius, as was Baudelaire in the 19th century. Brueghel began his return to favor about 1890 and today he is one of the most popular of all Old Masters.

In the absence of firsthand documentary material, great artists' lives become the helpless prey of legend-mongers; Brueghel's is a typical instance. Because peasant life and carousals were stock themes of his paintings, it was taken for granted that he too was of peasant extraction. Then, more recently, when light was thrown on his familiarity with the Italian Renaissance, it was promptly assumed that Brueghel was a humanist of the Platonic school. But what do the paintings themselves tell us about the man? They tell us that he painted scenes of peasant life because he was an original artist of a refined yet lusty temper, highly conscious of his powers; they tell us, too, that, for all his intimacy with it, he reacted against the Italian Renaissance. Given the period and place in which he lived, Brueghel's art necessarily owed something to mannerism (an important point first made by Max Dvořák), but it was more in the nature of a counterblast to it. Even if he is not the "anthropologist and social philosopher" that Aldous Huxley (in *Along the Road*) sees in him, he is certainly a poet, adept in comedy and tragi-comedy, as well as a shrewd assessor of national character in the Netherlands (Friedländer). And, as we shall see presently, there can be no question of separating form and factual content (the "human comedy") in his work.

Brueghel's contemporaries, so Lampsonius informs us, looked on him as a kind of improved edition of Bosch, and this view, in the main, is still current. What Bosch had done—and he was the first artist in the Netherlands to take this step—was to paint religious and edifying subjects without the least regard to the long-established traditions of ecclesiastical art; he went out of the church, mingled with the people of his native Flanders, and voiced the feelings of the common man. So far as is known, Brueghel never painted a single picture intended to figure in a church, thus radically departing from a tradition that went back to Van Eyck; in this he took a liberty whose only precedent was that of Bosch. To Bosch, too, he owed his handling of color, in particular a nicety of tonal values brought out by contrasting touches of bright, pure hues. Unthinkable without Bosch is his way of patterning the composition with tiny figures arranged, not in depth, but on the surface—and this despite his thorough knowledge of perspective.

This, however, is not to say that Brueghel merely carried on and perfected the art of his great predecessor. Rather, he followed his own bent. Bosch had peopled the workaday world with visions of saints and demons; Brueghel left them out altogether, painting nature and daily life without any celestial or diabolic interventions, yet imparting to the passing moment an accent of eternity. Bosch, too, had treated nature as ever-present in man's daily life, but with an eye to stressing everywhere the conflict between good and evil. Brueghel, on the contrary, takes a broad, synthetic point of view of good and evil, thanks to his wider sympathy with human nature and the world around him, even its least pleasing elements.

A picture by Brueghel—in this he follows Bosch and medieval tradition—presents itself as a sequence in time, as against the Italian conception of a sequence in space rendered by perspective. But with Brueghel this chronological arrangement acquires a new efficacy owing to his presentation of the motifs as successive acts in a comedy, following each other like the happenings of a day. It was not from Bosch that he got this notion of an actuality without transcendence; it was Brueghel himself who, thanks to the climate of his time, achieved a new sense of reality, of the "mechanism of the world," as it then was called. This new viewpoint owed much to the Italian Renaissance, but even more perhaps to the typically Nordic conception of what Luther called the "*servum arbitrium*," i.e. the total subordination of human will to the inscrutable designs of Divine Providence. In this respect, then, Brueghel's art may be considered as a synthesis of the Middle Ages and the Renaissance, of the Reformation and the science of nature, of the moral life and freedom of thought. A child of the Middle Ages, Brueghel heralded the dawn of modern times.

PIETER BRUEGHEL (CA. 1525/30-1569). THE HARVESTERS, 1565. (46½ × 63¼″)
BY COURTESY OF THE METROPOLITAN MUSEUM OF ART, NEW YORK.

There is another antinomy in his art. Though patronized by Cardinal Granvella and the Emperor Rudolph II, Brueghel again and again portrayed the sufferings of the victims of catholic and imperial persecution in the Netherlands. Hence the stress usually laid on his friendship with Ortelius, who sympathized with the so-called "libertines" or Anabaptists, regarded as heretics by orthodox Catholics. At this time patriots all over the Low Countries were rallying against the Spaniards and beginning the fight for independence; so there is some justification for reading anti-Spanish —in other words patriotic—intentions into his pictures. This is borne out by a passage in Van Mander's life of the artist: "As some [of his drawings] were too biting and sharp, he had them burnt by his wife when he lay on his death-bed." It is impossible to come to a definite conclusion on the matter, but there is certainly no question that Brueghel's social satire, far more pointed and more daring than that of Bosch, was hardly likely to be appreciated by those responsible for the tragic plight of the Low Countries. Or was it simply that they took pleasure in the spectacle of others' sufferings, like the Roman aristocrats of the next century who so gleefully collected the low-life scenes painted by the "Bamboccianti"?

As suggested above, comedy is implicit in Brueghel's form no less than in his themes. His is neither the polished form of the Italians nor the grotesque extravagance of Bosch. Indeed it might be said that he lays little stress on form. Yet if we inspect his figures closely, we find that they are carefully built up in terms of volumes and adjusted to a geometric structure of cones, cylinders and the like. The results are, first, that their inherent energy as constructive elements of a whole is intensified; and, secondly, that their expressive power as individual forms is attenuated in the interest of compositional unity.

Precisely because he passes no judgment, moral or aesthetic, on the persons he depicts, Brueghel attains a reality beyond good and evil, beyond the beautiful and the ugly, the noble and the base. Human life writ large obliterates the individual and his personal aspirations; personality is submerged in anonymity, faces express neither joy nor fear, but dwindle to moon-like masks. There is here no intimation of destiny, for that is something operating from outside; each man bears his own fate within himself. Brueghel's attitude is that of a disillusioned observer, perhaps embittered, but assuredly resigned to the vagaries of the human situation. This impersonality inevitably led up to the genre scene; indeed both the *Procession to Calvary* and the *Conversion of St Paul* might be described as such, so completely are the figures of Christ and Paul merged into the mass of secondary figures. The "hero," idealized and set on a pedestal by the Italians, was eliminated from the field of art in Brueghel's work, and the historical picture shared his fate. Tolnay has pointed out the striking parallel between Brueghel's hordes of undistinguished figures and a passage in the writings of Sebastian Franck, the German freethinker, who died while Brueghel was still a boy: "Life is one and always the same on this earth. Every man is but a man. When we see a man as nature made him, we see all men."

As far as is known, Brueghel began his career by drawing and painting landscapes. In his quaint but telling style Van Mander writes: "On his journeys Brueghel did so many views from nature that it was said of him that, when he traveled through the Alps, he had swallowed all the mountains and rocks, and spat them out again, after his return, on to his canvases and panels." His pictures confirm these words. As a landscape painter, he aimed at an exact representation of reality, neither prettifying nor idealizing what he saw. Thus while a drawing in Berlin (1552) shows a featureless, quite ordinary mountain, another in the Louvre, dated 1553, shows a majestic, rugged mountain looming above a plain, with storm-clouds gathering overhead. When he was in Italy Brueghel must have seen one of those drawings by Leonardo which seem like pitched battles between natural elements. The earliest dated landscape painting (1553) is *Christ appearing to the Apostles at the Sea of Tiberias*; here the figures are so small that they almost pass unnoticed in the landscape, which, however, still owes much to Patinir.

Far more original is the *View of Naples* (Galleria Doria, Rome), in which the scene is viewed from above and forms are so well adapted to the circular sweep of a mountain range that the breakwater too—rectangular in reality—has become a semicircle. The city is placed far back so as to leave ample room for a fine seascape dotted with boats of various shapes and sizes and for a view of the crowded wharves. The presentation is still topographical, embracing a vast panorama, but the handling of the scene is painterly and strikingly effective.

In 1555 he began work on the *Large Landscape Series*, engraved by Hieronymus Cock. The variety of motifs—trees, mountains, rivers—and the deep spatial recession

PIETER BRUEGHEL (CA. 1525/30-1569). THE NUMBERING AT BETHLEHEM, 1566. (45⅝×64¾″) MUSÉE DES BEAUX-ARTS, BRUSSELS.

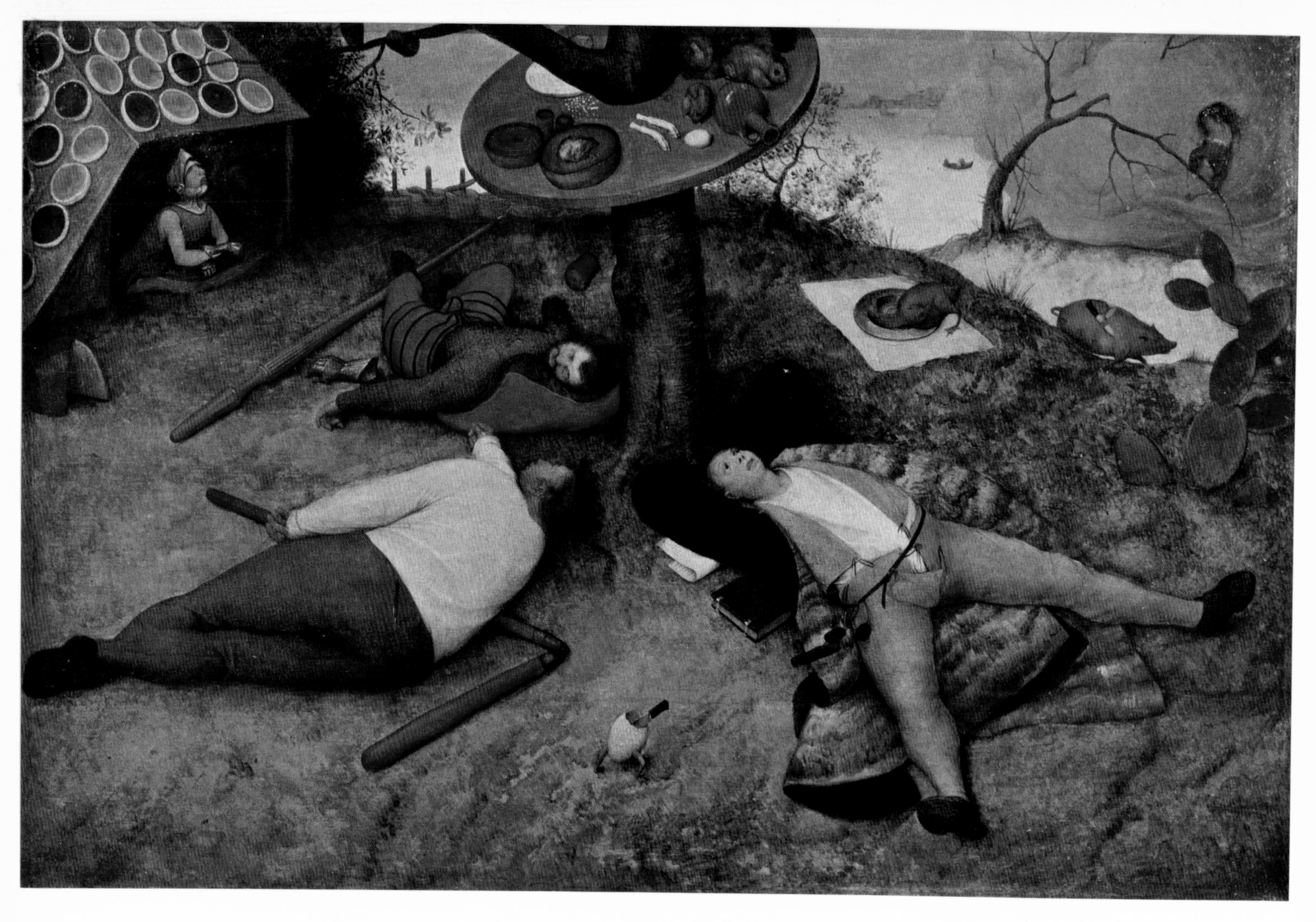

PIETER BRUEGHEL (CA. 1525/30-1569). THE LAND OF COCKAIGNE, 1567. (20½ × 30¾″)
ALTE PINAKOTHEK, MUNICH.

testify to the artist's desire to include as vast a prospect as possible. Then, to please his public with a touch of "human interest," he added figures, for example soldiers resting on the march, pilgrims on the way to Emmaus, or the Magdalen.

The expressive tension of the landscapes is stepped up by the colors. The *Fall of Icarus* (Brussels) is a case in point. Far from being the tragic scene suggested by the title, it is a lyrical depiction of a sunlit bay and foreshore. Here a high viewpoint helps to bring out the convexity of the sea stretching into the distance, while a subtle play of light vivifies and individualizes each element of the picture. Quite unaffected by the fate of the young flyer, who is seen sinking beneath the waves in the lower righthand corner of the picture, are the ploughman, shepherd and fisherman, but even more striking is the vast serenity of nature shown in all her smiling beauty. The other side of nature, her elemental fury, is illustrated in the *Storm at Sea* (Vienna). No human figure is visible; driven by the gale, ships are laboring in the troughs of gigantic waves that weave a sinuous linear arabesque across the picture surface, while gleams of livid light slash the blue-black expanse of sea and sky. This is not so much a representation of nature as the eye beholds her as the revelation of one of her moods.

Occasionally Brueghel forgoes the panoramic approach, as in a drawing at Brunswick, *Village Landscape* (1562), in which the subject is treated as a mere pretext for the rendering, in tiny lines of yellow ink, of the vibration of the light enveloping objects. The more he narrows down his subject-matter, the closer he gets to the life of nature. And it is this perception of the spiritual and eternal present behind the here-and-now that purifies and universalizes his art, and, differentiating him from Bosch and Patinir, links him up—as Van Mander rightly observed--with Titian.

Although the pictures he painted in the last decade of his life (1559-1569) form a group apart, we can trace in them a gradual evolution of his style—as was only natural, considering that the artist was still a relatively young man. The *Fight between Carnival and Lent* (Vienna) and the *Netherlandish Proverbs* (Berlin) date from 1559; the *Children's Games* from 1560. All three have much in common: the distribution of a number of small figures along an inclined plane running up to a high horizon-line, which reduces the problems of space representation to a minimum; a simplified type of composition,

PIETER BRUEGHEL (CA. 1525/30-1569). THE PARABLE OF THE BLIND, 1568. (33⅞ × 60⅝")
MUSEO NAZIONALE, NAPLES.

though in the last two pictures figures are grouped diagonally in order to suggest spatial recession. Notable is the union of ground and figures by means of color, and the scaling down of the latter to the aspect of automatons whose comic, apparently pointless antics are a perpetual source of surprise. The sudden beauty of certain figures and bits of landscape stresses the temporal values implicit in the motifs; we seem to be watching a comedy unfolding itself scene by scene.

One of the most remarkable of Brueghel's pictures, the *Triumph of Death* (Prado), differs radically from medieval versions of this subject in that here it is visualized as a pitched battle between the living and the dead—the victory of the latter being assured by sheer numbers. There are dramatic touches such as the bleak desolation of the background and gruesome acts of violence, but these are merely incidental. The message Brueghel sought to convey was one of forlorn resignation: "Such is the human condition, whether you like it or not."

Three major pictures date from 1562. The first of these, the *Fall of the Rebel Angels* (Brussels), is also a meditation on death, a theme which seems to have obsessed the artist at the time. The fallen angels are monsters worthy of Bosch, while the celestial angels are graceful figures carrying out their murderous task with joyous unconcern; the tragic drama of divine reprisal is submerged in comedy. The *Dulle Griet* or "Mad Meg" (Mayer van den Bergh Museum, Antwerp) represents a hag whose greed has emboldened her to visit Hell in quest of plunder. The disproportion between her tall ungainly figure and the Lilliputian creatures swarming around her is a throwback to medieval tradition, but the mordant satire of the scene as a whole, especially the group of shrews cudgeling a hapless pack of devils, is strangely modern in spirit. Presumably the *Two Monkeys* (Berlin) has some symbolic meaning yet to be elucidated. Meanwhile we can enjoy for its own sake this picture of two monkeys chained in a low dark archway opening on a sunlit view of Antwerp and the Scheldt.

We have another type of picture altogether in the *Suicide of Saul* (1562) and the *Conversion of St Paul* (1568), both in Vienna. In each a rugged Alpine landscape lends an epic grandeur to a scene of armies locked in battle or on the march. In a corner of the first we see Saul running himself through with his sword, while in the middle distance of the second Paul has just been thrown from his horse; but these incidents almost pass unnoticed, the artist's interest manifestly lay elsewhere. The *Procession to Calvary* (1564, Vienna) is a biting satire of the callous indifference of the crowd present at the tragic scene. In striking contrast is the delicately sensitive rendering of the little group in the foreground surrounding the weeping Virgin.

In 1565 Brueghel was commissioned to paint the series of *Months*, of which today only five are extant: *January* or *Hunters in the Snow* (Vienna), *February* or *The Gloomy Day* (Vienna), *July* or *Hay Making* (Prague), *August* or *The Harvesters* (Metropolitan, New York) and *November* or *The Return of the Herd* (Vienna). These rank among his finest works. We have seen him as a satirist, tilting at the follies of mankind, the futility of their griefs and joys. But he was a born landscape painter and if there was one thing he held sacred, one thing his satire spared, this was nature. Village

PIETER BRUEGHEL (CA. 1525/30-1569). THE MAGPIE ON THE GALLOWS, 1568. (18 1/8 × 20″)
LANDESMUSEUM, DARMSTADT.

life in the snow and gloom of winter, the lush exuberance of summertime, the wistful melancholy of autumn—these themes, in his hands, become so many evocations of the very soul of nature. Most popular of these scenes is *Hunters in the Snow*, in which dark silhouettes of peasants and ice-skaters, the descending line of tall bare trees and the structural perfection of the snowbound landscape give the full measure of his greatness. Broader and vaster is the landscape of the *Gloomy Day*; instead of standing out against the snow, tonal values melt into the prevailing grey, creating a sense of endless depth and distance. In *The Harvesters* the rendering of volumes in the half-reaped wheatfield and the sheaves is singularly "modern," while the figures of the harvesters seem strangely small and frail beside the monumental permanence of nature. Beyond them is a glimmering lake stretching out to the dim horizon. The poetic quality of Brueghel's landscape backgrounds is particularly striking in some slightly later works such as the famous *Magpie on the Gallows* (1568, Darmstadt), where the real theme is the wooded hillside in the foreground, sloping away towards a spacious valley.

Though in the *Numbering at Bethlehem* (1566, Brussels) the subject is given prominence, the landscape is no less fine than in the *Months*. Here there is more, far more, than satire, thanks to the moral and poetic elevation of the scene and the sensitive treatment of the poor folk flocking around the census-taker's table, amongst whom, unnoticed by anyone, is the Virgin.

In Brueghel's final phase we find a shift of emphasis from landscape to figures and individual expression. A new earnestness appears, though he still cannot refrain from an occasional fling at comical humanity, as in the *Wedding Banquet* (Vienna), the *Peasant Dance* (Vienna) and the *Land of Cockaigne* (Munich, 1567). The grotesqueness of the last-named is ingeniously heightened by the bird's-eye perspective and the quaint arrangement of the figures, disposed around the central tree like spokes of a wheel.

Dated to 1568, the year before his death, are *The Cripples* (Louvre), *The Misanthrope* (Naples) and the *Parable of the Blind* (Naples). In the first, the plight of the poor wretches is so poignantly conveyed that the grotesque merges into the tragic. The composition of the second is a masterpiece of simplicity. The picture is a tondo, in which the misanthrope, a somber figure slowly moving across a pale-hued landscape, is painted with illusionist realism. Beneath him the following explanation is inscribed in Flemish: "Because the world is so faithless I am going into mourning." But the world is already taking its revenge: a figure in a glass globe (symbol of vanity) is stealing the purse (symbol of earthly riches) which the misanthrope has been concealing under his voluminous cloak. The last, unquestionably Brueghel's most tragic and pessimistic work, illustrates the Gospel parable of the blind leading the blind. By increasing the number of blind men to six (there are only two in the parable) Brueghel "protracts our tension and fearful expectation of the fall we know to be inevitable for all" (F. Grossmann). And he points the moral of the parable by the contrast between the stumbling progress of the blind and the rock-like stability of the church in the offing.

Thus Brueghel's artistic evolution falls into three phases. After interpreting his responses to scenes of nature, he moves on to satirical depictions of the human comedy, the absurdities of men's private and public lives. And the satire is all the more convincing because he makes us feel behind these the iron hand of destiny. Then in the last phase he reveals the pathos of the human predicament with a poignancy rarely equaled and never surpassed by any other artist.

# PAINTING IN VENICE

GIORGIONE (CA. 1480-1510). PORTRAIT OF A YOUNG MAN, 1505-1507. (22¾ × 18″)
KAISER FRIEDRICH MUSEUM, BERLIN.

# 4

# FROM GIORGIONE TO VERONESE

For an understanding of the development of Venetian painting in the 16th century, we have to take into account various factors other than those of a strictly aesthetic order. The art of the Venetians was relatively untouched by humanism since it had no direct contacts with classical antiquity and, above all, because it stemmed from an outlook on the world very different from that which had prevailed in Florence during the previous century. Mantegna and Giovanni Bellini, it is true, assimilated Florentine art practice and adapted it to the artistic climate of Venice and North Italy in general. Nor must we forget that in the last decade of the 15th century Leonardo had given Florentine tradition a new direction and broadened the painter's field of activity. Before this, man had been the artist's chief preoccupation; henceforth he aspired to include the entire scheme of things in his domain. Ceasing to be a merely functional element of the composition, space was transmuted into landscape and atmosphere and became a living presence. And now that his form lay open to surrounding space, man was no longer an isolated unit but a fully integrated element of the picture. Sponsored by Leonardo and symbolized by his *sfumato*, this ideal was brilliantly realized by the color and light-and-shade effects of the Venetians, and by the new vision of reality implicit in their style. Thus as against the Florentines' insistence on outlines, proportions, structure and perspective, the Venetians saw the world in terms of colored masses, capable of absorbing human figures as well as things into themselves. This was not a Renaissance or a humanist conception in the sense in which these epithets apply to Michelangeol's or Raphael's art. It was, rather, a "modern" conception—as is proved by the fact that until the end of the 19th century it was, with rare exceptions, basic to all European painting.

This form of expression was not solely a creation of the genius of Giorgione and Titian; it linked up with the special conditions prevailing in Venice. At the beginning of the century it looked as if Venice was to come under a foreign yoke, but by heroic efforts she preserved her freedom and her victories fired the enthusiasm of all Italians. In 1544 Paolo Giovio declared that the banner of St Mark was the emblem of Italian liberty and nearly a hundred years later Bernardo Tasso extolled the Venetian achievement. "Is not Venice the shining symbol and consecration of Italian honor? What other light or glory remains to my poor Italy in the darkness of this troubled age? All the rest of us are serfs and tributaries of, I will not say barbarians, but foreign nations. Venice alone has kept her freedom, and owes obedience to none but God and her own well-framed laws." And, what was still more remarkable, Venice succeeded in maintaining a certain independence even in her dealings with the Papacy and the Council of Trent.

Another noteworthy fact is that—aside from politics—the genius of Venice expressed itself almost exclusively in painting. Florence is as famous for her architecture, sculpture and poetry as for her painting, and, when her fate hung in the balance, diverted her activity to scientific research. Venice, on the other hand, devoted all her energy, and all her wealth, to painting. We describe elsewhere the Europe-wide vogue of mannerism during this period (Brueghel alone was untouched by it). But though Venice dallied with certain mannerist procedures, she never let them get the upper hand—anyhow until after the deaths of Tintoretto and Veronese. The intellectual ferment which led to mannerism hardly affected Venice, whose age-old confidence in Church and State remained unshaken and where, for this reason, an atmosphere of buoyant optimism persisted longer than elsewhere.

Moreover the fact that they had kept their independence enabled the Venetians to appreciate, better than other Italians, the religious and artistic aspirations of the Germans and the Netherlanders. Dürer, Bosch and the northern engravers were familiar to Venetian artists and collectors; indeed it is not going too far to say that 16th-century Venetian painting reconciles the traditions of Florence with those of Bruges.

No Venetian artist, not even Titian, was an intellectual and to regard the Venetian painters as in any sense deep thinkers or philosophers would be to misjudge them. But certain affinities between the ideas of the school of Padua (the university town of Venice) and Venetian painting show that both thinkers and painters were in their respective manners—intuitively in the case of the painters—trying to express the *Weltanschauung* of the age. Although it is impossible to draw a hard-and-fast line between Florentine Platonism and the Aristotelianism of Padua and Venice, owing to the constant interactions between these schools of thought, there can be no doubt that the latter prepared the way for the "science of nature" that held the field at Padua during the 16th century. As early as its first decade the conception of "Immanence" was in high favor; sensation was regarded as the fountainhead of knowledge, more basic to it than even form, with the result that ever-increasing attention was directed to the "dictionary" of nature. The dialogue of Pietro Bembo (1470-1547), *Gli Asolani*, and *La Vita Sobria* by Alvise Cornaro (1475-1566) illustrate this attitude. Each in his own way stresses the benefits of living in the country and sees in nature a source of infinite delight. The steady increase in the number of country houses, the loving care with which they were planned and decorated, testify to the desire of the Venetians to escape from the artificial life of the city and return to nature. Echoes of these ideas can be found in various treatises on art, notably those of Pietro Aretino (1492-1556), Paolo Pino (first half of the 16th century) and Ludovico Dolce (1508-1568).

In his treatise published in 1548, Pino stages a meeting between himself and some beautiful women and the discussion centers on the best method of deciding which is

GIORGIONE (CA. 1480-1510). MADONNA AND SAINTS (FRAGMENT), AFTER 1504.
CHURCH OF SAN LIBERALE, CASTELFRANCO.

the most beautiful, that is to say on a problem of pure aesthetic sensibility. When a Florentine, Leon Battista Alberti for example, sought to work out a theory of art, his chief concern was to discover a scientific basis for it. Whereas the Venetian writer Dolce, instead of investigating, like the Florentines, the laws of ordered pictorial architecture according to perspective, declared (in 1559) that the basis of painting is something beyond "order" and that the arrangement of natural motifs in a picture should not seem studied or contrived but, rather, the work of chance. Pino, moreover, demurs at any law of proportions, holding that figures in a picture should be in movement and movement is independent of any such abstract law. Whereas the linear, plastic style of the Florentines called for meticulous finish, Michelangelo rebelled against this cult of finish—that was one of the tragedies of his stormy life. Aretino, too, knew that a smooth perfection destroyed the vitality of the image and praised Tintoretto's hasty execution, since it enabled him to give freer scope to his creative urge.

Alberti had formulated the principle of "composition"; Pino and Dolce replaced it by the theory of "invention"—which in some ways assimilated the artist's vision to the storyteller's role. The Venetians saw no distinction between form and content in the work of art since both were merged into their new conception of pictorial reality. Similarly they tended to rule out any distinction between form and color. To their thinking it was color that brought figures to life, effected contrasts between light and shade and determined perspective relations. But the contrasts should not be violent, nor the color over-strong. Flesh-tints, above all, should be subdued, not too bright, the colors being handled in such a way as to give the texture of the skin a gentle radiance. These methods corresponded to a sensuous vision of reality, essentially human and intuitive, irreducible to any logically precise definition. Alberti had formulated an aesthetic; the Venetians relied on preferences of taste.

This relative indifference to art theory (as compared with Florence) was fundamental to the new way of seeing that arose in Venice. Implicit in the humanists' ideal of due proportion and perspective representation of space was a residue of the medieval and Platonic notion of transcendence. Nothing of this existed in Cinquecento Venetian art. Ordered beauty and pure form were replaced by the splendors of life at its most luxurious; mysticism by ritual observance. *Maestria* of touch and color conjured up the whole gamut of reality, almost without discrimination, thanks to a happy concord between the senses and the mind—thus ushering in the modern vision of reality.

**GIORGIONE**

Although no exact information as to the life of Giorgio da Castelfranco, commonly called Giorgione, is forthcoming, one thing is certain: that he was the originator of the Venetian style of painting as we see it in the work of Titian, Sebastiano del Piombo and many others. Nothing definite is known about his early training or the chronology of his works. He died of the plague in 1510, in his early thirties.

The *Madonna and Saints* in the Cathedral of Castelfranco (near Treviso, in Venetia), probably painted a little after 1504 for Tuzio Costanzo, is a very early work. One of the striking things about it is the loftiness of the throne, whose top is out of sight, rising beyond the upper edge of the picture towards the zenith. The Madonna and the two saints stand out clearly against the background formed by the throne (behind which is a landscape prospect) and a sort of wall draped in red velvet. Though perhaps a little unsure, the composition is beautifully conceived, while the elongation of the figures, the elegance of their postures and even the artificial character of the separation between figures and landscape reveal the poetic quality of the young artist's genius. Here we find nothing of the austerity or deep religious fervor of Giovanni Bellini; the pervading mood is one of languorous enchantment and the figures, devoid of any plastic values, have a curiously dreamlike remoteness. Notable is the expression on the Child's face (this was something new in religious art) and the softness of the colors, giving Him the naïve charm of a very human babe. The throne, too, has none of the elaborate carvings dear to Bellini; it consists solely of color zones spread with richly patterned rugs. Drawing inspiration from Carpaccio, Giorgione lavished a wealth of spellbinding colors on this picture. The landscape, like that of the two small scenes, *The Trial of Moses* and *The Judgment of Solomon* in the Uffizi, differs from Giovanni Bellini's landscape backgrounds; less carefully built up and elaborate, it has a melting suavity of color, reminiscent

GIORGIONE (CA. 1480-1510). THE THREE PHILOSOPHERS (DETAIL), 1506-1508.
KUNSTHISTORISCHES MUSEUM, VIENNA.

GIORGIONE (CA. 1480-1510). THE THUNDERSTORM, CA. 1505. (30 5/8 × 28 1/4") GALLERIE DELL'ACCADEMIA, VENICE.

of the painting of Northern Europe. But it is in his three major works, the *Thunderstorm* (Venice), the *Three Philosophers* (Vienna) and the *Sleeping Venus* (Dresden) that the tendencies adumbrated in the *Madonna and Saints* reach their culmination. None of these three pictures has a well-defined theme, whether religious or philosophical. The *Venus* was for Giorgione merely a pretext for painting a woman in the nude, and he treated the *Three Philosophers* and the *Thunderstorm* as "free fantasies." When in Venice (1541-1542) Vasari saw Giorgione's frescos—no longer in existence—in the

Fondaco dei Tedeschi, he admitted that he could make nothing of what they represented. And in evaluating his art, we do well to bear in mind this absence of any traditional, identifiable theme; also the fact that, apart from certain "show-pieces" made for churches, the Ducal Palace and the Fondaco dei Tedeschi, Giorgione painted chiefly for private persons. Ferriguto, an authority on humanist literature, suggests that Gabriele Vendramin, Taddeo Contarini and Girolamo Marcello who, between 1525 and 1530, owned the three pictures named above probably commissioned Giorgione to paint them,

GIORGIONE (CA. 1480-1510). THE THREE PHILOSOPHERS, 1506-1508. (47⅝ × 55¾")
KUNSTHISTORISCHES MUSEUM, VIENNA.

when they were all quite young men. This is borne out by what Vasari says: that Giorgione worked for "three young members of the Venetian aristocracy," friends whom he met at parties and musical evenings.

X-ray examination has shown the way in which Giorgione went about these pictures. In the *Thunderstorm* are two figures whom Marcantonio Michiel (an early authority on Giorgione) described as "a soldier and a gypsy," but they might easily be named quite otherwise, since the "soldier" is unarmed and the "gypsy" so called simply because she has nothing on. X-rays show that the artist originally painted a woman going down to the river to bathe at the spot where the soldier stands now. Obviously if he had started out with any definite program in mind, Giorgione could not have made such a drastic alteration. The reason for it was purely aesthetic; the composition was better balanced by the figure of a standing man at this point than by that of a woman. Also, by so doing he added a touch of mystery that would have been lacking in a "straight" picture of two women bathing. Thus Giorgione's thematic material was a product of the free imagination; the *Thunderstorm* was painted for the pleasure it gave the artist in creating it and his friends in looking at it.

In the *Three Philosophers*, too, X-ray examination has revealed some interesting pentimenti; for example, the central figure was originally a Moor and those on the right and left were likewise exotic types, one wearing a big diadem, the other an oriental hat. As the Magi came from the East and one of them was a blackamoor, it may be that Giorgione's original intention was to depict them on their way to Bethlehem. True, there was no iconographic precedent for this—all "Nativity" pictures showed the Kings of the East at or near their journey's end—but Giorgione may have been inspired by an apocryphal text in which the three kings were described as "addicts of celestial mysteries," that is to say astrologers, watching for the promised star. In any case he totally discarded any such allusion in his final version, and merely painted three—unspecified—philosophers. But we must remember that at this time, as Ferriguto has pointed out, the three chief schools of philosophy in vogue at Venice were medieval Aristotelianism, Averroism and the new "science of nature." So it seems clear that Giorgione wished to symbolize medieval Aristotelianism by the bearded old man, Averroism by the Oriental, and the new philosophy by the young geometrician.

Giorgione completed neither the *Three Philosophers* nor the *Venus*; that was left to Sebastiano del Piombo and Titian. But there are grounds for thinking that his death was not the reason for these pictures' being left unfinished. They are not in keeping with his final style and, in any case, he failed to complete several other works. He began a picture without knowing exactly what form it would take, and improvised as he went along. And such was his impatience with the drudgery of manual labor that he often left the finishing of it to some brother artist who understood what he was after. This, as we have seen, was also a habit of Leonardo and Michelangelo who, like Giorgione, were in many respects precursors of modern art. It was by this disdain of "finish" that they disowned the medieval identification of the artist with the artisan and emphasized the fact the former created more with his mind than with his hands.

Since, as Giorgione saw it, the "subject" was merely a vehicle for expressing his way of seeing and feeling, he was naturally led to bring his figures into close association with their setting and, as in the pictures we have been discussing, to express his personal reactions as much by the landscape as by the figures. In the *Thunderstorm* we have, for the first time, a landscape with figures instead of figures with a landscape. When an artist takes for his field not only man and the works of man, but nature as a whole, he cannot enclose the human figure in a contour-line that isolates it from surrounding space. On the contrary, he has to create figures capable of being immersed in atmosphere and acquiring from it the modifications that light and shadow bring to bodies. But Giorgione showed some hesitation in choosing between closed and open forms. Giovanni Bellini had taught him to appreciate the beauty and elegance of the circumscribing line, and the splendid oval of the Dresden *Venus*, though it belongs to a world of dreams—so magical is the play of light—was still a closed circuit. But by the time he painted the "soldier" in the *Thunderstorm*, Giorgione had moved towards purely pictorial form, unenclosed and treated sketch-wise.

What we have named purely pictorial form and "unfinish" are two aspects of a style that holds a well-nigh perfect balance between imagination and perception. Giorgione was careful not to define his themes because he wished to give free play to his emotions and imagination; to modify his subjects as the fancy took him. Hence his brilliant improvisations and his practice of regarding as completed, works which might at first sight look unfinished, provided they fully corresponded to his inner vision.

Thus Giorgione's painterly imagination and his sense of the oneness of things led him to open forms, to reject the limitations of the finite and even to view drawing in terms of color. It also led to the expression of states of mind rather than of specific emotions. Nor must we overlook his sensuality, a sensuality free from any sense of sin though curbed by an almost superstitious awe of nature. For Giorgione's art stems from a feeling of participation in all life, an instinctive not an intellectual response, and a poetic contemplation of the universe. Hence that dreamworld in which his figures have their being, the rapt entrancement of their faces, half asleep or lost in wandering thoughts, and the gentle light that bathes them, the light of that enchanted hour when nature is just awakening or on the verge of sleep. In his portraits, too, we see the same magical transfiguration, for example in the Berlin *Portrait of a Young Man* and in the Brunswick *Self-Portrait*.

Finally mention may be made of a problem perhaps never to be solved, that of Giorgione's activity during the last two years of his life. The Dresden *Venus* is probably contemporary with the frescos of the Fondaco dei Tedeschi (finished in 1508). But some pictures traditionally ascribed to Giorgione seem to belong to a rather later phase; we have in mind chiefly the *Concert champêtre* (Louvre) and the *Concert* (Pitti). These works are certainly by his hand, as is proved not only by the style but also by their depth of feeling and that dreamlike atmosphere which, while characteristic of Giorgione, was not achieved by Titian until a much later date. In these final works we find a new quality of emotion, a sublimation as it were of his creative personality.

We will begin with a few facts that may help to the understanding of Titian's place in the evolution of European art. In 1508 Giorgione and Titian were still young men, rich in promise for the future, and the former, without being the acknowledged master of the Venetian School, was the artist to whom above all his generation looked for guidance and inspiration. The frescos he and Titian did together in the Fondaco dei Tedeschi have always been regarded as the starting-off point of the new style of painting described above. Barely two years later, in 1510, Giorgione died; Titian was destined to outlive him by sixty-six years.

Until quite recently it was assumed that the two artists were practically contemporaries; the current opinion is that Titian was Giorgione's junior by ten years. But, in view of the conflict of evidence on the subject, it would be rash to draw any conclusions from the supposed age difference.

Born at Pieve di Cadore in northern Venetia, Titian came of a family renowned for its prowess in the field of battle. Michelangelo, too, came of a near-noble family and he too lived to a great age (a little less than Titian's, however), reaching the zenith of his powers late in life, when he was a weary, soured old man. Though not directly bearing on their art, this longevity may suggest how it was that these two men came to be precursors of modern art. For significantly enough, it was towards the end of their lives that their paths tended to converge. Michelangelo's classical, humanistic tendencies are evident in his early *David,* whereas Titian's first dated work, the frescos in the Scuola di Sant'Antonio at Padua (1511), far from having any kinship with classical art, is full of dramatic movement and juvenile brio. Indeed what differentiates his work from Giorgione's is precisely a tendency to dramatize reality so as to make it more "alive." However, at the height of his renown, Titian had to face the charge of not being able to draw as well as the Florentines. As a result he applied himself to learning the secret of Michelangelo's draftsmanship—with untoward consequences, since an exact rendering of the model cramped his natural style, which was essentially allergic to classical form.

Still it would be a mistake to call Titian an impressionist; that would certainly be to overstate the case. The art he aimed at, which had little in common with that of the classicists, was of a social, not to say imperial order; Titian's truth was an actuality seen through aristocratic eyes. We may find it difficult to subscribe without demur to an ideal of this kind; Brueghel's peasants seem nearer to us today than does the equestrian portrait of the Emperor Charles V. Yet we cannot shut our eyes to the grandiose role played by that great monarch in world history. The world he personified, which he saved from anarchy and united under his rule, found its befitting style in the art of Tiziano Vecellio, Count Palatine and Knight of the Golden Spur. Once they discarded the conception of the artist as an artisan, the Florentines had realized that by grace of their genius such men as Leonardo, Raphael and Michelangelo were entitled to a high place in the social order. But it was left to Titian to be the peer of princes and emperors. To have a portrait of oneself by his hand was a patent of nobility; a "Pietà" by him was tantamount to a social "indulgence," and a "Venus" to a proof of sensual

TITIAN (1477/87-1576). THE THREE AGES OF MAN, CA. 1515. (41 3/4 × 71 1/2")
COLLECTION OF THE EARL OF ELLESMERE, NATIONAL GALLERY OF SCOTLAND, EDINBURGH.

refinement. If he so generously satisfied the wishes of his patrons, this was because his own tastes were the same as theirs, and because he had a unique knack of bringing their painted forms to life. He could treat with foreign monarchs from the neutral ground of Venice and paint the French king no less readily than the Emperor Charles V and Philip II of Spain. When in 1513 Leo X suggested he should come to Rome he declined the offer. He had not yet won his spurs and he guessed that like Sebastiano del Piombo he would be forced to truckle to the Holy See. When twenty-two years later he went to Rome he was famous throughout Europe and he was accorded Roman citizenship.

On Giovanni Bellini's death in 1516 he was appointed official painter of the Venetian state and began to work for Alfonso I of Ferrara; in 1523 he became painter to Marquis Federigo Gonzaga of Mantua, thereafter to the Dukes of Urbino and the House of Farnese. In 1530 at Bologna he painted the first portrait of Charles V, who invited him to Augsburg for the Diets of 1547, 1548 and 1550-1552. He was the first artist to have a sort of publicity agent—for this in fact was the role of Pietro Aretino, who sent a steady stream of letters to all the great personages of the day, partly to further his personal interests but also to make known the genius of his painter friend.

In 1531 Titian settled into a house in the north of Venice, in the district called Birri Grande. From his new home he could see the Dolomites, the rugged mountains he had so often roamed as a boy, in the far distance. His garden became famous and was a favorite resort of all distinguished visitors to Venice. In 1540 Titian invited to his house the writer Priscianese, along with other intellectuals, for the August 15 holiday. His guests duly admired the master's paintings, then the garden; at sundown dinner was served on the terrace to the accompaniment of music and singing by youths and pretty women in gondolas weaving over the lagoon. This shows that Titian was by now a man of independent means and assured position. He could rub shoulders without constraint with princes, kings, the Emperor and the Pope himself and paint with equal self-confidence the works of piety they commissioned and the decorations of their bed-chambers. He passed no judgment on the subjects he depicted but devoted himself wholly to presenting them with the utmost vitality and to the most grandiose effect. And with his superb color, spiritual penetration and abounding vigor he created as it were a synthesis of the many-sided life of the age.

In the frescos of *The Life of St Anthony* (1511) at the Scuola di Sant'Antonio in Padua, we can see that already Titian had completely shaken off Giorgione's influence. Here there is nothing of the romantic, dreamy languor of his predecessor but a gift for direct narrative seen at its best in the scene of the *Miracle of the New-born Child*. There are a good many figures, but grouped in such a way that the child seems isolated in the center of the composition, visual and psychological pivot of the scene. Forms are brought forward to the surface but that surface is deepened and filled with movement by the juxtaposition of the figures. There is a well-marked distinction (as in Giorgione) between full and empty spaces, the latter suggesting illimitable distance. But most striking of all is the vigor of the color, stepped up by sharp contrasts between light and dark to an extent that would have been impossible with chiaroscuro. The figure of the elegant young man whose dark complexion is foiled by a light-hued cloak is a stroke of genius. Dramatic though it is, the scene has a wonderful serenity. In a different vein is the fresco whose theme is a jealous husband stabbing his wife. This purported to show "St Anthony healing the wounded woman" but Titian relegated the healing to the background, placing the act of violence in the forefront of the scene. Movement is stressed by a foreshortening of the fallen woman's body and the lifted dagger, and the artist shows much skill in suggesting action, without actually showing it, by the man's uplifted arm.

In this very early work we find what were to be the characteristics of Titian's art: free rendering of gestures, intricate composition, rich color orchestration, vital actuality, contrasts of light and dark, highlights on figures. But though in the Padua frescos he turned away from Giorgione's themes he reverted to them subsequently—in, for example, the *Three Ages of Man* (Edinburgh) and *Sacred and Profane Love* (Galleria Borghese, Rome). The far-flung landscape, the nude or draped figures, the pure, brilliant colors saturated with light fully justify the vast popularity of these noble pictures. Yet though motifs and colors derive from Giorgione, Titian has failed to impart to them the singular poignancy infusing Giorgione's art. He responds to the beauty of human forms and depicts it to perfection, but he cannot invest them with the glamour of a dreamworld—because he is no dreamer.

The Uffizi *Flora* is typical in this respect. There is no landscape, no aura of mystery to distract attention from the physical charms of the young woman, a blonde beauty whose opulent forms tell out delightfully against a uniform background. Botticelli had called on tall, willowy figures to set off his subtle, sinuous line. But Titian found in an amply molded, fair-haired type of womanhood the perfect medium for his rich, effulgent color.

Three mythological scenes fall into the same category. Painted for Alfonso d'Este, they are titled *The Worship of Venus* (1518-1519), *The Bacchanal* (1520), both in the Prado, and *Bacchus and Ariadne* (1522-1523) in the National Gallery, London. Noteworthy in the first of these three works is the effect of restless, exuberant movement conveyed by the frolicsome children, the gay, flower-like profusion of the flesh tints. In the other two pictures, too, there is much animation—some of it, one cannot help thinking, rather purposeless—but the charm of the landscape and colors fully justifies these aberrations, if such they are.

The grandiose expressive power of the *Assumption of the Virgin* (1516-1518), painted for the Church of the Frari in Venice, shows Titian in a different mood. Raphael had succeeded in creating a unity between earth and sky by means of plastic values; Titian does the same thing by means of movement. Despite the fullness of the Virgin's form she soars effortlessly heavenwards, borne aloft by an inner force that gives her body a sinuous movement, harmonizing with the attitudes of the two groups of apostles at the bottom of the picture. A feverish unrest pervades the scene, while the grey-blue of the air behind the apostles melts into the orange-yellow sheen of the celestial regions towards which all are gazing rapturously. Though anything but a mystic, Titian has evoked the scene as vividly as if he had seen it with his own eyes. And it is a token of his total mastery of his means even at this relatively early stage of his career that with light, color and movement, he could body forth his imaginings with such complete verisimilitude.

Light and color effects are even more emphatic in the Ancona *Virgin in Glory* (1520). Here, too, no distinction exists between earth and heaven; in the distance we have an enchanting glimpse of the lagoon, while in the foreground rises the stately figure of St Francis—one of the first of Titian's figures to be imbued with that profound spiritual dignity whose presence makes itself felt in so many of his portraits. In 1522 he painted a triptych for the church of Santi Nazaro e Celso in Brescia; whereas the light effect in the central scene is wholly admirable, one of the side panels—that representing *St Sebastian*—must be written down a failure; here Titian tried to imitate Michelangelo, with lamentable results.

He worked seven years (1519-1526) on the *Pesaro Madonna,* in which he employed the form of composition best suited to his handling of color, light and movement. This involved an unusual placing of the Virgin, well on the right, so as to provide for more

TITIAN (1477/87-1576). FLORA, CA. 1515. (31 × 24¾″)
UFFIZI, FLORENCE.

TITIAN (1477/87-1576). PORTRAIT OF A MAN WITH GLOVES, 1523-1524. (39 ¼ × 34 ¼″)
LOUVRE, PARIS.

open space and a diagonal line ascending towards her, emphasized by two tall pillars shooting up towards the sky. While there is no special beauty or religious feeling in the forms, this *Madonna* has a wonderful emotive power and we sense an aspiration towards an ideal which, though undefined, is fully achieved.

TITIAN (1477/87-1576). PORTRAIT OF POPE PAUL III WITH HIS NEPHEWS ALESSANDRO AND OTTAVIO FARNESE (DETAIL), 1546. MUSEO NAZIONALE, NAPLES.

The famous *Venus of Urbino* (1538) in the Uffizi is altogether different. Despite the picture's title, this is the likeness not of a goddess but of a very human, enchantingly beautiful young woman waiting on her couch for the maid to bring her clothes. And it is not a pagan vision but a faithful portrait sublimated by its gorgeous colors.

Titian was the inventor of a new style of portraiture, thanks to his objective, wholly unbiased vision of reality and his prodigious skill in creating harmonies of form and color. An excellent example of this is the anonymous *Man with Gloves* (Louvre), which not only "registers" to perfection a certain type of man but also has the immediacy of a likeness done from the life, a pictorial snapshot so to speak. Raphael's superb portrait of his friend Castiglione was also that of an individualized type figure but it had not this verisimilitude. Titian's peculiar gift was that of recording a moment of a life. Hence the unique forthrightness of his portraits, frank to a degree, yet invested with a noble dignity.

Brief mention may be made of some other portraits: *Andrea Gritti* in Vienna, remarkable for its dynamism and color; *Diego de Mendoza* in the Pitti Gallery, with its amazing color orchestration realized solely by effects of black on a dark grey ground; for here, by a strange alchemy of which he had the secret, Titian conjures up with these simple means colors that are, in the literal sense, "not there." No less magical is the way in which, while presenting figures full face and without real movement, he instills into them, by deft, almost imperceptible touches, the vibrancy of life. We see this in that wonderful portrait in the Pitti Gallery which has so often changed its name; once known as *The Englishman*, it next was called *Ippolito Riminaldi*, and finally, with better justification, *Ottavio Farnese*.

Paul III gave Titian the opportunity of making what is perhaps one of the most dramatic portraits known to art. The Pope is admonishing his "nephew" Ottavio in the presence of another "nephew," Alessandro Farnese. Ottavio is bending with feigned obsequiousness towards the man who is, in fact, his grandfather. The Pope's anger had been aroused by the news that the young man was intriguing against his father Pier Luigi, the Pope's son. The fiery indignation of the venerable pontiff, bowed and decrepit though he is, dominates the scene. The fact that the picture was left unfinished intensifies its emotive impact. Titian often painted dramatic scenes, but in no other did he reach this Shakespearian height of tragic power.

It must have been harder for him to break away from the tradition of official portraiture when his model was a prince or emperor. Yet it is these works that best reveal the independence he so jealously safeguarded in his dealings with the great ones of the earth and his feeling that his creative powers entitled him to rank beside them. An example is the *Portrait of Charles V with his Dog* (1532-1533) in the Prado. Without losing anything of the majesty befitting it, the Emperor's figure is humanized by the presence of the dog and the palpitating life that animates the picture. This is all the more remarkable when we remember that all Titian had to go on in this case was a portrait by the Austrian painter Jacob Seisenegger.

The bold originality of Titian's portraiture is even more conspicuous in the Munich *Charles V* of 1548. Though the background may have been added by some other hand, the general conception was assuredly Titian's—and it is superb. Charles is quite simply dressed, in black, like any ordinary citizen and like all the Venetians of the day, even the richest. Indeed this could be described as a Venetian, almost bourgeois portrait

TITIAN (1477/87-1576). THE EMPEROR CHARLES V AT THE BATTLE OF MÜHLBERG (DETAIL), 1548.
PRADO, MADRID.

study, were it not that the haughty expression of the face and a certain grimness in the gaze reveal the Emperor, conscious of his august prerogative. An even more famous portrait of the same year (Prado) shows him on horseback at the Battle of Mühlberg. The horse is black, the sky mottled with angry red; one might almost think the painter had a presentiment of the future when he made this picture—for, despite the rider's kingly mien, it might well be a celebration not of triumph but of death.

But Titian was too much a man of the Renaissance ever to repudiate the appeal of physical beauty. In the Prado *Adam and Eve* he celebrates the virile strength of Adam and the loveliness of Eve, weaving the movement of their arms and bodies into a graceful arabesque. Titian's rendering of their figures is quite different from Michelangelo's. Turning to account his studies of anatomy, Michelangelo took the bony structure of the bodies as his starting-point, then clad the framework of the skeleton with a softly undulating sheath of flesh and skin. Titian, however, viewed the model from outside, in its atmospheric environment, with the result that the beauty of the bodies he painted is never abstract or isolated, but that of living, breathing human beings.

TITIAN (1477/87-1576). VENUS WITH THE ORGAN-PLAYER, 1547-1548. (53½×86½")
PRADO, MADRID.

TITIAN (1477/87-1576). ACTAEON AND DIANA, 1559. (74¾ × 81½″)
COLLECTION OF THE EARL OF ELLESMERE, NATIONAL GALLERY OF SCOTLAND, EDINBURGH.

Titian painted many Venuses in his long career, but (as was perhaps to be expected) those of his last period are the loveliest, an example being the famous Prado *Venus with the Organ Player*. In the *Venus of Urbino* he had struck a realistic note, heightening this effect by introducing servants into the scene. In later life he lifted the picture on to another plane, that of a purely imaginary, not to say unreal, world. He depicted a nude woman reclining on a terrace overlooking a park, with a small dog and an organ-player beside her. Yet Titian's "best of impossible worlds" is not the fabric of a dream and it differs from Giorgione's in his "Concerts" by being far more objective.

In his portraits Titian made an end of those concessions to mannerist design in the Michelangelo manner which were the undoing of an earlier work, the Brescia *St Sebastian* (1522). But he was always haunted by notions of this order, for the good reason that none of his admirers ever dreamt of telling him that Florentine chiaroscuro and Michelangelesque line were alien to his genius; that his path lay elsewhere, towards a pictorial architecture in terms of light and color. In 1548 Paolo Pino voiced the eclectic theory of art then in vogue when he said that what an artist should aspire to was a combination of Michelangelo's form with Titian's color. Needless to say, Titian was quite aware that in his handling of form it was best to follow his own bent. Yet he could not always shake off Michelangelo's influence, especially in his nudes. This is why three pictures in the Salute, Venice, rate among his most conspicuous failures: *Cain and Abel*, the *Sacrifice of Isaac* and *David and Goliath* (1542-1544). But when in 1548-1549 he painted *Sisyphus* and *Tityus* (Prado), he completely integrated plastic form with light and shade; these works teem with cosmic energy and dramatic life, untrammelled by any would-be academicism.

After his return from Augsburg, Titian never left Venice again. He was now at the peak of his career and had little more to expect of life. He had created a style that harmonized exactly with the ideal of the aristocracy of his time, and he was adulated by the highest in the land. Though constantly short of money and often harassed by domestic worries, he was free to paint exactly as he liked, with the flattering assurance that each new picture would be greeted as a masterpiece. Yet even in his imaginative freedom there was a strain of sadness due perhaps to life-weariness but also to a too close acquaintance with the greatest men of the day. He had come to know that milieu, its pomps and vanities, all too well; the glamour had departed. Clear-sighted enough to see the calamities which involuntarily, driven by destiny, he had brought on Europe, the Emperor abdicated in 1556 and retired to a convent in Estremadura. Titian's escape from life was to engross himself still more deeply in his art and it was now, in his last years, that he took a bold forward stride towards a wholly new style of painting. Naturally enough Vasari, a Tuscan, was baffled by this startlingly "modernistic" art in which he saw only patches of color so disposed that the picture looked meaningless unless viewed from a considerable distance. Like many who came after him he could not conceive of forms devoid of contour lines and built up by light alone.

The mythological scenes might be described as poems inspired by Titian's cult of light and sensual relish of his medium, the gorgeous luxuriance of his palette. The *Danaë* (Prado), *Perseus and Andromeda* (Wallace Collection, London), the *Rape of Europa* (Gardner Museum, Boston), *Actaeon and Diana* (Edinburgh), the *Nymph and Shepherd* (Vienna) are examples of these pure poems of light and color, pervaded by the aerial vibrations which traverse the "mythologies" of his last period.

But he also had moods of profound depression whose influence makes itself felt in his *Crucifixions*, in the *St Sebastian* (Hermitage, Leningrad) and even in some religious pictures which in earlier days he would have treated with a bland serenity, such as the *Annunciation* (Venice, Church of San Salvatore) or the *Virgin and Child* (National Gallery, London), where a gentle play of light creates an atmosphere of tender, faintly nostalgic intimacy.

Some comparisons will indicate the change of style that took place in this, Titian's final phase. The Louvre *Entombment* (ca. 1525) is composed in terms of the movement needed to carry the dead Christ's body, and while the swiftness of the action heightens the dramatic effect, it gives the scene a purely external significance. The figures of Mary Magdalen and St John the Evangelist have much beauty, but the bodies in the foreground are over-modeled to the point of seeming ponderous. Though an admirable illustration of an incident, the scene lacks spiritual insight. Very different is the Prado *Entombment* (1559), where the composition is in depth, line is absorbed by color, detail subordinated to general effect. Modeled by gradations of light, the figures seem like weightless phantoms glimmering against the darkness of the background. This picture is not an illustration but a meditation on the Divine Tragedy, and is imbued with an intense emotion, absent in the Louvre *Entombment.*

No less revealing is the difference between the two versions of *Christ crowned with Thorns*, one in the Louvre, the other in Munich. The former was painted round about 1560, the latter some ten years later. In both alike light is the unifying principle. But in the Louvre picture the light strikes on solid bodies—Christ's limbs and arms for example —which cut it short abruptly. While there is no questioning the dramatic effectiveness of this procedure, it certainly tends to overstress action at the expense of the spiritual content. In the Munich picture, on the other hand, light roves freely through the composition, creating its own medium of expression, and is not cut short by any obstacle in the setting—thus the wall at the back and the bust of a Roman emperor included in the earlier work have been omitted. It is the light, and not the brutal conduct of the crowd, that creates the atmosphere of tragedy. For it is no normal illumination, though seemingly accounted for by the flaring lamps above, nor does it issue from them; this light is like an emanation of the malevolence of the mob surrounding Christ.

The *Martyrdom of St Lawrence* (Jesuit Church, Venice) marks perhaps the climactic point of Titian's researches in the domain of light. A dim penumbra, shot with broken gleams that flicker into life and die away abruptly, shrouds the scene in a mysterious gloom. Here we certainly have the point of departure for that "luminism" which, subordinating all things, even color, to the vagaries of light, was to be used to such magnificent effect by Rembrandt.

Titian pictured himself several times. In the Berlin *Self-Portrait* (ca. 1555) we see him full of dauntless energy, eager for new fields to conquer. Painted many years later, the side-face portrait in the Prado shows us a man worn out by the efforts of a long, crowded life, yet one within whom burns unquenched the sacred flame, source of that apotheosis of light which is the crowning glory of his art.

The vision of reality inaugurated by Giorgione and masterfully carried to its logical conclusion by Titian impressed contemporaries as a new, momentous discovery. Figures were no longer isolated but participated in the world around them, form was no longer linear but integrated into the texture of the picture, and the vibrancy of color made itself felt no less in full light than in semi-darkness. Needless to say, the Venetian painters were quick to explore the possibilities of this new art language that every artist could make use of individually, adapting it to his personal means of expression and thus taking another forward step on the path leading to the autonomy of art.

TITIAN (1477/87-1576). THE ENTOMBMENT, 1559. (54 × 68¾″)
PRADO, MADRID.

TITIAN (1477/87-1576). SELF-PORTRAIT, CA. 1555. (37¾ × 29½″)
KAISER FRIEDRICH MUSEUM, BERLIN.

TITIAN (1477/87-1576). CHRIST CROWNED WITH THORNS, CA. 1570. (110¼×71″)
ALTE PINAKOTHEK, MUNICH.

**SEBASTIANO DEL PIOMBO**

It was Sebastiano del Piombo who introduced this new way of seeing to the Roman art world, whilst Lotto made it known at Bergamo and in the Marches. And as was to be expected, Venice witnessed an influx of artists from provincial towns, amongst them Palma from Bergamo, Pordenone from Friuli, Dosso from Ferrara, Savoldo and Romanino from Brescia. True, at Brescia Moretto displayed a certain independence, as Moroni did at Bergamo. But, for that matter, all the artists named above made personal and significant contributions to Venetian painting as a whole.

Sebastiano Luciani, better known as Sebastiano del Piombo, was born in Venice about 1485; if Vasari is to be trusted, his death took place in 1547. Like Titian, he undertook the task of completing several pictures left unfinished by Giorgione—notably the *Three Philosophers*—and thus was one of the first artists to practise the "new style." After the master's death he moved to Rome where he did much to propagate the discoveries of the Venetian school. Indeed, though Lotto and Dosso also went to Rome, it was he above all who initiated Roman artists into the secrets of Venetian color and the new manner of painting. When we remember that Raphael was so much impressed by the innovations of the Venetians as to modify his style when he moved on from the *School of Athens* to the *Mass of Bolsena*, it is easy to understand Sebastiano's prompt success in Rome. But he in turn was influenced by what he saw in Rome, where Raphael and Michelangelo were adding to their laurels, and he set out to amplify Giorgione's achievement by infusing it with the Roman sense of plastic values. Gifted with an amazing power of assimilation, he went far towards combining beauty nearly as perfect as Raphael's with a monumental style little short of Michelangelo's. Having championed the cause of the latter in his rivalry with Raphael, he came to be regarded as the exponent *par excellence* of the Michelangelesque ideal. Except for a three years' stay in Venice (1526-1529) he spent the rest of his life in Rome. In 1531 he was appointed Custodian of the Papal Seals (hence his sobriquet "del Piombo") and in virtue of this post took the habit. Once he had become a monk, his activity as a painter diminished considerably.

The paintings made on the organ shutters of the church of San Giovanni Crisostomo show that when he was living in Venice he almost equaled Titian. In these paintings we see already certain characteristics differentiating him from Giorgione; a striving for monumentality, the fusion of light into color and (as Vasari noted) a tendency to accent relief. Given these characteristics, the course of his evolution once he was in Rome was a foregone conclusion. All the same his first work in that city, the paintings on the lunettes in the Villa Farnesina, was not a success. He employed the fresco technique and, though on the whole the colors blend harmoniously, the lay-out seems improvised and sketchy. But he quickly became acclimatized in Rome and, giving up elaborate compositions, devoted himself chiefly to portraits. Two, *La Fornarina* (Uffizi) and *Dorothea* (Berlin), show that, after a stay of little more than a year in Rome, he had already succeeded in combining the virtues of Raphael and those of Giorgione with the happiest results, in a style that was both delicate and forceful. The *Violin Player* of about 1515 (Rothschild Collection, Paris), in which the Raphaelesque element is more pronounced, is certainly one of the most attractive works of the Renaissance.

SEBASTIANO DEL PIOMBO (CA. 1485-1547). DOROTHEA, AFTER 1512. (30 × 23 ½″)
KAISER FRIEDRICH MUSEUM, BERLIN.

While Sebastiano del Piombo quickly mastered Raphael's elegance and plasticity, he had more trouble over Michelangelo's form and monumentalism. Nevertheless he succeeded in embodying these in the Viterbo *Pietà* (ca. 1517-1518). Here Christ's body forms the basis of a pyramid culminating in the Virgin's face, which thus acquires a monumental grandeur, as of an ageless effigy of grief, a grief that permeates the night-bound desolation of the landscape, one of the most tragic in all Italian art. There is no question that the figures were inspired by Michelangelo (even perhaps taken direct from one of his drawings) but the color is typically Venetian and moreover links up by effects of contrast the figures in the background. So it matters little that the structure of the human forms and the *contrapposto* in that of the Virgin derive from Michelangelo; though borrowing other painters' motifs, Sebastiano has achieved a wholly personal creation of the highest order.

Between 1517 and 1519, when he painted the *Raising of Lazarus* (London), a change came over his style. Its composition is frankly mannerist; the crowd of figures bears no relation—whether of harmony or contrast—to the background, and the color, while it retains the Venetian ripeness and juiciness, seems like a film applied to a prefabricated form. The same is true of the *Birth of the Virgin* (Santa Maria del Popolo, Rome), where the plastic values of the figures are too strongly marked for them to fit naturally into the perspective lay-out.

Best of the works of the painter's last period are his portraits: *Anton Francesco degli Albizzi* (Duveen Collection, New York), *Andrea Doria* (Galleria Doria Pamphili,

LORENZO LOTTO (CA. 1480-1556). THE CONDEMNATION OF ST LUCY, 1532. ($12\frac{1}{2} \times 27\frac{1}{8}$″)
PREDELLA SCENE OF THE SANTA LUCIA ALTARPIECE. PINACOTECA, JESI.

Rome), *Pope Clement VII* (Naples) and *A Cardinal* (Vienna)—imposing figures standing boldly out against the backgrounds thanks to a skillful use of chiaroscuro and color contrasts. Self-conscious virtuosity there certainly is, but also remarkable vitality; qualities that reveal at once this painter's strong points and his limitations.

**LORENZO LOTTO**

Born in Venice about 1480, Lotto was a contemporary of Giorgione, Titian and Sebastiano del Piombo, but as an artist he stood outside the main currents of the age. In early youth he left Venice and found employment in various Italian towns where his works were fairly well received; not well enough, however, to prevent his dying a poor man, an inmate of the convent of Loreto. He was probably self-taught and while (like so many contemporary artists) borrowing much from other painters, he always struck a personal note in all he set his hand to. To start with, he looked to Giovanni Bellini, Alvise Vivarini, Dürer and Giorgione for guidance; then, in 1509, when he was commissioned to paint some rooms in the Vatican and moved to Rome, he came under the influence of Leonardo and Raphael—but not Michelangelo—and changed his manner, though without losing any of his originality. In the course of his long life he traveled widely, staying in 1495 (when he was a mere boy) at Recanati, then from 1503-1508 at Treviso. Following his Roman sojourn he lived at Bergamo from 1513 to 1526 and after a year in Venice he settled down at Jesi (near Ancona, in the Marches) where, apart from brief trips to Venice and Treviso and various towns in the Marches, he remained until his death in 1556.

LORENZO LOTTO (CA. 1480-1556). ST LUCY AT THE TOMB OF ST AGATHA, 1532. (12 ½ × 27 ⅛")
PREDELLA SCENE OF THE SANTA LUCIA ALTARPIECE. PINACOTECA, JESI.

LORENZO LOTTO (CA. 1480-1556). PORTRAIT OF A YOUNG MAN, CA. 1525. (18 ½ × 14 ¾″)
KAISER FRIEDRICH MUSEUM, BERLIN.

Unlike so many other painters of various degrees of eminence who left their hometowns in search of inspiration, fame and fortune at Venice, Lotto did not yield to the lure of the island city and its dazzling art; his interests lay elsewhere. Once in later life he reverted to the art tradition of his youth and fell under the spell of Titian, but the allegiance was short-lived. This unrest was not merely temperamental; it was, rather, an outcome of Lotto's innate piety. In him the religious sentiment took the form of a wholly personal, instinctive yearning towards God, and was very different from the official piety, sponsored by the Church, which was *de rigueur* in Venice during the first half of the Cinquecento and his pictures, imbued with the simple faith of the common people, found relatively little favor in the city of the Doges. Thus it was natural enough he should take over the religious motifs favored by Dürer, who certainly could not be accused of orthodoxy. "As good as goodness and as virtuous as virtue" (so Aretino described him), Lotto abstained from any polemic against tendencies he disapproved of, led a lonely life without family or pupils, launched no school, and was content with painting pictures after his own heart, many of them masterpieces. The first generation of mannerists, too, could be described as non-conformist. But whereas they stood for an intellectual approach, leading to abstract forms—a visual interpretation of the Platonic "idea"—Lotto kept very close to life, such was his devotion to natural forms and colors. Seldom pausing to take thought, he created with a fluent ease and fantasy rare in the history of art. He was more interested in details than in general effect and added wholly novel accents to a flower, a branch, light falling on a short flight of steps, a timid face, a look of contemplation, the gesture of the child St John stooping to stroke his lamb. So strong was his feeling for the natural world—a sort of Christian animism—that even in the light playing across foliage or weaving through the dark, even in stones and folds of garments, we seem to sense a soul within. Like Antonello, Lotto tends to give a cylindrical conformation to his figures, and often he recaptures the wistful grace of Bellini's Madonnas; but sometimes he blocks out the features of old men and even those of the Child Jesus with the extreme nervous acerbity that we instinctively associate with Dürer.

This failure to control his sensibility was at once a handicap and an asset to the artist. It enabled him to bring off some refreshingly spontaneous effects, unique of their kind and of their time, but it also prevented him from producing the large-scale works which were then the order of the day. Whereas by common consent one of the greatest achievements of the Renaissance was unity of vision, the integration of all the parts of a picture into a coherent whole, Lotto reverted to a lay-out that had obtained in the 14th century, and sometimes painted disconnected scenes on one and the same panel (at Trescore and Cingoli, for example). Though acceptable two centuries earlier, this method was bound to lead to confusion when the painter sought to reconcile two conflicting exigencies: that of a sequence of scenes on the one hand and, on the other, the principle of perspective and the subordination of all the elements to an over-all play of light. But sometimes Lotto turned this difficulty in his own manner by rendering details in so enchanting a way that one overlooks defects in the compositional scheme.

Starting out from the 15th-century Venetian tradition (still medieval in many ways) of the closed, precise and solid image, Lotto explored new and diverse fields of art, in each of which he scored brilliant successes, but he could not bring himself to keep to any single path. Revolutionary though it was, Giorgione's and Titian's art practice had been based on balance and good order. Lotto rejected these, followed the call of his creative fancy and took no account (or very little) of what his contemporaries were saying or doing.

The altarpiece he painted in 1505 for Santa Cristina al Tiverone, near Treviso, and the Recanati triptych of 1508 are typical of his first period. While inspired by Bellini, the composition is more dynamic. And the wonderful *St Jerome* in the Louvre (1506) proves that he was one of the finest landscape painters of the century.

His portraits form a class apart in his output; in them exceptional psychological insight is allied with much finesse of execution and a happy knack of handling form and color. Noteworthy, too, is the very human sympathy between the artist and his models; he not only observed their personalities but could enter into their feelings. In this context mention may be made of the three portraits of young men, in Vienna, Berlin and Venice, that of *Andrea Odoni* (Hampton Court) and above all the *Gentleman with Gloves* (Brera, Milan) in which it is not the outward man that commands attention but the revelation of the soul within.

On his return from Rome in 1514 Lotto painted an *Entombment* (Pinacoteca, Jesi); this must be written down a failure, since, in attempting to vie with Raphael, he lost sight of the need for building the composition into harmonious form. The same is true of the *Virgin and Child* in San Bartolomeo at Bergamo; in the predella, however, we see him at his best as a narrative painter and interpreter of sacred scenes on "modern" lines. Datable to the same period as the frescos in the Suardi Chapel at Trescore (1524) are several Madonnas and *Sacre Conversazioni* in which we see once again the warmth and tenderness of feeling which make Lotto one of the most endearing artists of his age. In a scene of the *Santa Lucia Altarpiece* (1532, Jesi) the animation and spontaneity are such that it might represent a quarrel among villagers in any Italian hamlet. At this time he was relying less on a variety of colors and painting chiefly in shades of grey, as is particularly noticeable in the predella. In the *Presentation in the Temple* (Palazzo Apostolico, Loreto) we have the culminating point of his spiritual and artistic evolution. There is something quite new to Renaissance art in the manner in which the scene is depicted—as no more than a gathering of some poor, humble folk in a vast, shadow-filled expanse; more than any contemporary Italian picture, it foreshadows the art of Rembrandt.

**PALMA PORDENONE DOSSO DOSSI**

Propitious to experiments in style, the art climate of Venice enabled painters to develop their personalities to the full, and there were many who, while lacking the originality of such a man as Lotto, produced work of lasting value. Notable among these were Palma, Pordenone and Dosso Dossi.

Palma Vecchio ("the Elder") was born near Bergamo in 1480; he died in 1528. A highly expert technician, he was nothing of a dreamer. From Titian he acquired his taste for painting attractive women in the flower of their youth and the true subject of the *Three Sisters* (Dresden) is the blonde beauty of his models, while his *Two Nymphs* (Frankfort) marks the climax of that unromantic sensualism which prevailed in Venice after Giorgione. In his religious works, such as the *Sacra Conversazione* (Academy, Venice), he succeeded in combining dignity with popular appeal. The Brunswick *Adam and Eve,* however, is one of his outstanding successes, forms being located in space with a firmness and solidity rare in Venetian painting of the period.

Giovanni Antonio de' Sacchis (1483/84-1539), commonly known as Pordenone, the name of his birthplace, after trying out various manners, elected to follow in the path of Giorgione. Then, in 1516, he went to Rome and henceforth showed more concern for plastic values, violent movement, and monumental effects. After working at Cremona and in Emilia he moved to Venice where in 1537 he was commissioned, in preference to Titian, to do some paintings in the Ducal Palace—not so much on his artistic merits as because, unlike Titian, he could be relied on to deliver the work at the due date. No less remarkable than his rapidity of execution was the boldness of his composition and a tendency to press his stylistic innovations to extremes; but we cannot help feeling he often gets his effects without much discernment or finesse and that his work has little real charm. Nevertheless his painting played an important part as one of the formative elements of Baroque.

Dosso Dossi, one of Titian's pupils, came of a family from Trento in northern Venetia. The first documentary reference to him is dated 1512—which places him in the group of Giorgione's immediate successors. In 1514 he was given a commission for work in the Este castello at Ferrara, and thereafter he was employed by that famous family for the greater part of his life. He died in 1542. His brother Battista, with whom he often collaborated, was a follower of Raphael rather than Titian, whereas Dosso, though occasionally borrowing from Raphael, rarely departed from the Titianesque manner. *Circe* (Galleria Borghese, Rome) is perhaps his finest work; color is stepped up to a flame-like intensity and form dissolves into it so thoroughly that the whole scene acquires an aura of mystery and magic. Hardly less striking are the *Nymph and Satyr* (Pitti, Florence), the *Court Jester* (Modena) and the *Holy Family* (Hampton Court), whose landscapes have a dreamlike charm. Unfortunately Dosso soon got into a rut, his inspiration flagged and his colors tended to lose their warmth and luster.

**SAVOLDO**
**ROMANINO**
**MORETTO**

Gian Girolamo Savoldo was born about 1480 at Brescia, where as a young man he studied under Vincenzo Foppa. In 1508 he joined the painters' guild of Florence. He had a thorough grasp of both the new style sponsored by Leonardo and of traditional Flemish techniques with which he became acquainted chiefly through the work of Hugo van der Goes. There are good grounds for believing that he resided in Venice from 1521 to 1548, the year of his death. If the dating of his *St Anthony Abbot and St Paul the Hermit* (Venice) to 1510 can be relied on, it is clear that, after mastering Giorgione's and Titian's handling of light and shade, Savoldo had already developed a personal and highly accomplished style. In 1548 we find Paolo Pino, his pupil, complaining that his teacher was not appreciated as he should be and indeed shamefully neglected; which suggests that Savoldo had much the same experience as Lotto. Still, unjust as this may seem, we must remember that in a city dominated as Venice was by the prestige of Titian and his associates, there was little chance for any other painter, however meritorious, to make his mark. In any case Savoldo, unlike Lotto, did not even try to align himself to Titian who, at the time when Pino made his protest, was at the height of his fame and worldly success. Moreover, whereas Lotto was a born experimentalist drawing inspiration from very diverse sources, Savoldo after some early ventures settled down into a style of his own from which he never departed. But it was an admirable style, and he did well to keep to it. Though we can sense behind it no mean intelligence, his form has a massiveness and simplicity that give his art a popular appeal; while his colored shadows reveal a fusion of Flemish tradition with the discoveries of Leonardo and Giorgione. But he handles form and color in his own way, stripping them of merely ornamental beauty in order to render appearances in terms of his personal vision. Modern critics have done well to stress Savoldo's contribution to the art of the future and the fact that if he cut an isolated figure it was because he was an artist ahead of his time and as such neglected by contemporaries.

It is in the light of these observations that we best can understand the modifications Savoldo brought to Giorgione's treatment of his subjects. He transformed the narrative picture into a genre piece so as the better to envelop landscape and figures in the dusk of evening or nocturnal darkness. His favorite themes were the Nativity, the Adoration of the Shepherds and the Rest during the Flight into Egypt. But he also painted isolated figures: a woman richly clad or half hidden under a flowing mantle, a shepherd, a flute-player, St Matthew visited by the angel. Whether he places his figures in a landscape setting or an interior, he always employs light of a special kind, limited in range and striking through a veil of shadows.

In the Crespi-Morbio *Nativity* and the various versions of the *Flight into Egypt* (Munich, Ragusa, Milan), certain details, such as the shepherd beside the fire in the first-named picture and the glimpses of the sea, mountains and ruins in the others, are, despite the precision given their forms, merely evocative recalls of the leading themes. In the *Magdalen* (National Gallery, London) Savoldo has transformed a very ordinary, not to say prosaic, scene—that of a woman wrapped in a big shawl walking by in the evening shadows—into a romantic vision, and in the *Flute-Player* (Contini-Bonacossi Collection, Florence) the relations between the room, the objects and the figures are stated with such ease and forthright realism that, despite touches of the elegance inseparable from Renaissance art, they anticipate the luminist procedures and crystal-clear precision of the 17th-century Dutch painters. For not a few independent-minded Venetian artists, looking beyond the Renaissance, prepared the way for some of the most valuable discoveries of the succeeding epoch.

Mention may be made of two other Brescian artists, Romanino and Moretto. Girolamo di Romano, called Romanino (1484/87-1566), seems to have had his early training in Venice in the milieu of Bellini and Giorgione whose influences are evident in the *Deposition* of 1510 (Academy, Venice). When in 1513 he painted the large *Santa Giustina Altarpiece* (Padua), he displayed complete mastery of Giorgione's synthesis of form and color, though tending here and there to exaggerate the color factor. On the other hand the paintings made for the Duomo of Cremona in 1519-1520 show that he here was aiming at grandiose effects and elaborate composition, accompanied by some highly curious innovations in the handling of form.

Moretto (ca. 1498-1554), whose real name was Alessandro Bonvicino, was a little younger than Savoldo and Romanino. In his early phase he seems to have come under Foppa's influence, doubtless at second hand, by way of one of his pupils, since Foppa (who died in 1515 or 1516) could hardly have been his teacher. Next, he was drawn to Titian, but to Roman art as well, being particularly attracted by Raphael's form and Lotto's use of it in some of his pictures. Indeed it may be said that no other Lombard painter departed so widely as he from the orthodox Venetian tradition, this independence being due to his desire for an essentially formal beauty—hence his predilection for tender, silvery colors as being most suitable for harmonizing form with chiaroscuro. One of his happiest achievements is the Vienna *Santa Giustina*, which has a sedate grandeur all its own. While at first sight his art gives the impression of being more archaic than Romanino's, the unity and solidity of his color-form structure, far from being reactionary, pointed to the future. His *Feast in the House of Levi* (Santa Maria della Pietà, Venice), painted in 1544, anticipates the banquet-pictures which Veronese brought to such perfection. The altarpiece of *St Nicholas of Bari commending Two Children to the Madonna* (1539, Brescia) might be a scene of family life; indeed this gift for giving elevated subjects a homely flavor and a local setting is one of the charms of Moretto's art.

**MORONI**

Giovanni Battista Moroni (1529/30-1578), a native of Bergamo, probably studied under Moretto, but he also drew inspiration, if with extreme caution, from Savoldo, Titian and Lotto. In his many religious pictures the execution is dull and lifeless; their one redeeming feature is a skillful use of color. It was with his portraits of notables of Bergamo that he made his name. All these people spring to life under his brush. He displays a rare insight into character and employs a technique that brings out the figures more effectively than would any detailed treatment, while silvery light seeping into the colors creates a subtle, all-pervasive radiance. Nothing of the artist's personal feelings about his sitters is allowed to intrude; hence the exceptional verisimilitude of his portraits. Best known is *The Tailor* (National Gallery, London), which doubtless owed its prompt success to the unusual nature of the subject; instead of painting a pope or emperor, or even a local celebrity, Moroni showed a tailor at work, scissors in hand. Thus portraiture, in which by definition the sitter's personality is all-important, was reduced to the condition of a genre scene. It is a noteworthy point that even the portraits on which he has inscribed the name of the model and the date, give the same impression of anonymity. Moroni's "truth," in short, is something more than factual or historical exactitude; it is of a purely artistic and, in the Aristotelian sense of the epithet, universal order.

TINTORETTO

It is impossible to evaluate the three great masters of the second half of the 16th century—Tintoretto, Bassano and Veronese—without taking into account the wave of mannerism that traversed Venetian art between 1540 and 1550. In the next chapter we shall attempt to define the nature of mannerism, but meanwhile we may prepare the way by isolating such of its elements as enter into the art of the three painters named above. Differing from other art historians, we do not think that any of them can properly be described as a mannerist; all three far overshot the confines of that movement, largely owing to the content of their pictures.

The motives which led Tintoretto, after some hesitation, to strike out in another direction, were of various kinds. A mannerist artist is, by his very nature, an intellectual; the making of a mannerist picture involves studious preparation, hard brainwork, painstaking research. Tintoretto was the opposite of an intellectual; he was a man of the people who happened to have a genius for painting, and when he took over some of Michelangelo's procedures, he gave no thought to the ideas that lay behind them. From Titian he may perhaps have learnt some methods of handling light, form and color, but always he adapted them to his own ebullient temperament, simplifying them to the point of changing them entirely.

At the time when throughout Italy the distinction between artist and artisan was becoming ever more pronounced, with the result that painters were growing class-conscious—Titian's elevation to the rank of Count Palatine was a symbol of their new prestige—Tintoretto still saw himself as an artisan, and took pride in being one. The fact, however, should be noted that the merit of the artisan consists in the pains he takes in giving finish to his work, and that Tintoretto's "slapdash" execution has become a byword. Aretino and Vasari were startled both by the headlong speed at which he worked and by his "almost infernal cleverness," but took him to task for his careless drawing. Yet this was Tintoretto's great discovery. After Michelangelo and Titian, painters needed to reacquire the craftsman's touch, that habit of leaving the maker's imprint on every stroke of the brush and substituting light for line so that the painting acquired the simple, natural aspect of the sketch. This may throw light on Tintoretto's conduct when at the San Rocco competition he submitted the finished picture instead of a cartoon. Leonardo's improvisations were limited to a few pencilled lines on paper; Tintoretto's took the form of gigantic canvases. Thus he made the decisive step towards the "unfinished" work of art which, ceasing to seem a mere preparatory sketch, exists in its own right and thanks to the uninhibited imagination that has gone to its making does not need to produce the effect of being completed. But the basic cause of Tintoretto's anti-mannerism was the religious sentiment which, evident chiefly in his later work, distinguishes him from all other artists of the day.

Titian had worked for a pope and two emperors and his pictures fall into two well-marked categories, sacred and profane. But Tintoretto worked for the Venetian Scuole Grandi of San Marco and San Rocco, institutions whose function it was to befriend the poor, and these confraternities took no notice of class differences. They accepted gifts of money from all and sundry and gave help to everyone who needed it. Being very wealthy, they commissioned mural decorations and these dealt exclusively, as in the Middle Ages, with sacred subjects. Thus a religious scene by Tintoretto was like a pictorial "talk" addressed to the populace, intended to make known to them the underlying message of the biblical episodes represented, and to exalt their faith.

It would seem that in his youth Tintoretto had learnt much about the practice of art but that he lacked general culture. The driving force of his work derives, we feel, from his belief in God, the Virgin, the saints, the Christian legends and the mission of the Scuole—but still more from a profound faith in the value of what he was doing. He painted in a fine frenzy of creation, never standing back to appraise his work, and drawing on all the resources of an exceptionally fertile imagination. In this respect he outdid even Rubens, type figure of the artist who gives himself up, unreservedly, not to say exuberantly, to his creative impulse.

Tintoretto was a man of the people, worked for the people and shared their simple faith. At that time, when the Counter-Reformation was in full swing, when popes, emperors and Venetian ruling class were using religion as a means to shore up the temporal power, the masses took no interest in fine points of dogma, in Socino's theories or the problem of liberty of conscience. They left such matters to the intelligentsia, dutifully went to Mass, prayed, and yielded happily to the spell of the old legends that transported them so far from their drab, everyday lives. They were not so much ignorant as naïve, and the Bible stories appealed to them less for the lessons they inculcated

TINTORETTO (1518-1594). JOSEPH AND POTIPHAR'S WIFE, CA. 1544. (21 1/4 × 46")
PRADO, MADRID.

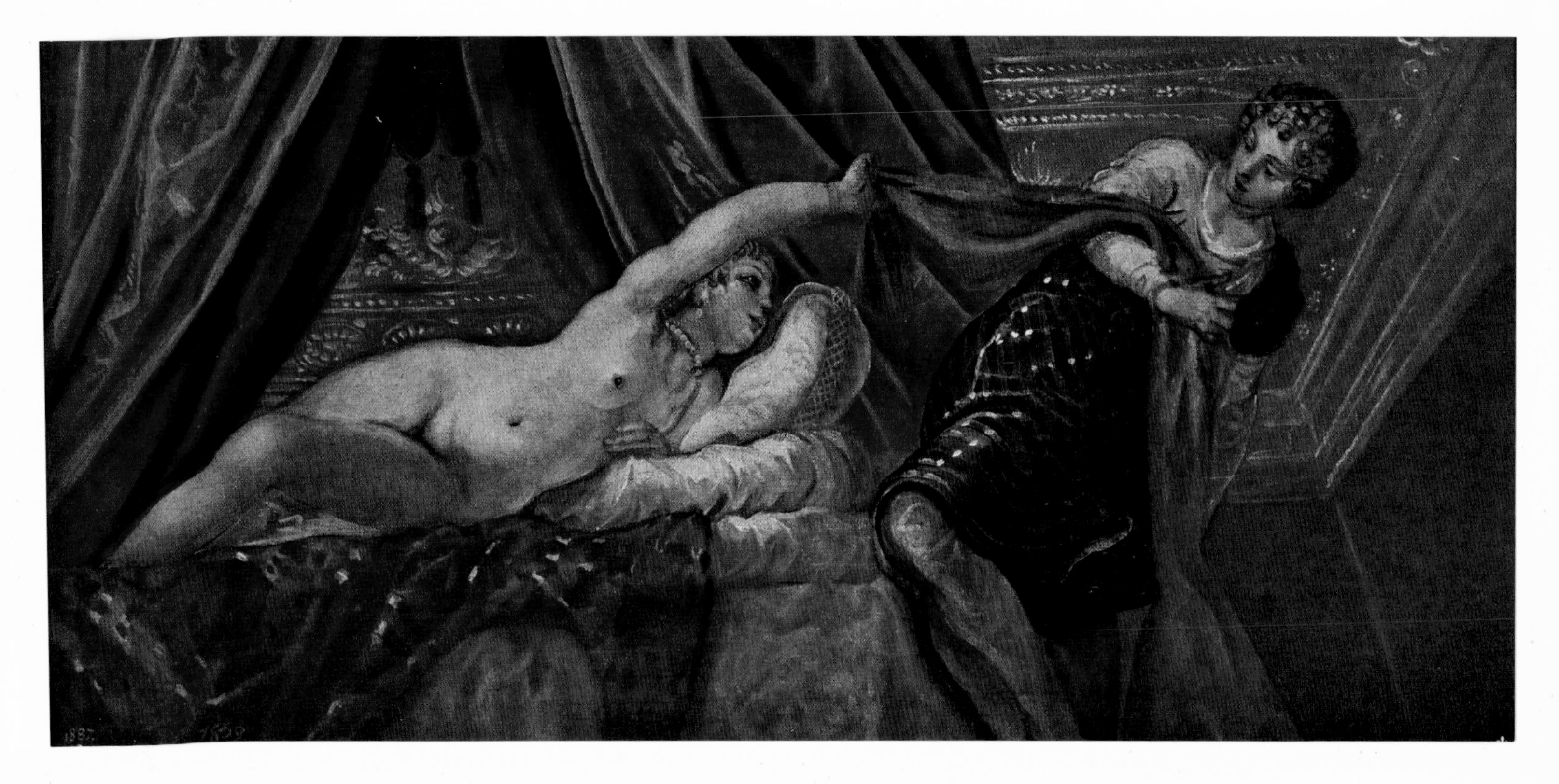

than as poetry. No other artist felt so strongly as that true son of the people, Tintoretto, the ever-present actuality of the world beyond our ken or lived on such familiar terms with the people of the biblical stories.

This was obviously what might be called a primitive approach to religion and it is not surprising that Tintoretto has always been in high favor with admirers of the so-called Primitives. For he was not only a great narrative painter but also an inspired illustrator with the gift of imparting, as Ruskin pointed out, mysterious overtones to the most ordinary things, stones, leaves and shadows, and of opening windows on a super-real world.

The hugeness of his paintings is another striking feature of his œuvre. The conception of the Sublime may account for the relation between the notion of "great art" and the actual size of a work; in Tintoretto's case such are the dimensions of some of his pictures that they have the overwhelming power of a natural phenomenon when it assumes the aspect of a cataclysm. In this sense he is a man of the Renaissance; though he humanizes God and brings Him near to us, his universe is peopled with Titans and traversed by stresses of whirlwind force.

Jacopo Robusti, nicknamed Tintoretto because his father was a dyer (*tintore* in Italian), was born in 1518 at Venice, where he lived until his death in 1594. His life was uneventful, a long round of unremitting service to his art. Enrolled as a Master Painter in 1539, he soon assimilated not only the art of Titian but also that of Michelangelo and the foreign mannerists who had come to Venice. In 1545 he won the admiration of Aretino, but it was not till 1548 that his first triumph came with the *Miracle of St Mark,* painted for the Confraternity of St Mark. He entered into relations with the Scuola di San Rocco (Confraternity of St Roch) in 1549, and thereafter was employed by them until his death. In 1553 he received a commission for pictures for the Ducal Palace; in 1562 he dispatched a picture to the Gonzagas at Mantua, and in 1587 another to King Philip II of Spain. His last commission was to fresco a wall of the Council Chamber of the Venetian Senate, but he died before the work was actually begun. So far as we know, the only time he left Venice was when he made a trip to Mantua in 1580.

His contemporaries formed very different estimates of his art. Vasari said that his drawing was haphazard, improvised, and showed little discernment or mastery of design. Titian disapproved of him and, though one of his admirers, Aretino found fault with his "lack of finish." One of the Brothers of the Scuola di San Rocco offered to contribute fifteen ducats provided that any artist other than Tintoretto was employed for the decoration of the Sala dell'Albergo. When Tintoretto presented a painting as a gift in 1564, twenty-one out of fifty-one members of the Scuola were for declining it. Some time after this, however, the painter had his revenge, being made a member of the Brotherhood. In 1577 he was even allotted a fixed salary for life, on condition that he delivered a stated number of pictures per year.

Tintoretto's output was so vast and varied that only a partial account of it can be given here. First of his early works that calls for mention is a ceiling decoration made about 1544, now in the Prado. It consists of Old Testament scenes painted in

TINTORETTO (1518-1594). THE WASHING OF FEET (FRAGMENT), CA. 1550. PRADO, MADRID.

bright colors, flecked here and there with a sort of dewy efflorescence. Bodies are elongated in mannerist fashion and gestures form graceful arabesques, creating a decorative rhythm rather than any sense of dramatic action. One of the best scenes is *Joseph and Potiphar's Wife*, where the woman's nude body is saturated with light and emphasis is laid on empty space rendered in illusionist perspective so as to stress, by contrast, the figures and their movement.

Very different in conception is the *Washing of Feet* (Prado), which is built up by oppositions of light and shade that, together with the general lay-out, create a sense of drama all the more instant because in this picture Tintoretto ceased to trouble about decorative effect. The dramatic element here is essentially pictorial, that is to say independent of the subject; it stems wholly from the artist's unfettered imagination. There is a tonal relationship between the light hues of the background and the penumbra of the foreground, telling out dark upon light, in which glittering touches form glancing aureoles around the bodies. These are so arranged as to allow of empty spaces giving the composition a rhythm neither linear nor plastic, but composed of sudden apparitions, the figures seeming like so many flashes of light. Any massing of the personages or the use of perspective would have hampered that free play of the imagination to which this picture owes its intriguing power.

On its appearance (in 1548) Tintoretto's *Miracle of St Mark* (now in the Academy, Venice) was hailed as a masterpiece, though there were some who qualified their admiration. Its merits are so conspicuous that we can easily understand its prompt

TINTORETTO (1518-1594). THE MIRACLE OF ST MARK (ST MARK DELIVERING A SLAVE), 1548.
(13 FT. 7 IN. × 17 FT. 9 IN.) GALLERIE DELL'ACCADEMIA, VENICE.

XVI 115

TINTORETTO (1518-1594). ST AUGUSTINE HEALING THE LEPERS, 1549-1550. (100 ½ × 67″)
MUSEO CIVICO, VICENZA.

success and even today there could be no better point of departure for an appraisal of Tintoretto's art. Pallucchini has rightly observed that this picture was not due to a sudden flash of inspiration, but the outcome of long years of study and research. It has something grandiose about it that is absent in the earlier works, and reveals a greater harmony between the style and the essentially dramatic theme. But in adapting the style to such a theme there was always the risk of lapsing into rhetorical effect and we are conscious of the struggle it must have cost the artist to bring his task to a successful conclusion. Working in this manner, he had no time for reflection; he boldly identified movement with action, and the presence of the crowd ruled out those empty spaces which had set the rhythm of, for example, the *Washing of Feet*.

But after bringing off this triumph, Tintoretto could afford to let his imagination run free, and in *St Augustine healing the Lepers* (Vicenza) he achieved a *contrapposto* between the groups and the open spaces, between tracts of light and pools of darkness, that creates a world of magical enchantment. *Adam and Eve* (now in the Academy, Venice), one of his best works, belongs to the cycle of Old Testament scenes made for the Scuola della Trinità and dates probably to the middle of the century. Here "subject" is reduced to a minimum: two bodies rendered with an extreme textural richness, vibrant with inner life; and it is the landscape—nature idealized—that plays the leading part in creating the poetic atmosphere of the scene.

From 1564 to 1588 Tintoretto was employed almost continuously on the decorations of the Scuola di San Rocco.

The *Crucifixion* (1565) covers forty feet of wall; the size made it possible to represent a great throng of people, while allowing for empty spaces and imparting to the groups a movement extending to the far horizon. All compositional elements are caught up in a vast gyration centering on the sublime image of the Cross; nothing is static, earth and sky seem to participate in the divine tragedy. By a special handling of light even the open spaces are made to contribute to the general effect; they are given an organic life of their own and act as sources of a weird illumination that strikes through the darkness falling from a lowering sky. In *Christ before Pilate* the entire composition is dominated by the pale form of the Savior. Tintoretto has not sought to personalize the emotions of either of the leading figures, but to convey the atmosphere of the tragic scene, the purity and truth symbolized by the tranquil, white-stoled figure, while those whose eyes are blind to that purity and truth are relegated to the shadows. In *Moses striking Water from the Rock* no stress is laid on the miraculous aspect of the event, the water gushing forth is the leading motif, paralleled by the swirling movement of the crowd of onlookers. The *Adam and Eve* in the Scuola di San Rocco, datable to 1577-1578, is quite different from the picture in the Academy of Venice on the same theme made twenty-five years earlier. Tintoretto's joy in painting bodies bathed in light is of the past; the atmosphere of the scene deprives it of any sensual appeal and brings home to us only the momentous significance of the Fall. The setting of the *Adoration of the Shepherds* is a hut, divided into two stories so as to isolate the Nativity proper from the scene below and to differentiate the divine from the human elements.

TINTORETTO (1518-1594). THE CRUCIFIXION, DETAIL: THE TWO MARYS, 1565.
SCUOLA DI SAN ROCCO, VENICE.

TINTORETTO (1518-1594). THE CRUCIFIXION, DETAIL FROM THE LEFT SIDE, 1565.
SCUOLA DI SAN ROCCO, VENICE.

TINTORETTO (1518-1594). THE CRUCIFIXION, 1565.

TINTORETTO (1518-1594). THE CRUCIFIXION, DETAIL: ST JOHN THE BAPTIST, 1565.
SCUOLA DI SAN ROCCO, VENICE.

17½ FT. × 40 FT.) SCUOLA DI SAN ROCCO, VENICE.

TINTORETTO (1518-1594). THE CRUCIFIXION, DETAIL FROM THE RIGHT SIDE, 1565.
SCUOLA DI SAN ROCCO, VENICE.

◀ *Folding plate: entire panel.*

Some luminous touches bring out the awe-struck look on the faces of the participants. In the *Baptism of Christ* the distant crowd beyond the half-light of the foreground and middle distance where the action is taking place is plunged in sunlight so vivid as to make it look like a fantastic trelliswork of quivering filaments of light.

In the *Last Supper*, owing to the composition in depth, Christ is placed at the near end of the table. The apostles form an agitated group, appalled by the Master's terrible announcement. Eighty years had passed since Leonardo painted his fresco in Santa Maria delle Grazie, Milan. In Tintoretto's rendering of the scene nothing remains of the spirit of the Renaissance; of its architectural composition, its plastic values, its stress on individual character. Such a tempest of emotion surges through this scene that there could be no question of individualizing expressions. In the dim light the apostles form a somber mass, dramatically lit by a few rare gleams. The Renaissance is over, mannerism left behind; Tintoretto's handling of light in this *Last Supper* is unequivocally Baroque.

But in the *Ascension* we find another mood. The dancing lights and shadows breathe rapturous joy, and flails of light edging the angels' wings seem to be bearing the Savior heavenwards.

In 1582-1583 Tintoretto painted two quite different pictures: the *Annunciation* and the *Massacre of the Innocents*. In the former Gabriel, swooping down through an opening in the wall, cuts a rather material figure and the picture seems a mere bravura piece, devoid of any transcendental intimations. On the other hand, in the *Massacre of the Innocents*, greatly admired by Ruskin, Tintoretto refrained from depicting isolated acts of brutality, agonized expressions, streaming wounds and the livid hues of death; he transmuted the human tragedy into a catastrophe on the cosmic level, its horror rendered solely by effects of light and shade.

The *Flight into Egypt* belongs to the same period. On the left is the slow procession on donkey-back and on the right one of the loveliest landscapes ever painted, owing its beauty less to the actual scenery than to an exquisitely balanced play of light. About a year later came *St Mary of Egypt* and the *Magdalen*; the setting in each case is a vast, enchanted landscape and here again it is light that quickens our sense of mystery, peoples the solitude and imbues wild nature with friendly life. Last of Tintoretto's San Rocco paintings was the *Visitation* (1588) in which, after so many scenes of crowded life, he returned to the reposeful composition, with few figures, of his youth. All the *Visitation* shows us is two women, simple, humble forms in front of a deep spatial recession—the painter's farewell, touching in its modesty, to the gigantic picture cycle he had worked on for over twenty years.

In the course of his long life Tintoretto lavished peerless treasures, pictures charged with that sublime magic of which he had the secret, on various Venetian churches and confraternities. The Scuola di San Marco, which had provided him with the opportunity of scoring his first success with the *Miracle of St Mark*, gave him a commission, in 1562, for three more pictures. In the *Removal of St Mark's Body* (Academy, Venice) and the *Finding of St Mark's Body* (Brera, Milan), the rendering of space dominates the theme.

And it is to light yet again that these scenes owe their dramatic power; the light flooding a vast public square in the first picture and, in the second, striking on a row of tombs. In the *Adoration of the Golden Calf* (Madonna dell'Orto, Venice) the incantatory power of the picture and its dramatic effect stem from the clouds encircling the mountain top where Moses is being given the Tables of the Law.

Although constantly employed on large-scale works, Tintoretto found time to paint many portraits, in which the figures, dashed off in feverish haste, spring to vivid life against dark backgrounds with the instantaneity of lightning flashes. The very rapidity of the effect obtained individualizes the personage represented. Unlike Titian and Lotto, he did not aim at bringing out the inner life of his models—but surely it is a mistake to regard the "psychological portrait" as the *nec plus ultra*; as Baudelaire observed, the portrait may be history and it may be art. Tintoretto's imagination was too fertile and too active for him to content himself with "history." He intended his images to make an immediate, convincing impression on the beholder, and in this he succeeded. Examples are the unforgettable *Portrait of a Man* (1553, Vienna), the *Young Nobleman with a Golden Chain* (Prado), *Vincenzo Zeno* (Pitti), *Jacopo Sansovino* (Uffizi), *Alvise Cornaro* (Pitti), *Doge Pietro Loredano* (National Gallery, Melbourne) and *Nicolò Priuli* (Frick Collection, New York).

In his justly famous *Susanna and the Elders* (Vienna) we feel that the artist has only just shaken off the influence of mannerism. The nude body is even more brilliantly illuminated than the one in *Joseph and Potiphar's Wife*, and this light builds up a form that is more solid and in stronger contrast with its surroundings than any of Titian's figures. All the rest—glimmering background, hedge of rose bushes, trinkets, fallen garments and so forth—serves merely to bring into prominence the woman's body emerging in lonely splendor. This picture is exceptional in Tintoretto's œuvre; in it he has concentrated his attention on light rather than on color, which here performs an essentially formal role. Though the subject is biblical, it is transposed into a frankly pagan key, thanks to the airy lightness of the brushwork. In some of his "mythologies," such as *Mercury and the Graces* and *Ariadne, Bacchus and Venus* (ca. 1578, Ducal Palace, Venice), Tintoretto seems to have drawn inspiration from the elegantly spontaneous rhythm of the Vienna *Susanna*. Reminiscences of it can also be traced in his strangely fascinating *Deliverance of Arsinoë* (Dresden), where the nudes, the hero in full armor, the ship, the sea, the distant light and nearby shadows conjure up before us a poet's vision of a romantic dreamland.

Tintoretto's inventions and discoveries defy enumeration. In the *Crucifixion* (1568) in San Cassiano, Venice, the crosses are foreshortened so as to heighten the effect of the storm that is breaking overhead and the lances fretting the horizon. In the Berlin *Annunciation* the figures act as guide-marks leading the eye towards a central burst of light. And it is light on sea and sky that gives its dramatic instancy to the miracle in the *Vocation of St Peter* (National Gallery, Washington). In the Louvre *Paradise* the movement set up by the many-colored masses of figures disposed, circle within circle, around the vast effulgence of the sky gives the scene an overwhelming emotive power, though individual figures are hardly distinguishable. The same theme is treated, on a colossal scale, in the famous canvas in the Ducal Palace (1586-1590), which proved, if proof were needed, that at the age of seventy Tintoretto was far from having exhausted the resources of his copious imagination.

Between 1591 and 1594, that is to say in the last three years of his life, he painted, for San Giorgio Maggiore, a *Last Supper*. The general effect is even more eye-filling

TINTORETTO (1518-1594). ARIADNE, BACCHUS AND VENUS, CA. 1578. (57½×61¾″)
DUCAL PALACE, VENICE.

than that of any of the earlier works, so dazzling are the sudden bursts of light, so dramatically bold the rendering of infinite space. This is, in fact, an early example of the exuberant vision of Baroque.

On a general survey of Tintoretto's œuvre, what strikes one most perhaps is the incantatory quality of his art; almost we feel that he is deliberately trying to cast a spell on the beholder. Then, looking deeper, we perceive the profound religious feeling that led him to present biblical and saintly personages, even God himself, under an aspect that was human and intelligible, yet conveyed intimations of transcendence, of the godhead immanent in all things. Light and shadow, space and movement are his means of expression and a masterly use of one of the richest palettes known to painting makes them live before us. Characteristic of his art are its warm humanity, its combination of popular appeal with a sense of the otherworldly, the mystery and magic he imparted to the facts of visual experience. Abandoning Titian's style and leaving mannerism behind, he blazed a trail towards the "luminism" of the next century.

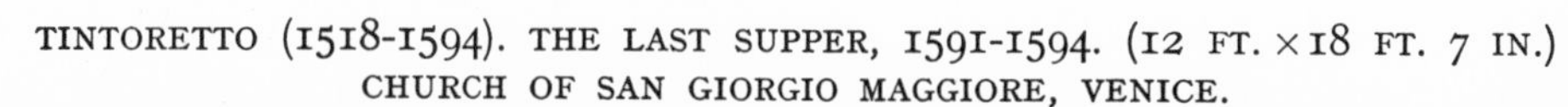

TINTORETTO (1518-1594). THE LAST SUPPER, 1591-1594. (12 FT. × 18 FT. 7 IN.)
CHURCH OF SAN GIORGIO MAGGIORE, VENICE.

JACOPO BASSANO (1510/15-1592). THE ADORATION OF THE SHEPHERDS, 1568. (94 ½ × 59 ¼″)
MUSEO CIVICO, BASSANO.

JACOPO BASSANO

Another great Venetian painter was Jacopo da Ponte, called "Il Bassano," who devoted himself to representing the life of peasants and shepherds, using as its setting the countryside around the small market-town of Bassano, in Venetia, from which he got his name. Before this, however, he had drawn on various sources of inspiration and it was only after much experimentation that he realized he could give freest play to his imagination and highly personal style in scenes of country life. One of his characteristics was a feeling for the intrinsic beauty of color, which led him to break up the outlines of forms in order to adapt them to this new conception of color and give it full effect. And this special sensitivity enabled him to put the physical properties of his medium to the service of spiritual values in works that amply justify the high esteem in which contemporaries held them.

Writing in the 17th century, Marco Boschini said that Bassano's brushstrokes and touches of color were "like so many gems: rubies, emeralds, turquoises and diamonds that sparkle even in darkness." But what appeals to us today is not merely the iridescent sheen of his colors but also his gift for instilling their very texture with a vibrant life no previous painter had achieved and which indeed remains unequaled.

Though living in a small, out-of-the-way town, Bassano enjoyed immense success, and this he owed not only to his exquisite colors but also to his novel interpretation of religious themes. Pictures of legendary figures divinely beautiful but rendered with a rhetorical, hollow magniloquence were beginning to pall. So it is easy to understand why Bassano's presentation of the biblical stories in terms of everyday peasant life and with complete sincerity was so readily welcomed; it must have come as a relief after the high-flown showpieces of the late Venetian School.

It is perhaps a little saddening that Masaccio's and Alberti's visions of man as an heroic figure, center of the universe, should have dwindled, less than two centuries later, into amiable scenes of pastoral life and peasants' kitchens cluttered with pots and pans. But the course of art history is paved with such regrets, and there could be no turning the clock back. The Renaissance, one of the most brilliant eras of European culture, had had its day and we see here the humble beginnings of that long, slow evolution which was to lead up to the flowering of 19th- and 20th-century art.

Born at Bassano some time between 1510 and 1515, Jacopo da Ponte produced his first work in 1531 when still a pupil of Bonifazio dei Pitati. His five years' training under that master (1530-1535) enabled him to shake off the provincialism inculcated by his father Francesco da Ponte the Elder. When the latter died, he became head of the family and received official recognition from the municipal authorities of his hometown. His talent ripened slowly; in a picture made in 1540, the *Supper at Emmaus* (Cittadella), his interpretation of the face of Christ is uncouth to the point of ugliness, though he was more successful in making a convincing figure of the innkeeper. This was in fact an early token of his true vocation. Moreover, in a slightly previous work, the *Flight into Egypt* (Bassano), datable about 1537, he had, it seems, already realized the necessity of striking a realistic note. But, once he had outgrown Bonifazio's influence, he turned towards the Italian and foreign mannerists then in vogue in Venice, assimilating their methods with remarkable skill. Evidently he hoped to acquire from others the qualities he lacked: beauty, elegance, and also a certain sleight of hand.

But what he still needed was to effect a fusion between his innate naturalism and the mannerist procedures he had espoused so wholeheartedly; to break his line so that color could make play with the intervals; and to learn that through the medium of color he could give entire expression to his creative impulse. Subsequently to 1562, the year in which he painted in his new style the *Crucifixion* for the church of San Teonisto at Treviso, he produced a series of masterpieces, amongst them *Pentecost*, the *Manger*, the *Baptism of St Lucilla, Podestà Sante Moro commending a Donor to the Virgin, St John the Baptist* (all in the museum at Bassano), *Jacob's Journey* (Hampton Court), *St Peter and St Paul* (Modena), *St Jerome* (Venice), *Adam and Eve* (Pitti). While differing in composition, all have in common a treatment of space enabling the artist to present figures in depth and to submerge mannerist elements with his glorious color.

His health broke down in 1581 and thereafter, until his death in 1592, he produced little work of his own. His four sons, Francesco, Giambattista, Leandro and Girolamo took over his themes and exploited them with much success.

**PAOLO VERONESE**

Titian, Tintoretto and Bassano had made haste to discard mannerism, after it had served their turn, and to integrate their linear and plastic form into the new vision of reality as color, light and shade. After 1550 all three tended to restrict their range of colors and to stress the role of light; this "luminism," a tendency to see the world in terms of light and dark, was premonitory of the spiritual malaise of the 17th century.

But Paolo Veronese, last of the great Venetian painters of the Renaissance, felt no such qualms; in his art all is *joie de vivre*, serenity and certitude, frank enjoyment of the contemporary scene. For though born in Verona, Paolo was the most brilliant interpreter of the aristocratic, luxurious life of Venice in her Golden Age. Like other great painters of the time, he set much store on color, but used it in a very different way. Once he had discovered its exact relationship to light, he gave each hue its utmost brilliance, with the result that shadows dwindle into a vague penumbra, often hardly perceptible, and the color sings. Other artists, Tintoretto in particular, had taken the obvious course and employed dark shadings so as to throw light into relief; Veronese succeeded in making his light tell out on a bright ground. The painter's black is always darker than any black in nature, and his white far less luminous than natural light. But if even the darkest tone is kept relatively pale, it is possible, by bringing it into relation with the brightest tone, to produce an effect of intense luminosity, approximating to the light of day. This is one of the reasons why Veronese, after being little understood in the 17th century, was so much appreciated and imitated in the 18th, when *peinture claire* came into vogue again.

Paolo Caliari, commonly called Veronese, was born at Verona in 1528. At the age of thirteen he began studying under Antonio Badile, and he remained in his hometown until 1553. After he had thoroughly mastered his art, he settled (in 1555) in Venice where, except for a few brief journeys, he resided until his death in 1588.

In 1560 Francesco Sansovino wrote: "Paolo is beginning to make a name for himself both as an excellent painter and also as an agreeable talker, a young man pleasant to consort with." Looking at his pictures, we can see why this was so. Tradition has it that even Titian, hard to please as he was, liked Veronese. And the instant appeal of his paintings, coupled with his personal charm, was rewarded by a career of unruffled success, a happy marriage and many children, a trip to Rome, close friendship with the great architects Palladio, Sansovino and Scamozzi, and lucrative assignments.

Newly arrived from a provincial home, the young artist was dazzled by the colorful life of Venice at her apogee, the round of brilliant festivals, the beauty of the costumes of both men and women, the spacious palaces and loggias, and the elegance of the Venetian nobility. Tintoretto had always remained a man of the people; the outlook on life of Veronese, a stone-breaker's son, was that of an aristocrat born to the purple—as indeed is evident in all his work.

When the Inquisition arraigned him in 1573 for having introduced into his *Feast in the House of Levi* such incongruous figures as dwarfs, people dressed like Germans (i.e. protestants) and buffoons, he retorted that painters, like poets and madmen, were entitled to take liberties and that anyhow, in this picture, his commission was "to ornament it as seemed good to him." But the worldly pomp and splendor of his compositions, notably his great banquet-pictures, and the lack of feeling in his renderings of Christ show that, with some rare exceptions,

PAOLO VERONESE (1528-1588). ST MENNAS, AFTER 1560.
(97 ¼ × 48″) GALLERIA ESTENSE, MODENA.

the alleged religious theme counted for relatively little in his painting. His last big work was the *Triumph of Venice*, and we might almost say that, whatever the ostensible subjects of its predecessors, Venice had always been their source of inspiration.

In expressing his untrammelled joy in the splendors of Venetian life and in building up his gorgeous color-orchestrations governed by a rhythm that never falters but gathers strength continually no matter how great the picture surface to be covered, Veronese deliberately dispensed with several of the elements made use of by other painters, such as overt movement. True, he is capable of making his figures move in space and renders perspective with skill, but it is "pose" that determines the movement of the figures and their balanced distribution within the limits of the picture. For though he has no difficulty in producing effects of depth and spatial recession, he prefers to spread out the images upon the surface, and in a good many of his works places a crowd of figures in the extreme foreground against a backdrop of buildings and open sky.

PAOLO VERONESE (1528-1588). YOUTH BETWEEN VICE AND VIRTUE, CA. 1570. (40⅛ × 60⅛″)
PRADO, MADRID.

PAOLO VERONESE (1528-1588). THE ADORATION OF THE MAGI (DETAIL), 1573.
CHURCH OF SANTA CORONA, VICENZA.

PAOLO VERONESE (1528-1588). THE MARTYRDOM OF ST JUSTINA (DETAIL), 1575.
MUSEO CIVICO, PADUA.

Other exceptional qualities of his art are its smiling grace, emotional detachment and a serenity that in his day seemed somewhat out of date. This has recently led some to affiliate his work to the classical art of the High Renaissance. But though Veronese is as serene as Raphael and this fine tranquillity is a quality of the very greatest art, his style, far from being classical, is more in line with our modern sensibility than with that of the Renaissance during the first half of the 16th century. The art of Veronese is not a throwback but, more perhaps than that of any of his contemporaries, points the way to the future. Therein lies his strength. The serenity of his art is the outcome of a gift for absorbing the most diverse elements and uniting them in a coherent whole bearing the imprint of his style. There is nothing of the artisan in his make-up; nowhere in classical art do we find that consciously patrician air which makes its first appearance with Veronese and was to characterize the new aristocratic art of the Baroque period.

In his early efforts we see how many and how varied were the sources he drew on. The Bevilacqua-Lazise altarpiece (1548, Verona) shows the influence of Antonio Badile, his teacher; the decoration of the Villa Soranza (1551, Castelfranco) that of Giulio Romano's mannerism; and the *Transfiguration* (1555-1556) in the cathedral of Montagnana (like all the works of this period) reveals the combined influences of Raphael and Titian.

But by 1555-1556, when he painted the frescos in the sacristy of San Sebastiano, Venice, Veronese was in full possession of his style. Notable in the *Crowning of Esther* is his success in solving the problems of formal structure; the scene is viewed from below, the play of light brings out the density of masses, while colors acquire a deep-toned resonance against the luminosity of the sky. Esther is one of the first truly beautiful women he painted and the magnificence of the setting is worthy of her beauty.

Given his temperament, it was natural that Veronese took every opportunity of painting scenes of feasts and banquets, and these in fact are his most famous works. Since in them he had not to use the "frog's-eye view" needful in ceiling decorations, he could give vivacity to these pictures without detriment to the harmonious distribution of the figures, and thus achieve a satisfying balance between the vitality basic to movement and the tranquillity appropriate to contemplation. These feast scenes also gave him opportunities of filling the background with architectural features, in which his friendship with leading architects led him to take a special interest. Though on the face of it mere accessories, these architectural elements, thanks to a double play of light, have an important part in the color-scheme. A glowing flood of light sweeps over the images in the foreground; then becomes paler, more attenuated, as it glances across the architecture in the distance, investing it with a remote, dreamlike glamour.

Most effective of these banquet-pictures are the *Feast in the House of Simon* (ca. 1560, Turin), the *Marriage at Cana* (ca. 1562-1563, Louvre, and 1571, Dresden), the *Feast of St Gregory* (1572, Monte Berico, Vicenza) and the *Feast in the House of Levi* (1573, Venice). In the last-named picture, above all, the rhythmic arrangement of figures and architecture, their alternate presentation in depth and on the surface, the delicate sheen of the background, the balanced disposition of colors across the luminous

PAOLO VERONESE (1528-1588). THE MYSTICAL MARRIAGE OF ST CATHERINE, CA. 1575.
(12 FT. 4 IN. × 8 FT.) GALLERIE DELL'ACCADEMIA, VENICE.

expanse have an effect on the beholder that is well-nigh overwhelming. Though the themes are religious, there is no religious emotion in these pictures and it is noteworthy that the figure of Christ is the one that, as usual, Veronese renders least successfully. Since he was called on to paint "feasts" he thought fit to depict those he had seen with his own eyes, the spectacular banquets that were then a feature of Venetian life. But the fascination he found in these scenes led him to picture them under an ideal aspect and to invest them with a compelling grandeur unique in this genre.

Veronese liked painting surfaces of vast dimensions whose width much exceeded their height (as in these "feasts") and which permitted him to present his subject on the surface against a luminous ground. Some of the most striking of the pictures in which he used this format are the *Family of Darius before Alexander* (National Gallery, London), the *Adoration of the Magi* (Dresden), and the *Madonna with the Cuccina Family* (ca. 1571, Dresden).

With Palladio as architect and Veronese as painter the luxurious Villa Giacomelli built at Maser (near Treviso) by the Barbaro family became the "finest pleasure-house of the Renaissance." The landscapes on the walls seem like so many windows open on the countryside and harmonize perfectly with the figures beside the doors, on the balconies and ceiling. But Veronese did not aim at any illusionist realism; there is an airiness and vivacity in these scenes that make them seem like glimpses of some lovely, lost Arcadia. Most remarkable of his decorations is that in the Audience Chamber of the Ducal Palace, painted between 1575 and 1577. In *Venice attended by Justice and Peace* and the figures of "Virtues"—*Meekness* and *Simplicity* especially—we see visions of feminine beauty which, for glorious color and delicate handling of shadows and volumes, have never been surpassed by any other artist.

Towards the end, Veronese lost something of his serene detachment. Conscious of the tragic side of the age he lived in, he gave expression to his new sense of compassion and fellow-feeling for suffering humanity in Pietàs and Crucifixions. Also in some works of this period, for example his *St Helen* (National Gallery, London), where the saint robed in white believes she sees angels carrying the Cross, he strikes a visionary note; but such works are adventitious, half unwitting revelations of his belated change of heart. For his true vocation was to hymn the glories of Venice, her pomp and pageantry. More than any other artist it was Veronese who created the legend of Venice in the sunset glow of her splendor and opulence, before the hard times came—a legend whose glamour will endure, whatever changes time may bring.

# MANNERISM

JACOPO PONTORMO (1494-1556/57). THE DEPOSITION, 1525-1528. (123 × 75 ½″)
CAPPONI CHAPEL, CHURCH OF SANTA FELICITA, FLORENCE.

# 5

## FROM PONTORMO TO EL GRECO

FROM about 1515, when Pontormo, Rosso and Beccafumi came on the scene, until 1614, the year El Greco died, the art style known as "mannerism" was in the ascendant. During the 17th century it fell into disrepute and until quite recently the term "mannerist" always conveyed disparagement—an injustice which modern critics, very rightly, refuse to countenance. Vasari when he used the word *maniera* was merely thinking of an artist's personal style; for Bellori, however, it implied "mannered," or "resulting solely from the artist's 'fantasy,' not from imitation (of nature)." And thereafter, until the end of the 19th century, this absence of the element of nature-imitation was the reason why mannerism was frowned on. But today when so much stress is laid on the creative imagination, the fantasy so brilliantly present in the work of mannerist painters has no lack of admirers.

However, before turning to study the art of some typical mannerist painters regarding whose merits there can be no doubt, we must try to find an answer to the question: "What exactly is meant by 'mannerism'?" Actually it is as hard to define as the epithets Baroque and Gothic. These movements were too vast, too complex, to be resumed in any cut-and-dried definition; the most that can be done is to describe their salient characteristics and to set forth the ideas on art prevailing amongst the painters who took part in them.

Since it is usual to describe the art of Raphael, Fra Bartolomeo and Michelangelo (in his early phase) as classical, we may say that one of the distinctive features of mannerism is its anti-classicism. Whereas the three artists just named were admired for the balance they struck between the ideal and the real, the mannerists sacrificed the representation of reality to an ideal of elegance, refinement and delicate perfection quite other than the Raphaelesque conception of the beautiful. Since naturalness was the least of their concerns, they may be described as "formalists"—but in no pejorative sense; their interest in form was so intense that its realization became in effect the content of their art. Moreover they practised an illusionist realism peculiar to themselves, of a kind we are tempted to describe as "surrealistic."

This cult of form gave rise to a conception that has had much importance in the history of art: the conception that art is not the imitation of nature but a product of the mind and a creation of the "inner eye." Leonardo, too, regarded painting as an intellectual activity. But to his thinking the function of the intellect was to elicit and interpret the secrets of nature; the mannerists, on the other hand, regarded the operation of the mind, begetter of forms that have only an indirect relation to nature, as an end in itself. In short, the artist was enjoined to create without spontaneity, without *laisser-aller* or concessions to popular or religious sentiment; his work was to be subjective through and through. But art cannot operate *in vacuo*, and for their raw material, so to speak, the mannerists turned to the great masters, Raphael and Michelangelo, and not to nature. Thus their contacts with nature were at second hand. So great was their aversion from imitation that, when they could not succeed in creating, they felt compelled to "invent." This invention exercised itself chiefly in their figures and motifs, and with these they crowded their compositions; for they had little relish for depicting space since this would have forced them to give their figures a more natural expression. So studied an art was bound to be intellectual. Even in their happiest moments, when by charming flights of fancy these painters succeed in making us forget their intellectual bias, this is not due to any instinctive sensuality but to that calculated action on the senses known as erotism. Thus the gulf between them and the great Venetians is apparent. When Titian achieved his new vision of reality there was no question of divided purposes or any intellectual problems to be solved, and his discovery of color values owed as much to his senses as to his mind.

Given their refinement, the mannerists tended to shut their eyes to "base reality," and as was to be expected they had most success in the courts of Francis I and Henry II, then the most elegant in Europe. On the other hand, however, we must not forget that, owing to its development over a long period and in different places, mannerism had to adapt itself to a great diversity of local conditions. To begin with it reflected the discontent of certain Tuscan artists who could neither accept classical form and its immobility, nor ecclesiastical art, then no less stagnant as compared with the new modes of religious expression discovered in Germany and made known to the Italians chiefly through Dürer's engravings. But this first wave of revolt soon came to a halt, inhibited by court etiquette and the exigencies of the social order of the day. Of this the Counter-Reformation was quick to take advantage; until the end of the century it imposed on mannerist art appropriate disciplines, more concerned with decorum than with moral considerations. Soon, however, it became clear to the ecclesiastical authorities that mannerism was not acceptable enough to the populace at large to play the propagandist part they asked of it and accordingly they turned towards the Baroque, then in its early phase, an art form that exactly met their requirements.

During the second half of the Cinquecento, in fact, the mannerists lost ground; they had kept too close to the forms of Michelangelo and Raphael, rule-of-thumb had replaced invention. It was they who founded the first academies, at Florence in 1563 and in Rome in 1578, which, though doubtless helpful to the artists personally—since they raised their social standing—did nothing for art itself. And it was in Spain that Renaissance mysticism found its true pictorial expression; El Greco's visionary genius and his impassioned inward drive realized to perfection the mannerist ideal; no other artist had conjured up so compellingly a world transcending visual experience.

ROSSO FIORENTINO (1495-1540). THE DEPOSITION, 1521. (147 ¼ × 77″)
PINACOTECA, VOLTERRA.

This brief account of the type forms of mannerism will explain, we hope, our reason for not speaking of mannerist tendencies in the case of such men as Brueghel, Bassano and Tintoretto who, by and large, saw the world through the eyes of the ordinary man and were in no sense "intellectuals." Whatever paths they followed, their art belonged to a world in which no possible distinction could be drawn between style and reality, between the thinking mind and the creative imagination.

**PONTORMO AND THE TUSCAN MANNERISTS**

Jacopo Carrucci, called Pontormo after the town where he was born in 1494, launched the mannerist movement in Tuscany. When, after studying under Leonardo, Piero di Cosimo, Mariotto Albertinelli and Andrea del Sarto, he set up as an independent painter in 1513 or 1514, he had prompt success. The Medici family commissioned him to make the decorations in their country house at Poggio a Cajano. In 1530 Michelangelo sent him some cartoons to use as models for paintings. After the return of the Medici to Florence he continued working for them and in 1546 was given an assignment to fresco the choir in the church of San Lorenzo, on which task he was engaged until his death in 1556/57. This work (now destroyed) was universally condemned by those who saw it as a hopeless failure.

In the *Sacra Conversazione* (San Michele Visdomini, Florence), painted in 1518 in his early youth, all the characteristic features of Pontormo's style are already present. There is no attempt to render space, figures are assembled in such a way as to come flush with the picture surface, "representation" gives place to "presentation." But these figures have no beauty in themselves, they are badly proportioned and twisted into preposterous attitudes so as to convey a sense of emotion wrought up to fever pitch. Yet it was with this work that a young artist aged twenty-four, dissatisfied with the moral and intellectual climate of the day, gave a new direction to Renaissance painting. In 1518 it was no longer possible to feel the simple religious faith of the Middle Ages, and in any case the Platonic Idealism then in vogue precluded direct relations with nature and any such intimate association between mind and matter as was attained by Titian—who in this same year was painting his *Assumption* for the Frari church. In his *Commentary on Plato's Symposium* Marsilio Ficino, stressing the incompatibility of mind and nature, declared that beauty was a revelation of the secret consonance of all things with an ideal order, and of a spiritual rather than a corporeal nature, a proportion of parts, not beautiful *per se*, within a perfect whole. Spiritual values, in short, had to be isolated from sensations and the mind debarred from placing any reliance on nature. Another of Ficino's dicta was that "we must forget what we have learnt because in learning it we renounced the study of ourselves." By dint of heroic efforts Michelangelo succeeded in overcoming this antagonism between mind and nature. Pontormo was a different type of man; no fighter but sensitive and high-strung, he preferred to retire from the struggle and give himself up to his soul-searchings. He invites the spectator to fill out in his imagination the hints, allusions and curious implications present in his works; hence their undoubted charm, a charm that is, however, a total negation of the rationalism practised by the humanists.

The *Supper at Emmaus* (1525, Uffizi) and the *Visitation* (ca. 1530, Carmignano) are typical of Pontormo's art; there is no action, the motionless figures look like disembodied spirits. He does not strive for any dramatic effect; on the contrary, settings and atmosphere are those of some fabled land of dreams, giving the impression that Pontormo knew his incapacity for treating such subjects on the plane of actuality. Between 1522 and 1525 or thereabouts he frescoed scenes from the Life of Christ in the Carthusian monastery of Galluzzo, employing motifs culled from Dürer's prints. Vasari—and probably most of Pontormo's contemporaries—resented this; the idea of discarding the "Italian manner" and drawing inspiration from a relatively little known artist of the far North struck them as ill-advised, to say the least of it. But today we can easily see why Pontormo was drawn to Dürer; he found in him a fidelity to reality that had ceased to exist in Florentine art, and moreover a religious and moral earnestness now confined to those who were in sympathy with the Reformation, whether inside Italy or abroad. Thus the Galluzzo frescos have a distinctive quality of their own, absent in the general run of Florentine painting. In *Christ before Pilate* the figures are rigid, open spaces emphasize the tragic isolation of Christ, his anguished suspense and the sublime significance of the event. But these frescos are in too poor a condition for us to form an opinion of their original color. The *Deposition* in Santa Felicita, Florence, has stood up much better against the ravages of time. Despite the theme the colors are bright and pure, devoid of chiaroscuro, at once delicate and brilliant as jewels touched by sunlight. A restless movement animates the figures, its purpose being solely to implement the sensuous rhythm of a tantalizingly intricate arabesque.

Pontormo's portraits are usually complete successes; in these the very nature of the subject forced him to take notice of the facts of visual experience. But there can be no doubt that he pointed the way to mannerism by the clean-cut distinction he drew between the Idea and the physical world, between mind and matter, an antithesis he felt so acutely that in the end his mind became unhinged—yet it is precisely this spiritual unrest that gives his art its very real greatness.

Giovanni Battista di Jacopo di Gasparre, commonly known as Rosso Fiorentino, was born at Florence in 1495. After entering the painters' guild in 1517 he was given a commission to fresco the *Assumption* in Santa Annunziata, Florence. In 1521 he painted the Volterra *Deposition* and in 1525 *Jethro's Daughters* (Uffizi). In that year he moved to Rome where he lived until 1527, becoming a close friend of Michelangelo. The sack of Rome compelled him to leave that city and he visited several Italian towns —Perugia, Borgo San Sepolcro, Città di Castello, Arezzo—before setting out for France in 1530. Given the appointment of court painter to the king, he decorated, in collaboration with Primaticcio, the Pavilion of Pomona (1532-1535); also, between 1534 and 1537, the Galerie François I at Fontainebleau. He made many designs for costumes, silverware and "Triumphs," notably one in celebration of the visit of the Emperor Charles V. He died in France in 1540.

Rosso's art, like that of many other painters of the day, shows the joint influences of Leonardo, Fra Bartolomeo, Michelangelo and the Germans, Dürer in particular.

Thus it bears the mark of that cultured sophistication which characterizes Florentine painting after the first decade of the Cinquecento. All the same, his style is more original than that of Pontormo, with whom he was closely associated at one time. His work has none of the complexity and feverish tension that give Pontormo's art its curious appeal, but his forms have greater actuality and he brings off some striking effects of color. Yet, while endowed with more facility and fluency than that highly temperamental artist Pontormo, he remains always on a slightly lower level.

In the *Deposition* the monochrome background is painted a dark blue—not the blue of the sky—against which the other colors stand out violently, keyed up to their maximum intensity. Stressed by forms built up in facets and by extravagant gestures, they acquire the shrillness of a cry of despair, but a despair that, lacking co-ordination, is all on the surface. Another outstanding feature of this picture is the strongly centrifugal impulse given the lines of force governing the composition. Here the painter has replaced both the monumental conceptions of Renaissance art and the expression of Christian sentiment by a fantasia of forms, products of a brilliantly fertile, often willfully bizarre imagination, and interpreted the subject on boldly symbolic lines. Symbolism is even more conspicuous in *Jethro's Daughters.* Two prostrate figures are being struck by a third, while a young girl stands aloof in an attitude of studied indifference suggesting she is the cause of the affray. Space is non-existent, so crowded is the scene with bodies telling out strongly against the background, though the contrast between lights and darks is due more to the colors than to any attempt at modeling. *Jethro's Daughters* and the *Deposition* show Rosso at his best. Had he stayed in Italy, he would certainly have worked in isolation; as it was, by going to France he became the founder of the School of Fontainebleau. For his work on the Galerie François I he had many French and Italian helpers. The technique of this decoration in which painting and stucco ornamentation are combined to happy effect was quite original, though it may have been suggested by a decoration carried out by Raphael and his assistants in Rome. Notwithstanding the fact that this work has suffered much from the injuries of time and rough handling, the unity of lines, colors and volumes, despite a rich variety of motives, is such that it ranks high as an example of a large-scale decorative ensemble governed by free fancy, yet executed with consummate artistry.

Domenico Beccafumi was born near Montaperti, probably in 1486; after receiving his early training at Siena he went to Rome to perfect his style by a close study of the works of Raphael and Michelangelo. Returning to Siena in 1512, he came under the influence of Sodoma, whom he sought to outdo on his own ground. After this he worked at Pisa and Genoa. He was also a sculptor and executed a marble pavement in *commesso* work for the cathedral of Siena. He died in 1551.

His sensitive handling of light and his *sfumato* implemented by a dexterous use of lights and darks qualify him to rank as a mannerist. His *Communion of St Catherine* (Siena) is imbued with poetic emotion, and an exquisite sensibility makes itself felt in the handling of light and shade in his *Nativity* (San Martino, Siena). It is clear that to begin with he shaped his style on Leonardo; then, when in Rome, he turned

AGNOLO BRONZINO (1503-1572). PORTRAIT OF UGOLINO MARTELLI, 1537-1538. (40 × 33 ½″)
KAISER FRIEDRICH MUSEUM, BERLIN.

DOMENICO BECCAFUMI (CA. 1486-1551). THE BIRTH OF THE VIRGIN (FRAGMENT), 1543.
PINACOTECA, SIENA.

towards Raphael, and at Siena towards Sodoma and other painters. But better than any of his contemporaries he saw how Leonardo's *sfumato* could be carried a stage further, and it was this in fact that led him to the discovery of "luminism." Thus he is entitled to a leading place among the Central Italian painters of the first half of the century.

Born at Florence in 1503, Agnolo di Cosimo, better known as Bronzino, brought to its extreme conclusion the Florentine mannerists' cult of abstract forms. He died in 1572. Pupil and assistant of Pontormo, and much influenced by Michelangelo, he became court painter to Duke Cosimo de' Medici and inaugurated that series of portraits of members of the Medici House on which all 16th-century court portraits were modeled. In the early *Portrait of Ugolino Martelli* (1537-1538, Berlin) he already employed his characteristic lay-out of dark, contrasting forms against a bright background, an arrangement that ran counter to the practice of the day. We find in his handling of form a sense of tension and solidity that enables him to combine successfully geometrical abstraction and concrete reality. However, when in 1545-1546 he painted the famous *Portrait of Eleonora de Toledo and her Son* (Uffizi) he relaxed the tension with the result that here the form seems over-abstract and essentially decorative. Noteworthy in this portrait is the painter's new, aristocratic vision, leading him to treat the subject almost like a sacred effigy standing on an altar. In the allegorical picture of *Venus, Cupid, Folly and Time* (National Gallery, London) form is solidified to the point of absurdity; not only the faces but bodies, too, seem mask-like, unnatural. In fact when he had not the living model to impose a salutary restraint, as in the portraits, Bronzino tended to let his imagination get out of hand.

MANNERISM IN NORTH ITALY

Like the Florentines, a Parma artist Francesco Mazzola (1503-1540), known as Parmigianino (i.e. the little Parmesan), tended to the use of abstract forms, but, less doctrinaire in his abstractionism than such men as Rosso and Pontormo, he achieved a fragile grace and delicacy, reminiscent both of Raphael and Correggio. His universal popularity contributed largely to the spread of mannerism in Europe.

The *Madonna of the Long Neck* (Uffizi, Florence) illustrates to perfection his aesthetic. Here elegance replaces beauty and the somewhat abstract treatment of the figure gives it an immaterial charm. His *sfumato,* his discreet allusions to reality, the elongation of proportions and the sinuous movement of his figures were enthusiastically followed up by many painters in the second half of the Cinquecento.

Primaticcio (1504-1570) might be described as Parmigianino's most accomplished disciple, though he never actually studied under him and was closely associated with Giulio Romano and his group at Mantua. After being employed for six years by Duke Federigo Gonzaga, he was sent by his patron, in 1532, to the court of the French king. He quickly won the favor of Francis I, was appointed court painter, and worked on the Fontainebleau decorations. Architect and sculptor as well as painter, he lacked perhaps the high originality and forcefulness of Rosso but his work has more spontaneity and a refined distinction all its own and he played an important part in the founding of the School of Fontainebleau.

Niccolò dell'Abbate, born at Modena in 1509 or thereabouts, was Primaticcio's collaborator at Fontainebleau, where he died in 1571. Influenced by Dosso Dossi and later by the Flemings, he took over their imaginary landscapes but re-interpreted them in a quite original manner. In Niccolò's art we find a graceful sinuosity of line, a tendency to elongate figures and a subtle handling of *sfumato*. Thus he was well qualified to accompany Primaticcio to France (1552), where he consolidated his reputation, already well established when he left Italy. This was largely owing to his landscapes, which he ingeniously diversified with genre scenes—a procedure that provided mannerism with one of its most fruitful fields of action.

That remarkable *Landscape with Men threshing Wheat* (ca. 1555-1560) at Fontainebleau is now attributed to him. The composition is frankly anti-classical, the stack of straw being quite out of scale with the rest of the scene; still it makes a fine patch of color. In the figures, too, we find a satisfying blend of realism and stylization.

The œuvre of Lelio Orsi of Novellara (1511-1587) shows how comprehensive was the artistic culture of the day even in a small provincial town. For it reveals a host of diverse influences: those of Giulio Romano, Correggio, Parmigianino, Michelangelo as well as other painters. Orsi had a curious turn of mind and a knack of assimilating the idiosyncrasies of greater artists, in particular those tending towards an abstract expressionism, often with bizarre results. But his fantasies seem comparatively tame beside the extravaganzas of Giuseppe de Arcimboldi (1527-1593), who amused himself constructing human figures with fruit and vegetables; the result being greatly to the liking of the emperors Ferdinand I, Maximilian II and Rudolph II.

MANNERISM IN ROME

In the period after 1550 Rome became the headquarters of a type of mannerism that might be described as "imitative," as a result of the ever-increasing influx of artists from other parts of Italy and from abroad who came to study Michelangelo and Raphael. Though they oftener drew inspiration from the former, there was also a revival of Raphael's influence at this time. Raphaelesque mannerism was imported into northern Italy by Giulio Romano (1499-1546)—who acted as a sort of dictator of the arts at Mantua from 1524 onwards—and by Perino del Vaga (1500-1547) who decorated the Palazzo Doria at Genoa, where he settled in 1527. Unlike the Florentines and Parmigianino, these two artists had little use for theories, abstraction or studied grace, but practised a forthright realism sometimes needlessly aggressive.

Pellegrino Tibaldi (1527-1596) was born in Lombardy; as painter, sculptor and architect, he had much success at Bologna, at Milan and in Spain. After painting in the manner of Niccolò dell'Abbate, he turned for guidance to Michelangelo, and, by an exceptionally bold handling of forms, achieved an idiom that was largely original, with certain "surrealist" touches like those of the early Florentine mannerists.

Federico Barocci (1526-1612) took a different direction under the joint influence of Raphael and Correggio. Gifted with a delicate feeling for color and an unusual inventiveness in handling form, he might have developed into a front-rank painter but for his over-indulgence in a rather sentimental prettiness.

Towards the close of the century another mannerist painter, Federico Zuccari, who was born in 1542 near Urbino and died at Ancona in 1609, made a great name for himself at Venice and also in Spain and England. A number of influences can be detected in his work, which despite its limitations shows considerable skill. He is better known today as a writer than as a painter.

It might seem that mannerism in Florence was distinguished chiefly by its cult of abstract form, a direct consequence of that lofty intellectual ideal to which 15th-

PARMIGIANINO (1503-1540). THE MADONNA OF THE LONG NECK (DETAIL), 1534-1540. (85 × 52″)
UFFIZI, FLORENCE.

NICCOLÒ DELL'ABBATE (CA. 1509-1571). LANDSCAPE WITH MEN THRESHING WHEAT, CA. 1555-1560. (33½×44″) MUSÉE DE FONTAINEBLEAU.

century Florentine art had owed its greatness. But the most significant result of this movement was the appearance in Northern Italy of a luminist style put to the service of a naturalistic ideal—of which we shall have more to say hereafter. All we need point out at this stage is the gradual decline of creative activity in Central Italy at the time when painters from all over Europe were flocking to Rome. The new impetus given painting in Rome at the turn of the century was due to a Lombard, Caravaggio, and to a Bolognese of Lombard extraction, Annibale Carracci, the former a brilliant innovator and the latter an eclectic follower of the great tradition. As against these men the last champion of mannerist art, the Cavaliere d'Arpino, cut a futile and pretentious figure, quite incapable of demonstrating that mannerism was a force still to be reckoned with.

It was under the auspices of Francis I that the Renaissance came to France; during his reign (1515-1547) intercourse with Italy, which had almost died out in the second half of the 15th century, was actively revived and he summoned many Italian painters to his court. Frenchmen who had accompanied Charles VIII and Louis XII during their peregrinations in Italy had been much impressed by the works of art they saw there and, like Dürer, by the Italian artists' sense of "measure," that is to say order and proportion. Writing in 1529, in his *Champfleury*, Geoffroy Tory declared that the perfection of Italian art was due to their use of dividers and rulers. Between 1504 and 1508 Solario and another painter had come to work for Cardinal d'Amboise at the Château de Gaillon, near Rouen, in Normandy, and in 1513 Emilian painters were called in to decorate Albi Cathedral. But it was left to Francis I to consolidate these links with Italy; he began by summoning Leonardo to France and it was in that country that the great painter ended his life; then in 1518 came Andrea del Sarto, Rosso in 1531 and, a year later, Primaticcio.

Since the French king was constantly traveling from one château to another, the French court had lacked a center where an intellectual life worthy of the Renaissance could develop at leisure. Fontainebleau supplied this need and, with its palaces decorated by Rosso, Primaticcio and Niccolò dell'Abbate, became a very mirror of Renaissance culture. In the court of Fontainebleau conversation bulked as large as hunting among the recreations of the nobility and for the first time women played a part in it. "No courtier can undertake any gallant enterprise of chivalry, unless he be stirred by the conversation and love of woman." Francis I took Castiglione's advice to heart and the presence of women at his court fostered the taste for elegance and witty repartee which was to become a trait of the French character.

What is known as the School of Fontainebleau was launched by the joint efforts of the three painters named above. But they had many French and foreign assistants, some of whose names are known, though it is impossible to distinguish their works from that of the three Italians who set the style of the decorations as a whole. In any case these paintings are in too damaged a condition for us to form any clear idea of the personalities of the various painters; these can be better seen in their drawings and prints. Nevertheless we can discern certain new elements differentiating the Fontainebleau paintings from contemporary Italian works of the same class: notably a special emphasis on elegance and a greater range of decorative effects.

But in his efforts to acclimatize foreign art in France the king did not confine himself to Italian painters; the *bella maniera* might be admirably suited for decorations, but, to his thinking, portraiture called for that minute attention to details, deriving from the miniature, which was peculiar to Flemish art. Jean Clouet (father of François Clouet) was probably of Flemish origin—in any case he never acquired French nationality—and Corneille de Lyon was a Dutchman from The Hague. Yet despite the presence of these foreign elements in the French portrait and the diverse influences contributing to shape the taste of the French king's court, we find a uniformity of style reflecting, we may be sure, the personal predilections of this enlightened monarch.

JEAN CLOUET (CA. 1505-CA. 1541). KING FRANCIS I ON HORSEBACK, CA. 1540. ($10\frac{1}{2} \times 8\frac{5}{8}$")
UFFIZI, FLORENCE.

FRANÇOIS CLOUET (BEFORE 1522-1572). PORTRAIT OF KING CHARLES IX, 1563. (87 ¼ × 45 ¼")
KUNSTHISTORISCHES MUSEUM, VIENNA.

To him was due the "modernistic" trend of the art of Fontainebleau, the taste for refined yet sumptuous elegance, the quick-wittedness and liberal outlook on life which were to enter into the pattern of French life at large. The king's sister, Marguerite of Navarre, took part in this cultural movement, not only encouraging writers but doing much to foster that love of nature which found such exquisite expression in the poems of the Pléiade group.

But after the death of Francis I (1547) the Counter-Reformation put an end to these careless raptures; light-heartedness gave place to strait-laced piety.

The most famous portrait painter in France during the first half of the 16th century was Jean Clouet. In 1516 he was appointed court painter at Tours and became the king's *valet de chambre*. In 1529, or soon after, he moved to Paris where he lived until his death, which took place in 1541 or shortly before. Among the portraits that can be more or less certainly ascribed to him are *Claude de Lorraine, Duke of Guise* (ca. 1525, Pitti Palace, Florence) and *Francis I on Horseback* (ca. 1540, Uffizi). Whereas the former has all the characteristics of the 15th-century miniature, a new, essentially decorative style can be seen in the portrait of the king. For between 1525 and 1540 the concepts of Italian mannerism had been gaining ground in France and, though these had no direct influence on Clouet, he felt a need to renovate his art. Unlike his famous contemporary Corneille de Lyon, appointed Painter to the Dauphin, whose court portraits have the gemlike luster of enamel work, he broke with the tradition of the illuminators and developed a personal manner owing little to the past.

On his death his son François took over his official post of king's painter, holding it from 1541 onwards, during the reigns of Henry II, Francis II and Charles IX. He died in Paris in 1572. Three works signed by him are extant: the apothecary *Pierre Quthe* (1562, Louvre), *Charles IX* (Vienna) and *Diane de Poitiers* (National Gallery, Washington). With Diane are her two children and a nurse, and a maidservant can be seen in the background. These works give a good idea of François Clouet's style. The figure of Pierre Quthe is located in its spatial context with a dignity akin to that of Italian portraits, but the meticulous execution is typically Flemish, and Clouet has succeeded in combining the two styles on remarkably ingenious lines. In *Diane de Poitiers* we find a mannerism more in the Flemish than the Italian style, and there is a marked contrast between the studied formalism of the nude and the realistic, free-and-easy rendering of the nurse. A similar anomaly can be seen in some of his court portraits. The disposition of the figures in *Charles IX* (Vienna) and *Henry II* (Louvre and Pitti Palace, Florence) recalls that of Titian's *Charles V* and *Philip II*, but here too the attention given to details, the exquisite nicety of handling and studied elegance strike a new, original note. Mention may also be made of Clouet's *Elizabeth of Austria* (1571, Louvre) in which the sumptuously clad figure is treated in a style much more Flemish than Italian, as is evident if we compare it with, for example, Bronzino's *Eleonora de Toledo*.

The unidentified artist known as the Master of Flora, to whom are attributed, amongst other works, the *Triumph of Flora* (Feilchenfeldt Collection, Zurich) and the

FRANÇOIS CLOUET (BEFORE 1522-1572). DIANE DE POITIERS, BETWEEN 1560-1570. (36 1/4 × 32″)
NATIONAL GALLERY OF ART, WASHINGTON (SAMUEL H. KRESS COLLECTION, LOAN).

MASTER OF FLORA (OP. CA. 1540-1560). THE TRIUMPH OF FLORA. (51 ½ × 43 ¼″)
MRS W. FEILCHENFELDT COLLECTION, ZURICH.

MASTER OF FLORA (OP. CA. 1540-1560). THE BIRTH OF CUPID. ($42\frac{1}{2} \times 51\frac{3}{8}''$)
BY COURTESY OF THE METROPOLITAN MUSEUM OF ART, NEW YORK.

*Birth of Cupid* (Metropolitan, New York), was evidently a highly cultured man, gifted with a nimble wit and not a little originality—despite the fact that his technique recalls Primaticcio's, some of his motifs are taken from Bronzino and the colors owe something to Correggio. For this artist's exquisite refinement, his defiance of the rules of composition and his knack of getting charming effects by happily inspired inaccuracies of drawing and proportion are both a reflection of the French spirit in those golden years and a synthesis of the aspirations of the School of Fontainebleau.

ANTOINE CARON (1521-1599). AUGUSTUS AND THE SIBYL OF TIBUR, CA. 1580. (49¼ × 66¾″)
LOUVRE, PARIS.

About Antoine Caron, unlike this nameless master, much is known. He was born at Beauvais in 1521 and died in Paris in 1599. After working for Francis I until 1540 and collaborating with Primaticcio and Niccolò dell'Abbate on the Fontainebleau decorations, he was appointed court painter to Catherine de' Medici. The decorations he made to celebrate the return of Henry III from Poland in 1573 and for the festivities in connection with the wedding of the Duc de Joyeuse in 1581 were universally admired. Jean Dorat and Louis d'Orléans wrote verses in his honor. A complete list of his works is now available, largely owing to recent research-work by J. Ehrmann.

A signed painting by Caron in the Louvre depicts the *Massacres under the Triumvirate,* in which we may perhaps see an allusion to the bloodshed attending the Wars of Religion then in progress. His best picture is probably *Astronomers studying an Eclipse* (Anthony Blunt Collection, London), which unmistakably alludes to the Huguenots; for in 1571 an eclipse actually took place accompanied by a rain of fire, which was interpreted as a token of divine displeasure. *Augustus and the Sibyl of Tibur* is a pictorial transcription of one of the Incarnation and Nativity mystery plays performed in the Tuileries in the presence of Catherine de' Medici. The abstract symbolism of these pictures, reconstructions of the life of ancient Rome—one sometimes has an impression that the artist wishes to parade his erudition—gives them a certain frigidity. Though Caron was the most famous French painter of his age, he is not the best; he owed his success most likely to the fact of being a *persona grata* at court. A change of heart and a new type of artist were needed if French painting was to regain its former eminence.

BARTHOLOMEUS SPRANGER (1546-1611). VENUS AND ADONIS, CA. 1592. (53×43")
RIJKSMUSEUM, AMSTERDAM.

ANTONIO MORO (CA. 1519-1576). SELF-PORTRAIT, 1558. (44 ½ × 34 ¼″)
UFFIZI, FLORENCE.

LUMINISM
AND REALISM

We have already seen that Brueghel's journey to Rome had no effect on his style; his attitude to art remained throughout his life far closer to that of Bosch than to the classical ideal deriving from Greek sculpture. Jan van Scorel, on the other hand, was profoundly influenced by what he saw in Rome and, turning his back on the art tradition of his homeland, took over the Italian manner and even sought to prettify it. Dominicus Lampsonius, author of *Pictorum aliquot celebrium Germaniae inferioris effigies*, published in 1572 at Antwerp, inscribed Scorel's portrait with the legend: "To me shall be accorded evermore the merit of having made known to the Belgians that none may aspire to the name of painter unless he has seen Rome and learnt there to ply a thousand brushes and lavish color, so as to create works worthy of renown." Similarly in his *Descrittione di tutti i Paesi Bassi* (1567), Ludovico Guicciardini explained that when painters and sculptors of the Low Countries went to Rome they did so with an avowed intention of discarding traditional Flemish style and learning that of the Italians. Carel van Mander (1548-1606) declared that by taking the Ancients as exemplars, Rome and Florence had "recaptured nature as she truly is," whereas the Flemings had kept to "vulgar" nature.

Among Scorel's pupils was Antonio Moro, who was born about 1519 at Utrecht and died in 1576 at Antwerp. After visiting Rome in 1550 and 1551, and Portugal in the following year, he became the portrait painter most in demand at the courts of Brussels, Lisbon, Madrid and London. The *Portrait of Mary Tudor, Queen of England* (Prado) is typical of his "official" style. His presentation of the figures as a real mass existing in space shows a capacity much like Titian's for producing an effect of actuality. But he cannot bring himself to omit any detail, with the result that in his portraits the new Titianesque vision, blurred by a plethora of accessories, loses much of its vitality. All the same he had quite amazing technical ability and portrayed his models with an objective precision rarely equaled. Moro's sitters were on several occasions the same as Titian's and he must have realized the peril of competing with the Master on his own ground. Nevertheless all but an understanding few were loud in admiration of these portraits, more detailed and materialistic than those of the great Venetian. But there is no denying their convincingness, and it is on his portraits that Moro's reputation rests, for his imaginative works are relatively feeble.

Pupil and rival of Jan van Scorel, Martin Heemskerck (1498-1574) spent most of his life at Haarlem. During a stay in Rome, some time between 1532 and 1535, he painstakingly sketched the Roman monuments and developed a passionate admiration for Michelangelo. But, having come to Rome relatively late in life, he kept his natural vision unimpaired, as can be seen in

PIETER AERTSEN (1508-1575). THE COOK, 1559. (63 ¼ × 31")
MUSÉE DES BEAUX-ARTS, BRUSSELS.

LUCA CAMBIASO (1527-1585). THE VIRGIN WITH A CANDLE, CA. 1570. (57 × 43″)
PALAZZO BIANCO, GENOA.

his admirably forceful portraits and the *St Luke painting the Virgin* (Haarlem), treated in the manner of a genre piece. St Luke in his outlandish costume, the angel holding a torch to light the scene, the winsome group of the Virgin and Child—all are elements answering to the ideal of the Netherlands, certainly not to that of Roman art. In the *Lamentation over the Dead Christ* (Delft), however, Roman influences are all too obvious; here the artist has reined in his imagination, though falling short of classical serenity.

Bartholomeus Spranger (1546-1611), who hailed from Antwerp, had much success in Rome and Prague. After visiting Paris in 1565, he went to Italy where he came under the influence of Primaticcio, Parmigianino and the Zuccari. In 1570 he was appointed official painter to Pope Pius V, in 1575 to the Emperor Maximilian II (at Vienna) and after that to the Emperor Rudolph II (at Prague). Propagated by engravings of his paintings made by Sadeler and Goltzius, his style won many imitators in the Netherlands, Italy and France. His art is the last manifestation of the mannerism of fantasy; the *Venus and Adonis* (Rijksmuseum, Amsterdam) is a typical example, notable being the sinuosity imparted not only to bodies but also to trees and mountains. With its artificial liveliness and surface elegance, this picture is a wholly intellectual creation, there is more artistry than art.

Pieter Aertsen (1508-1575) of Amsterdam, though his career followed much the same course as Heemskerck's, was more accessible to the new ideas then gaining ground in all parts of Europe. There is no proof that he ever went to Rome; he worked in Antwerp from 1535 to 1556, and after that in Amsterdam. Even in his religious pictures we can see a conflict between mannerist and realist tendencies, which, notably in the case of the *Adoration of the Magi* (Deutzen Hofje, Amsterdam), led to unsatisfactory results; to some of his other works, however, this apparent conflict lends an added interest. Aertsen specialized chiefly in pictures of fruit and, for this reason, has been regarded as one of the first exponents of the still life. He loved to "make the portrait" of everything he saw, and it was through the eyes of a portraitist that he painted fruit and vegetables or anonymous figures in genre-scene settings, such as *The Cook* (Brussels). In this famous picture he centered his attention on the color-light complex building up the woman's form; thus *The Cook* is out of line with Roman mannerist tradition, and may, rather, be assimilated to the Venetian trends sponsored, for example, by Tintoretto and Bassano.

It is thought that Aertsen migrated to Amsterdam so as to escape falling foul of Frans Floris, a thorough-paced mannerist, who was making a great name for himself in Antwerp, his birthplace, then the chief art center of the Netherlands. Floris was in Rome between 1541 and 1547 and his painting reflects an academic Romanism modeled on Michelangelo and Vasari.

The need felt by the Flemings to adjust mannerism to realism answered to an innate tradition of the race, and in the result the new realism came to be associated with luminist procedures. Already in the second half of the century mannerist painters were concentrating their attention on effects of light and shade suggested by those of Titian, Tintoretto and the Venetians in general. This can be seen in the work of various members of the Campi family of Cremona—Antonio Campi (1525 ?-1587) in particular—and even more noticeably in that of Luca Cambiaso (1527-1585), a Genoese painter who, following in the path of Beccafumi, used light to bring out the dramatic or intimate content of his subjects. Outstanding examples are his delightful *Virgin with a Candle* and *Christ before Pilate* (both in Genoa, Palazzo Bianco). Throughout the 17th century "luminism" was to advance from strength to strength in the wake of Caravaggio, its most spectacular exponent in Rome.

EL GRECO

In discussing the art of Titian, Tintoretto and Veronese we pointed out that these three painters, while assimilating the mannerist elements that had found their way to Venice, transformed them almost out of recognition and created a style of painting that was brilliantly original. Something the same is true of El Greco, but with a difference; he did not, like the Venetians, integrate the machinery of mannerism into his personal style, but juxtaposed it, stressing to the utmost their antinomy. Thus more and more as his genius ripened, and particularly during the last twenty-five years of his life, he played off mannerist line against constructive color, and with the resultant discords achieved an expressive power unsurpassed in the whole history of art. This is why, after excluding Tintoretto's art from the category of mannerism, we would include El Greco among the mannerists, though needless to say we are well aware that he left mannerism far behind and in fact contributed decisively to the formation and triumph of Baroque.

At the time when mannerism seemed to be lapsing into Roman academicism or Nordic quaintness El Greco harked back to its anti-classical, irrational elements—those that had characterized it at its birth. And it is hardly necessary at this time of day to emphasize the boldness and the genius with which he incorporated them into his art, an art singularly congenial to our modern taste.

Few painters are so closely studied and so universally appreciated at the present time; but El Greco's contemporaries, too, were fully alive to his genius. Then came an eclipse; until the advent of Romanticism he was dismissed out of hand as belonging to the "lunatic fringe" of art. It was perhaps the collection of his works made in Paris by King Louis Philippe that heralded his return to favor, and since then his reputation has risen steadily.

Domenikos Theotokopulos, known as "the Greek," was born in Crete in 1541 and died in 1614 at Toledo, in Spain. From 1565, perhaps earlier, he worked in Venice, as Titian's pupil; in 1569 he went to Rome, stopping on the way at Parma. While in the capital he was the guest of Cardinal Alessandro Farnese and his librarian Fulvio Orsini. After a longish stay in Rome, he migrated to Spain; the first mention of his presence in that country is dated 1577. He was then commissioned to paint a series of altarpieces for the convent of Santo Domingo el Antiguo in Toledo and he also made a picture, the *Espolio*, for the local cathedral. The only work he did for King Philip II was the *Martyrdom of St Maurice*, intended to be hung in the Escorial. In 1586 he started work on the *Burial of Count Orgaz* for the church of Santo Tomé at Toledo;

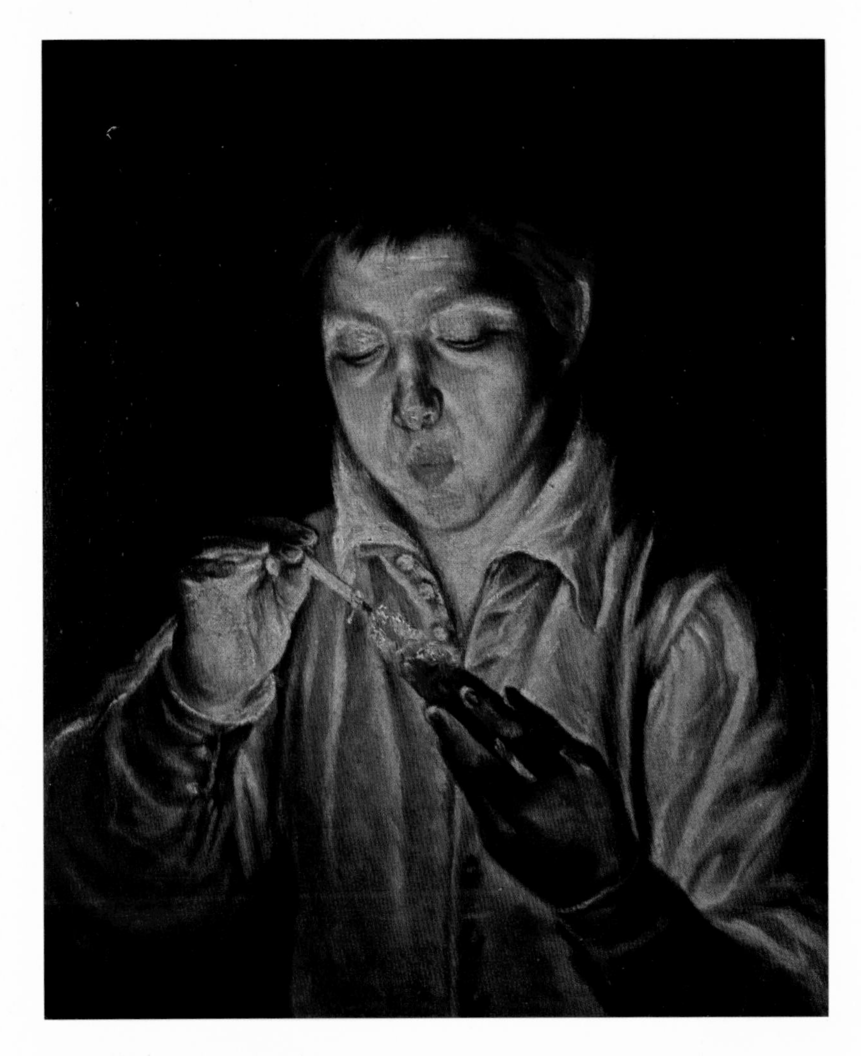

EL GRECO (1541-1614). BOY KINDLING A FLAME, CA. 1570-1575.
(23⅝ × 19⅝″) MUSEO NAZIONALE, NAPLES.

thereafter he was given many orders for paintings and sculpture by local ecclesiastical authorities and by churches in the neighborhood. A few days after El Greco's death his son Jorge Manuel made an inventory of the works left by his father; one hundred and twenty-six pictures figure in it.

Byzantine influence is strongly marked in the *Adoration of the Magi* (Benakis Museum, Athens), *Mount Sinai* (Baron Hatvany Collection, Budapest) and the *Modena Polyptych.* We have so far no means of deciding whether it was in Crete that El Greco acquired his "Byzantinism," or in Venice, where a whole group of Greek painters, known as "Madonneri," were turning out countless representations of the Virgin seen through Greek eyes. They may not have been great artists, but at least they transmitted the forms of Byzantine painting, as consecrated by its glorious past. Anyhow from the critic's point of view it is less important to determine whether the many paintings ascribed to El Greco are in all cases by his hand than to discern what Byzantine elements (other than innate traits due to his Greek origin) were "constants" in his art.

For many centuries Byzantine painting had no longer been based on visual experience; the Byzantine artist started out from an abstraction, an ideal concept, and went on to clothe it in material, individual form. His creative process was exactly the opposite of that of the classical artist, who made the concrete the point of departure in his pursuit of the ideal. For the Byzantines, the abstract model, being charged with mystical associations, was an indispensable basis to the concrete work of art. Obviously the mannerist approach to art had much in common with that of the Byzantines, the main difference being that whereas the latter started out from a predetermined archetype, the mannerist painter's ideal concept was a strictly personal creation, not imposed on him by others. Thanks to his Byzantine training El Greco could readily accept many of the procedures of mannerism.

As for his iconography, we must remember that Byzantine art was essentially ritual in nature. The Byzantine artist did not treat the episodes of sacred history as so many aspects of the human predicament but as a series of rites charged with symbolic meanings and emanating from an otherworldly source. This is why in Greco's art action is ruled out and stress laid on the psychological content of the scene. His color too—and this is one of the most striking features of his painting—stems from this tradition. In Byzantine art color values are created by the relations of hues between themselves, not by light-and-shade effects. And in El Greco's painting the colors play a leading part, clashing or harmonizing with each other, and stepped up to such intensity as to replace light.

These three concepts which El Greco took over from the Byzantine tradition—forms derived from abstract prototypes, composition within a ritual frame of reference, and color harmonies owing nothing to the play of light—were diametrically opposed to all the principles of Cinquecento Venetian art. But he had an amazing gift of assimilation and when he worked in Titian's studio quickly learned the secrets of tonal painting (the subtle variations imparted to each color by the action of light), dramatic composition (the relation between lay-out and theme) and, finally, the handling of

EL GRECO (1541-1614). THE ASSUMPTION OF THE VIRGIN, 1577. (13 FT. 2 IN. × 7 FT. 6 IN.)
THE ART INSTITUTE OF CHICAGO IN MEMORY OF ALBERT ARNOLD SPRAGUE.

EL GRECO (1541-1614). CHRIST DRIVING THE MONEY CHANGERS FROM THE TEMPLE, 1605-1614.
(41¾ × 41″) CHURCH OF SAN GINÉS, MADRID.

volumes and the movement of bodies (that is to say the art of disposing bodies in space): in short, the basic elements of Titian's style. He also learnt the virtues of the "touch" or aptly placed dash of color, of a judicious unfinish, and all the possibilities afforded by the new vision of reality.

But this assimilation was on a purely painterly level and did not involve any adhesion to Titian's attitude to life, which, ruling out all mysticism, led to a glorification of the material aspects of existence. Among the many conflicting tendencies El Greco had to reconcile, this antinomy between his innate mysticism, due to his Cretan upbringing, and the faith in nature revealed to him in Venice, was one of the most arduous problems he had to face in his formative years.

When working under the auspices of Titian, El Greco observed with interest what other painters, younger than the Venetian master but older than himself, were doing. Instinctively he was drawn to Tintoretto, with whose mystical outlook he had so much in common and who like himself put all his ardor into the depiction of sacred subjects. Greco had no trouble in taking over Tintoretto's light effects, more accentuated yet simpler than those of Titian. We also find affinities with Bassano; aside from certain similarities of composition (whose common source may be traced to engravings available to both artists), these affinities can be accounted for by the fact that Bassano's renderings of visual reality were less elaborate than Titian's.

However, stress must be laid on the mannerist factor, which played a vital part in the shaping of El Greco's art. While in Venice, he had opportunities of familiarizing himself with the mannerist procedures which had found their way there, as indeed to all art centers of the day; thus the elongation of figures, derived from Parmigianino, had become a common practice with Venetian painters. And the tendencies acquired in Venice were reinforced during his Roman sojourn; with the result that El Greco's mannerism is more pronounced than that of any other painter. We are inclined to agree with José Camón Aznar when he says that Michelangelo and Roman mannerism directly influenced him both in his preference for a certain type of figure and in his habit of constructing his composition in height, as also in his way of rendering garments. Thus it would seem that his contacts with Roman mannerism helped El Greco to free himself from the "tonalism" of the Venetians.

But apart from the influences operating in Venice and Rome, El Greco's mannerism may well be due to an instinctive sympathy with the anti-classical reaction. For as against Titian's materialistic vision of reality, mannerism stood for spiritual aspiration, a nostalgic yearning to return to the Middle Ages, to transcendence, to the abstract—in a word, to Byzantine tradition. Between the Byzantines who started out from the abstract and thence proceeded to the concrete and the mannerists who reversed the process, there is a connecting link: El Greco's art. As was only to be expected, he failed to attain his style at a moment's notice; long years were needed for its ripening and the discovery of ways and means of resolving his inner conflicts. Needless to say, an artist of genius can create masterpieces even though his style is still in the course of formation; nevertheless it was not until El Greco settled at Toledo that he found

EL GRECO (1541-1614). ST PETER, CA. 1606-1608. (81 ½ × 41 ½″)
CONVENT OF THE ESCORIAL.

himself, completely and triumphantly. This is evident when we compare the successive versions of *Christ driving the Money Changers from the Temple*. In the early ones, painted in Italy, forms are fully modeled, whereas in the later versions—that in the National Gallery, London (1600), and that in the Church of San Ginés, Madrid (the one we reproduce)—they are sublimated into wraiths of light, and the rendering of space is reduced to symbolic indications of its existence. And whereas in the early works we are still conscious of an uneasy interplay of different traditions, in the last their fusion is complete, the style harmoniously integrated.

EL GRECO (1541-1614). THE LAOCOÖN, CA. 1610-1614. (54 1/8 × 67 7/8")
NATIONAL GALLERY OF ART, WASHINGTON (SAMUEL H. KRESS COLLECTION).

When El Greco arrived at Toledo, the ancient capital had lost nothing of its prosperity despite the fact that Philip II had transferred his court to Madrid in 1561. There was a flourishing trade in silk and weapons—the famous "Toledo blades"—the Cathedral was one of the wealthiest in Spain and many of the most enlightened spirits of the age lived there, among them Cervantes, Lope de Vega, Góngora and St John of the Cross. The atmosphere of devout piety and mysticism then prevailing in Toledo was just what was needed to bring El Greco's genius to flower. In 1577, perhaps the year of his arrival in Spain, he painted the *Assumption of the Virgin*, central panel of one of the altarpieces in Santo Domingo el Antiguo (now in the Art Institute of Chicago). Sixty years had passed since Titian had painted his great *Assumption* in the Frari church, one of the earliest works in which he gave expression to his new vision of reality. But Greco, in Toledo, cast off his master's influence. He did away with space, brought forward the scene into the foreground and "presented" images instead of representing an event. True, a gust of emotion sweeps through those figures, we can sense their restlessness; but it is not co-ordinated in movement, still less in any action. Nevertheless this picture has tremendous expressive power and, though volumes of bodies are not suppressed, their physical aspects are wholly subordinated to the spiritual content.

El Greco was a superb portrait-painter, with a gift for probing into his model's soul and imprinting on the face what he discovered there. Looking at his *Cardinal Don Fernando Niño de Guevara* (Metropolitan, New York), we feel that here we have the typical Grand Inquisitor, shrewd, proud and wary, capable of being ruthless on occasion. No less unforgettable are the portraits of his Toledan friends, amongst others *Fray Hortensio Felix de Paravicino* (Boston), *Don Jerónimo de Ceballos* (Prado) and *Don Antonio de Covarrubias* (Louvre and Museo del Greco, Toledo). There was a phase in his evolution as an artist when El Greco struck a perfect balance between the grandiose vision of his large-scale compositions and the psychological insight of his portraits; I have in mind the time when he painted his most famous work, the *Burial of Count Orgaz* (Santo Tomé, Toledo). The burial scene itself centers on the blaze of gold and silvery light streaming from the vestments of the priests and the dead Count's armor, standing out against a dark background formed by the black-clad mourners. The upper half of the picture shows God surrounded by a splendor of light and fantastically shaped clouds. The composition may recall Byzantine art, but it is executed with an objective vigor worthy of Titian. Each detail, celestial or terrestrial, plays an exact and vital part in the composition and contributes to the flawless unity of the whole. This period of perfect equilibrium falls between the years 1585 and 1590.

During his final period, beginning about 1590, El Greco tended to give still freer play to his imagination and to lay yet more stress on emotive elements. The extreme elongation of bodies, devoid of any action, in which he now indulged, was perhaps a reminiscence of Italian mannerism and the climate of his 'prentice years, as was a special, flame-like lighting that seems an emanation of the soul within. To this period belongs the series of "imaginary portraits" of apostles and saints: St Francis, St John

EL GRECO (1541-1614). THE ASSUMPTION OF THE VIRGIN (DETAIL), CA. 1608-1613.
MUSEO DE SAN VICENTE, TOLEDO.

the Baptist amongst others. The *St Peter* in the Escorial is not only a magnificent piece of painting but also a striking demonstration of El Greco's gift for revealing the subject's inner life by means of wholly unrealistic forms.

Very few secular pictures figure in his œuvre. One of these is of exceptional interest: the *Laocoön* (National Gallery, Washington), dated to the last years of his life and mentioned in the inventory compiled after his death. The singular thing about the *Laocoön* is that it is obviously a caricature—of the famous Greek statuary group discovered in 1506 in Rome. Other caricatures had been made of it, for example one by the engraver Boldrini who depicted the ill-starred family as monkeys. El Greco contented himself with distorting the figures, placing on one side of the scene indifferent spectators and in the background, framed by a sort of human architecture, a view of Toledo (doing duty for one of Troy). The anti-classical bias manifest in this curious scene is characteristic of his last works, as it was of his earliest.

It was in religious scenes that El Greco had the subjects best adapted to the luminist style, the patterning in streaks of light, of his final period. Under his brush the *Immaculate Conception*, the *Nativity*, the *Baptism of Christ*, *Christ in the Garden of Olives*, the *Crucifixion* and the *Resurrection* were sublimated into mystical visions ranking beside those of Santa Teresa.

None of the treatises on art which El Greco is known to have written has come down to us. All we have is an inscription on the *View and Plan of Toledo* (Museo del Greco, Toledo) painted in 1609 or thereabouts. In it he explains that "so as to give the greatest possible size to the figures in the scene of the Blessed Virgin handing a chalice to St Ildefonso, I thought fit to show them as heavenly bodies, high in air, like lights which, though small and distant, seem larger than reality." This might equally apply, as Lopez Rey has pointed out, to the other *View of Toledo* (Metropolitan, New York), some of whose elements seem like leaping flames.

There in fact we have the key to El Greco's art. Whether his figures be terrestrial or celestial, they soar, patterned in light, illumined by the love divine, aspiring spirits freed from those bodies which the Renaissance had "discovered" and transmuted in a synthesis of mind and matter. This vision of a world of disincarnate, flame-like spirits was perhaps the necessary culmination of a genius like El Greco's; the remarkable vitality of Velazquez' color may have owed something to it, but it could not serve as a point of departure for the art of the future. On the contrary, if modern art was to come into being, it was incumbent on the artist to come down to earth again and return to the study of the living body, trying to elicit from it the secret of a human personality, without surrendering to the enchantments of a visionary world.

BIBLIOGRAPHY

INDEX OF NAMES AND PLACES

LIST OF COLORPLATES

# BIBLIOGRAPHICAL SUMMARY

### GENERAL

H. Wölfflin, *Renaissance und Barock*, Munich 1888. — Idem, *Die klassische Kunst*, Munich 1899. — Idem, *Kunstgeschichtliche Grundbegriffe*, Munich 1915. — H. Voss, *Malerei der Spätrenaissance*, Berlin 1920. — L. Dimier, *Histoire de la Peinture de Portrait en France au XVI^e siècle*, Paris 1924-26. — M. Dvořák, *Geschichte der italienischen Kunst*, 3 vols., Munich 1924-28. — A. Venturi, *Storia dell'Arte Italiana, La Pittura del Cinquecento*, vol. IX, tomes 1-6, Milan 1925-33. — E. Gothein, *Schriften zur Kulturgeschichte der Renaissance, Reformation und Gegenreformation*, Munich 1924. — G. de Ruggero, *Storia della Filosofia, Rinascimento, Riforma e Controriforma*, Bari 1930. — D. Cantimori, *Eretici Italiani del Cinquecento*, Florence 1939. — O. Benesch, *The Art of the Renaissance in Northern Europe*, Cambridge, Mass. 1945. — B. Berenson, *The Italian Painters of the Renaissance*, Oxford 1930. — K. Clark, *Landscape into Art*, London 1949. — M. J. Friedländer, *Essays über die Landschaftsmalerei und andere Bildgattungen*, The Hague 1947; in English, Oxford 1949. — *French Painting 1100-1900*, Catalogue of the exhibition at the Carnegie Institute, Pittsburg 1951. — E. Panofsky, *"Idea", ein Beitrag zur Begriffsgeschichte der älteren Kunsttheorie*, Leipzig 1924. — E. H. Gombrich, *Renaissance Artistic Theory and Development of Landscape Painting*, Gazette des Beaux-Arts, Paris-New York, May-June 1953.

## CHAPTER I · FROM LEONARDO TO CORREGGIO

### LEONARDO DA VINCI

G. Gronau, *Leonardo*, London 1903-Chicago 1915. — O. Siren, *Léonard de Vinci*, Stockholm 1911, London 1916, Paris 1928. — L. Beltrami, *Documenti e memorie riguardanti la vita di Leonardo da Vinci*, Milan 1916. — L. Venturi, *La Critica e l'Arte di Leonardo da Vinci*, Bologna 1919. — W. Bode, *Studien über Leonardo da Vinci*, Berlin 1920. — A. Venturi, *Leonardo Pittore*, Bologna 1920. — A. de Rinaldis, *Storia dell'opera pittorica di Leonardo da Vinci*, Bologna 1926. — E. Hildebrandt, *Leonardo da Vinci, der Künstler und sein Werk*, Berlin 1927. — W. Suida, *Leonardo und sein Kreis*, Munich 1929. — E. Verga, *Bibliografia Vinciana 1493-1930*, 2 vols., Bologna 1931. — Catalogue of the Leonardo da Vinci Exhibition, Milan 1939. — J. P. Richter, *The Literary Works of Leonardo da Vinci*, London, New York, Oxford 1939. — E. Panofsky, *The Codex Huygens and Leonardo da Vinci's Art Theory*, London 1940. — R. Langton Douglas, *Leonardo da Vinci*, Chicago 1944. — A. M. Brizio, *Scritti scelti di Leonardo*, Turin 1952. — K. Clark, *Leonardo*, Cambridge, Mass. 1952.

### SCHOOL OF LEONARDO

M. Salmi, *Una mostra di antica pittura lombarda*, L'Arte, 1923, p. 149. — W. Suida, *Die Jugendwerke des Bartolomeo Suardi*, Jahrbuch der Kunstsammlung d. Allerh. Kaiserh. XXV, Vienna 1906; *Die Spätwerke des B. S.*, idem XXVI, 1907. — Idem, *Bramante Pittore e il Bramantino*, Milan 1955. — K. Badt, *Andrea Solario, Sein Leben und seine Werke*, Leipzig 1914. — L. Beltrami, *Luini 1512-1532, materiale di studio*, Milan 1911. — G. Nicodemi, *Luini*, Florence 1916. — A. Ottino-Della Chiesa, *Luini*, Milan-Florence 1953. — C. Faccio, *G. A. Bazzi (il Sodoma) pittore vercellese*, Vercelli 1902. — C. Terrasse, *Sodoma*, Paris 1925. — F. Knapp, *Piero di Cosimo*, Halle 1899. — R. Langton Douglas, *Piero di Cosimo*, Chicago 1946. — E. Frantz, *Fra Bartolomeo della Porta*, Regensburg 1879. — F. Knapp, *Fra Bartolomeo*, Halle 1903. — Idem, *Andrea del Sarto*, Leipzig 1928. — J. Fraenkel, *Andrea del Sarto, Gemälde und Zeichnungen*, Strasbourg 1935. — A. J. Rusconi, *Andrea del Sarto*, Bergamo 1935. — H. Wagner, *Andrea del Sarto*, Basel 1950.

### RAPHAEL

Crowe and Cavalcaselle, *Life and Works of Raphael*, London 1882-85. — E. Müntz, *Raphaël*, Paris 1886. — O. Fischel, *Raffael's Zeichnungen*, Strasbourg 1898. — A. Colasanti, *Stanze di Raffaello*, Rome 1910. — A. Venturi, *Raffaello*, Rome 1920. — A. Rosenberg, *Raffael*, Stuttgart-Leipzig 1923. — H. Focillon, *Raphaël*, Paris 1926. — V. Golzio, *Raffaello nei documenti, nelle testimonianze dei contemporanei e nella letteratura del suo secolo*, Vatican City 1936. — F. Fosca, *Raphaël*, Paris 1937. — S. Ortolani, *Raffaello*, Bergamo 1942. — R. Vischer, *Raffaello e Rubens*, Bari 1945. — O. Fischel, *Raphael*, London 1948. — A. Venturi, *Raffaello*, Milan 1952.

### MICHELANGELO

A. Condivi, *Vita di Michelagniolo Buonarroti*, ed. K. Frey, Berlin 1887. — K. Frey, *Die Dichtungen des Michelagniolo Buonarroti*, Berlin 1897; *Sammlung ausgewählter Briefe an Michelagniolo*, Berlin 1899. — C. Justi, *Michelangelo*, Leipzig 1900. — K. Frey, *Michelagniolo Buonarroti*, Berlin 1907. — H. Thode, *Michelangelo und das Ende der Renaissance*, 3 vols., Berlin 1908-1913. — K. Frey, *Die Handzeichnungen Michelagniolos Buonarroti*, Berlin 1909-1925. — D. Frey, *Michelangelo Studien*, Vienna 1920. — E. Steinmann, *Michelangelo*; *Bibliographie 1510-1926*, Leipzig 1927. — R. Huyghe, *Michel-Ange*, Paris 1937. — C. de Tolnay, *La théorie de l'Art et Michel-Ange*, Le Congrès International d'Esthétique et de Science de l'Art, Paris 1937, p. 25. — M. Brion, *Michel-Ange*, Paris 1939. — H. Mackowski, *Michelangelo*, Stuttgart 1939-40. — E. Carli, *Michelangelo*, Bergamo 1941. — A. Bertini, *Michelangelo fino alla Sistina*, Turin 1942. — C. de Tolnay, *Michelangelo*: vol. I, *The Youth of Michelangelo*, Princeton University Press 1943; vol. II, *The Sistine Ceiling*, idem 1945; vol. III, *The Medici Chapel*, idem 1948. — Idem, *Werk und Weltbild des Michelangelo*, Zurich 1949 (from *L'Art et la pensée de Michel-Ange*, lectures at the Collège de France, 1948). — Idem, *Michel-Ange*, Paris 1951.

### CORREGGIO

J. Mayer, *Correggio*, Leipzig 1871, London 1876. — Q. Biagi, *Della vita e delle opere certe e incerte di Antonio Allegri detto il Correggio*, Modena 1881. — C. Ricci, *Antonio Allegri detto il Correggio*, London 1896. — H. Thode, *Correggio*, Leipzig 1898. — T. Sturge Moore, *Correggio*, London 1896. — G. Gronau, *Correggio*, Stuttgart and Leipzig 1907. — A. Venturi, *Correggio*, Rome 1927. — C. Ricci, *Correggio*, Rome 1930. — E. Mottini, *Correggio*, Bergamo 1934. — E. Bodmer, *Il Correggio e gli Emiliani*, Vienna 1942, Novara 1943.

## CHAPTER II · FROM GRÜNEWALD TO CRANACH

### GENERAL

For this and the following chapter we are much indebted to the book of OTTO BENESCH, *The Art of the Renaissance in Northern Europe*, Cambridge, Mass. 1945.

F. BURGER, *Die deutsche Malerei vom ausgehenden Mittelalter bis zum Ende der Renaissance*, Berlin 1913.

### GRÜNEWALD

H. W. HEGEMANN, *Matthias Grünewalds Isenheimer Altar*, Munich 1947. — W. K. ZÜLCH, *Grünewald*, Munich 1949.

### DÜRER

Our study of Dürer owes much to the exhaustive monograph of ERWIN PANOFSKY, *The Life and Art of Albrecht Dürer*, Princeton 1955.

A. SPRINGER, *Albrecht Dürer*, Berlin 1892. — L. CUST, *Albrecht Dürer, A Study of his Life and Work*, London 1897. — T. STURGE MOORE, *Albert Dürer*, London and New York, 1905. — E. A. WALDMANN, *Albrecht Dürer*, 3 vols., Leipzig 1916-18. — M. J. FRIEDLÄNDER, *Albrecht Dürer*, Leipzig 1921. — H. WÖLFFLIN, *Die Kunst Albrecht Dürers*, 5th ed., Berlin 1926. — W. WAETZOLDT, *Dürer und seine Zeit*, Vienna 1935.

### HOLBEIN

We made constant use of the excellent monograph of H. A. SCHMID, *Hans Holbein der Jüngere*, Basel 1948.

A. WOLTMANN, *Holbein und seine Zeit*, 2 vols., Leipzig 1874-76. — P. MANTZ, *Hans Holbein le jeune*, Paris 1879. — P. GANZ, *Hans Holbein der Jüngere*, Berlin and Leipzig 1911; Idem, *Hans Holbein, Die Gemälde*, with complete catalogue, Cologne 1949.

### LUCAS CRANACH THE ELDER

M. J. FRIEDLÄNDER and J. ROSENBERG, *Die Gemälde von Lucas Cranach*, Berlin 1932. — H. LILIENFEIN, *Lukas Cranach und seine Zeit*, Leipzig 1942.

## CHAPTER III · FROM BOSCH TO BRUEGHEL

### GENERAL

Dictionnaire des Peintres flamands, préface de Paul FIERENS, Brussels, n.d. — Max J. FRIEDLÄNDER, *Die Altniederländische Malerei*, vols. V-XIV, Berlin 1927-1937; Idem., *Essays über die Landschaftsmalerei und andere Bildgattungen*, Oxford-The Hague 1947. — A. LAES, *Le Paysage flamand, Notes, Remarques, Réflexions* in Miscellanea Léo van Puyvelde, Brussels 1949, p. 166. — J. VAN DER ELST, *L'Age d'Or Flamand*, Paris 1951. — C. LAURIOL, *Les Influences réciproques du paysage flamand et du paysage italien pendant la Renaissance*, in Les Arts Plastiques, no. 2, Brussels 1951, p. 105.

### BOSCH

P. LAFOND, *Hieronymus Bosch*, Brussels 1914. — C. DE TOLNAY, *Hieronymus Bosch*, Basel 1937. — M. BRION, *Bosch*, Paris 1938. — A. VERMEYLEN, *Hieronymus Bosch*, Amsterdam 1939. — L. VON BALDASS, *Hieronymus Bosch*, Vienna 1943. — J. COMBE, *Jérôme Bosch*, Paris 1946. — J. MOSMANS, *Hieronymus Bosch*, Bois-le-Duc 1947. — W. FRAENGER, *Hieronymus Bosch*, Coburg 1947; in English, *"The Millennium" of Hieronymus Bosch*, Chicago 1951. — J. DE BOSCHÈRE, *Jérôme Bosch*, Brussels 1947. — D. BAX, *Ontcijfering van Jeroen Bosch*, The Hague 1949. — G. VON CAMP, *Considérations sur le paysage chez Jérôme Bosch*, in Miscellanea Léo van Puyvelde, Brussels 1949. — J. LEYMARIE, *Jérôme Bosch*, Paris 1949. — W. FRAENGER *Die Hochzeit zu Kana, Ein Dokument semitischer Gnosis bei H. Bosch*, Berlin 1950. — W. VOGELSANG, *Hieronymus Bosch*, Amsterdam 1951.

### BRUEGHEL

C. DE TOLNAY, *Pierre Bruegel l'Ancien*, Brussels 1935. — A. L. ROMDHAL, *Le style figuré de Pierre Bruegel*, in Miscellanea Léo van Puyvelde, Brussels 1949, p. 121. — C. DE TOLNAY, *Bruegel et l'Italie*, Les Arts Plastiques no. 2, Brussels 1951, p. 121. — R. GENAILLE, *Bruegel l'Ancien*, Paris 1953. — G. C. ARGAN, *Cultura e realismo di Pietro Bruegel*, Letteratura no. 15/16, Rome 1955, p. 24. — F. GROSSMANN, *Tutta la pittura di Bruegel*, Florence-London 1956; idem, *Bruegel, The Paintings*, London 1955.

### LUCAS VAN LEYDEN

N. BEETS, *Lucas de Leyde*, Brussels-Paris 1913.

### JAN VAN SCOREL

Exhibition at the Central Museum, Utrecht, August-October 1955, catalogue by A. C. ESMEIJER and S. H. LEVIE, texts by Elisabeth HOUTZAGER and G. J. HOOGEWERFF.

## CHAPTER IV · FROM GIORGIONE TO VERONESE

### GENERAL

R. PALLUCCHINI, *La Pittura Veneziana del 1500*, 2 vols., Novara 1944. — R. LONGHI, *Viatico per cinque secoli di pittura veneziana*, Florence 1946.

### GIORGIONE

L. JUSTI, *Giorgione*, Berlin 1908. — L. VENTURI, *Giorgione e il Giorgionismo*, Milan 1913. — A. FERRIGUTO, *Il significato della Tempesta di Giorgione*, Padua 1922. — H. POSSE, *Die Rekonstruktion der Venus mit Kupido von Giorgione*, Jahrbuch der Preussischen Kunstsammlungen, Berlin 1931. — J. WILDE, *Röntgenaufnahmen der « Drei Philosophen » Giorgione's*, Jahrbuch der kunsthistorischen Sammlungen, Vienna 1932. — A. FERRIGUTO, *Attraverso i misteri di Giorgione*, Castelfranco 1933. — G. FIOCCO, *Giorgione*, Bergamo 1941. — A. MORASSI, *Giorgione*, Milan 1941. — L. VENTURI, *Giorgione*, Rome 1951.

### TITIAN

CROWE and CAVALCASELLE, *Life and Times of Titian*, London 1877. — O. FISCHEL, *Tizian*, Stuttgart, Leipzig and Berlin 1904. — G. GRONAU, *Titian*, London 1904. — W. SUIDA, *Tizian*, Rome and Leipzig 1933. — H. TIETZE, *Tizian, Leben und Werk*, Vienna 1936. — G. DELOGU, *Tiziano*, Bergamo 1940. — C. GAMBA, *Tiziano*, Novara 1941. — G. STEPANOW, *Tizian*, Zurich and Leipzig 1943. — G. A. DELL'ACQUA, *Tiziano*, Milan 1955.

SEBASTIANO DEL PIOMBO

L. DUSSLER, *Sebastiano del Piombo*, Basel 1942. — R. PALLUCCHINI, *Sebastian Viniziano*, Milan 1944.

LORENZO LOTTO

B. BERENSON, *Lorenzo Lotto*, London 1901. — Lorenzo Lotto Exhibition, catalogue by Pietro ZAMPETTI, Venice, June-October 1953. — A. BANTI and A. BOSCHETTO, *Lorenzo Lotto*, Florence 1953. — L. COLETTI, *Lorenzo Lotto*, Bergamo 1953.

SAVOLDO

R. LONGHI, *Cose Bresciane del Cinquecento*, L'Arte XX, 1917, p. 110. — G. NICCO FASOLA, *Lineamenti del Savoldo*, L'Arte II, 1940, p. 51.

MORONI

D. GUGINI, *Moroni Pittore*, with an essay by G. LANDORFF, Bergamo 1939.

TINTORETTO

J. RUSKIN, *The Stones of Venice*, 3rd ed., London 1874. — Idem., *Modern Painters*, ed. E.T. Cook, London 1903. — E. VON DER BERCKEN and A. L. MAYER, *Jacopo Tintoretto*, Munich 1923. — M. PITTALUGA, *Il Tintoretto*, Bologna 1925. — J. HOWARD WHITEHOUSE, *The Paradise of Tintoretto*, London 1931. — Tintoretto Exhibition, catalogue by NINO BARBANTINI, Venice 1937. — E. VON DER BERCKEN, *Die Gemälde des Jacopo Tintoretto*, Munich 1942. — *Mostra delle Tre Scuole*, catalogue by NINO BARBANTINI, Venice 1947. — H. TIETZE, *Tintoretto, Paintings and Drawings*, London 1948. — R. PALLUCCHINI, *La giovinezza di Tintoretto*, Milan 1950. — E. NEWTON, *Tintoretto*, London 1952.

JACOPO BASSANO

W. ARSLAN, *I. Bassano*, Bologna 1931. — *Dipinti dei Bassano nel Museo Civico di Bassano*, catalogue by L. MAGAGNATO, Venice 1952.

VERONESE

G. FIOCCO, *Paolo Veronese*, Rome n.d. — P. H. OSMOND, *Paolo Veronese, His Career and Work*, London 1927. — A. VENTURI, *Paolo Veronese per il IV Centenario della nascita*, Milan 1928. — A. M. BRIZIO, *Per il IV Centenario della nascita di Paolo Veronese*, L'Arte, 1928, p. 1. — Veronese Exhibition, catalogue by R. PALLUCCHINI, Venice, April-November 1939. — R. PALLUCCHINI, *Veronese*, Bergamo, 2nd ed., 1943. — G. FIOCCO, *Tiziano e Veronese*, Arte Veneta, 1948, p. 101.

## CHAPTER V · FROM PONTORMO TO EL GRECO

GENERAL

G. BRIGANTI, *Il Manierismo e Pellegrino Tibaldi*, Rome 1945. — I. L. ZUPNICK, *The "Aesthetics" of the Early Mannerists*, The Art Bulletin, December 1953, p. 302. — *The Triumph of Mannerism*, exhibition at the Rijksmuseum, Amsterdam, July-October 1955, catalogue by R. van LUTTERVELT, texts by B. MOLAJOLI, C. STERLING, J. ADHÉMAR, H. R. WEIHRAUCH, B. THOMAS.

ITALIAN MANNERISTS

P. CARPI, *Giulio Romano ai servigi di Federico II Gonzaga*, Mantua 1921. — L. FRÖHLICH-BUM, *Parmigianino und der Manierismus*, Vienna 1921. — A. MCCOMB, *Agnolo Bronzino, His Life and Works*, Cambridge, Mass. 1928. — L. BECHERUCCI, *I Manieristi Toscani*, Bergamo 1944. — G. NICCO FASOLA, *Pontormo o del Cinquecento*, Florence 1947. — C. H. SMYTH, *The Earliest Works of Bronzino*, Art Bulletin, Sept. 1949. — S. J. FREEDBERG, *Parmigianino, His Works in Painting*, Harvard University Press, Cambridge 1950. — Lelio Orsi Exhibition, catalogue by R. SALVINI and A. M. CHIODO, Reggio Emilia, July 16-September 30 1950. — B. SUIDA MANNINGS, *The Nocturnes of Luca Cambiaso*, The Art Quarterly, Autumn 1952. — B. GEIGER, *Arcimboldi*, Florence 1954. — P. ROTONDI, *Appunti sull'attività giovanile di Luca Cambiaso*, Genoa 1956. — Exhibition of Pontormo and Early Florentine Mannerism, catalogue by L. BERTI, Florence, March-July 1956.

For mannerist painting in Germany and the Netherlands, consult the bibliography of Chapters II and III.

MANNERISM IN FRANCE
AND THE SCHOOL OF FONTAINEBLEAU

E. MOREAU-NÉLATON, *Les Clouets*, Paris 1908. — R. ROSENBLUM, *The Paintings of Antoine Caron*, Marsyas vol. VI, New York 1950-1953, p. 1. — J. Ehrmann, *Antoine Caron, Peintre à la Cour des Valois*, Geneva-Lille 1955.

L. DIMIER, *Le Primatice*, Paris 1928. — Idem, *Le Château de Fontainebleau et la Cour de François Ier*, Paris 1930. — H. BADEROU, *L'école de Fontainebleau*, Geneva 1944. — J. ADHÉMAR, *French Sixteenth Century Genre Paintings*, Journal of Warburg and Courtauld Institute, vol. VIII, 1945, p. 191. — *Fontainebleau e la Maniera italiana*, catalogue by F. BOLOGNA and R. CAUSA, Naples 1952. — J. ADHÉMAR, *Pierre Milan et les origines de l'Ecole de Fontainebleau*, Gazette des Beaux-Arts, Paris-New York, May-June 1953, p. 361.

EL GRECO

J. F. WILLUMSEN, *La Jeunesse du peintre El Greco*, 2 vols., Paris 1927. — A. L. BUSUIOCEANU, *Les Tableaux du Greco de la Collection royale de Roumanie*, Brussels-Paris, 1937. — M. LEGENDRE and A. HARTMANN, *Domenikos Theotokopoulos called El Greco*, London 1937. — J. LOPEZ REY, *El Greco's Baroque Light and Form*, Gazette des Beaux-Arts, Paris-New York, August 1943. — J. CAMÓN AZNAR, *Dominico Greco*, 2 vols., Madrid 1950. — *Le Greco de la Crète à Tolède par Venise*, catalogue of the exhibition at Bordeaux, May 12-July 31 1953. — P. GUINARD, *El Greco*, Geneva 1956.

# INDEX OF NAMES AND PLACES

*Unless otherwise stated, pictures mentioned as being in the following cities are in the leading museum, as follows: Berlin, Kaiser Friedrich Museum; Dresden, Gemäldegalerie; London, National Gallery; Madrid, Prado; Munich, Alte Pinakothek; Paris, Louvre; Philadelphia, Museum of Fine Arts; Vienna, Kunsthistorisches Museum; Washington, National Gallery of Art.*

# THE COLORPLATES

*Plates at the head of each chapter:*



*On the dustjacket:*

Tintoretto: Ariadne, Bacchus and Venus (detail), ca. 1578. Ducal Palace, Venice.

# CONTENTS

I

## THE RENAISSANCE IN ITALY



2

## THE RENAISSANCE IN GERMANY



3

## PAINTING IN THE NETHERLANDS

4

## PAINTING IN VENICE



5

## MANNERISM

THIS VOLUME OF THE COLLECTION

THE GREAT CENTURIES OF PAINTING

WAS PRINTED BOTH TEXT AND COLORPLATES BY THE

SKIRA

COLOR STUDIO AT IMPRIMERIES RÉUNIES S. A., LAUSANNE, FINISHED THE TWENTIETH DAY OF AUGUST, NINETEEN HUNDRED AND FIFTY-SIX. THE COLORPLATES WERE ENGRAVED BY GUEZELLE ET RENOUARD, PARIS, EXCEPT THE ONE ON PAGE 173, ENGRAVED BY ALTIMANI, MILAN.

*The reproductions on pages 13, 79, 133, 165, 227 were executed by Roto-Sadag, Geneva, and the reproduction on page 9 by Imprimeries Réunies S.A., Lausanne.*

*The works reproduced in this volume were photographed by Louis Laniepce, Paris (pages 9, 15, 24, 25, 34, 35, 40, 41, 75, 94, 95, 111, 112, 113, 146, 152, 177, 181, 186, 225, 227), by Claudio Emmer, Milan (pages 3, 13, 14, 18, 19, 20, 23, 30, 31, 36, 37, 47, 48, 49, 52, 53, 53a, 56, 65, 74, 76, 77, 97, 114, 115, 125, 153, 161, 169, 172, 180, 182, 194, 195, 206, 207, 209, 210, 211, 211a, 212, 215, 216, 217, 220, 228, 231, 239, 250, 252, 255), by Hans Hinz, Basel (pages 10, 44, 61, 62, 63, 80, 85, 86, 87, 91, 102, 103, 104, 107, 108, 116, 119, 120, 122, 123, 124, 127, 128, 129, 130, 133, 134, 138, 139, 140, 141, 143, 148, 149, 163, 166, 184, 185, 189, 190, 191, 193, 203, 205, 221, 258, 260, 263), by Arte e Colore, Milan (pages 171, 173, 222, 223), by Henry B. Beville, Washington (pages 33, 117, 157, 245, 247, 257, 261), by Karl Meyer, Vienna (pages 99, 165, 243), by Walter Steinkopf, Berlin (page 196), by the photographic services of the Bibliothèque Nationale, Paris (page 79), and by the photographic services of Life Magazine, New York (page 64) and Anderson, Rome (photographs in black and white on pages 61a and 69).*

PRINTED IN SWITZERLAND